Information Seeking
and Subject Representation

Information Seeking and Subject Representation

An Activity-Theoretical
Approach to Information Science

BIRGER HJØRLAND

New Directions in Information Management, Number 34
Michael Buckland, Series Adviser

GREENWOOD PRESS
Westport, Connecticut • London

Library of Congress Cataloging-in-Publication Data

Hjørland, Birger.
    Information seeking and subject representation : an activity-
theoretical approach to information science / Birger Hjørland.
       p.   cm.—(New directions in information management, ISSN
0887–3844 ; 34)
    Includes bibliographical references (p.   ) and index.
    ISBN 0–313–29893–9 (alk. paper)
    1. Subject cataloging.   2. Indexing.   I. Title.   II. Series.
Z695.H694   1997
025.4′7—dc21   96–51136

British Library Cataloguing in Publication Data is available.

Library of Congress Catalog Card Number: 96–51136
ISBN: 0–313–29893–9
ISSN: 0887–3844

First published in 1997

Greenwood Press, 88 Post Road West, Westport, CT 06881
An imprint of Greenwood Publishing Group, Inc.

Printed in the United States of America

The paper used in this book complies with the
Permanent Paper Standard issued by the National
Information Standards Organization (Z39.48–1984).

10 9 8 7 6 5 4 3 2 1

Copyright Acknowledgments

The author and publisher gratefully acknowledge permission for use of the following:

Table 5.3 reproduced from *Information and Information Systems* by Michael Buckland. Copyright ©
1991 by Michael Buckland. Reproduced with permission of Greenwood Publishing Group, Inc., Westport
CT.

Figure 5.1 reproduced with permission from M. A. Forrester, *Psychology of Language: A Critical
Introduction*. Copyright 1996 by permission of Sage Publications Ltd.

Excerpts from *Reconstruction in Philosophy* by John Dewey. Copyright © 1920, by Henry Holt and
Co. Copyright renewed, 1947 by John Dewey. Revised and enlarged edition, copyright © 1948 by the
Beacon Press. Reprinted by permission of Beacon Press, Boston.

To Ida, Jesper, and Peter

Contents

Acknowledgments

This book reflects the current status of my theorizing about the foundation of information science. I would like to thank the people who have supported the research, the translation, and the publishing of this book.

First of all, thanks to the director of the Royal School of Librarianship in Copenhagen, Ole Harbo, who has supported my research by providing the time for me to do it. He has also supported the translation economically and introduced me to a very competent information scientist, Dr. Ylva Lindholm-Romantschuk, who has been a great help in the translation process.

I am also very grateful to my colleague at the Royal School of Librarianship, Hanne Albrechtsen, with whom I have had many fruitful discussions, and whose fine qualifications in both information science and in the English language have been of very great value in this process. Also thanks to information scientist Barbara Kwasnik, who during her time as a Fulbright professor has visited our school and offered kind comments on parts of the manuscript.

The formulation of some of the basic ideas in my theory are indebted to an initiative of Professor Erland Munch-Petersen. I would like to thank him and the people at the small, but very dynamic center for Library and Information Studies at the University of Göteborg for their kind support and interest.

Finally, but not least, thanks to Professor Michael Buckland for professional cooperation in the last few years, including recommending this book for publishing.

1

Introduction: Information Seeking and Subject Representation

AN ACTIVITY-THEORETICAL APPROACH TO INFORMATION SCIENCE

This work is a treatise on information science based on the author's combined background in psychology and information science (IS). It is based on the assumption that information seeking is the key problem in information science. Other problems, such as document representation, are subordinate to the problem of information seeking. A general theory of information seeking might therefore serve as a theoretical basis for IS.

IS has for a long time been drawing on the knowledge produced in psychology as well as in other fields. This is natural, since the central issue in IS concerns individual users navigating in information spaces such as libraries, databases, and the Internet. The problems of information seeking in IS seem related to problems in educational psychology, especially to the theory behind project-oriented teaching, where students are seeking information in relation to their projects. Both IS and educational psychology face the problems of how an individual acquires knowledge of a culture and a discipline. Therefore, there is a close connection between the fields, which, however, in my view has been impeded by the strong influence of positivist and rationalist trends.

In psychology, there was a well-known cognitive revolution started by the psychologist J. S. Bruner and the linguist Noam Chomsky around 1956–1957. This cognitive revolution regarded the human mind as a computer and linguistics as part of psychology, which studied the innate programs of the brain. In its development, this cognitivism has become less and less "hard": cognitivism has more and more tended to look at the individual mental states as social constructs. That is, today the machinery and programs of the brain are not seen as isolated from the sociocultural context as was originally believed.

The need for a less formal but a more social, cultural, and ecological orientation in psychology is now recognized by leading figures in this discipline (e.g., Bruner, 1990). The psychologist Ulric Neisser had a very important role in the development of the cognitive revolution in the 1960s. Ulric Neisser is professor at Emory University in Atlanta and a member of the American National Academy of Sciences. His book *Cognitive Psychology* (1967) was seen as a standard by followers of the computer model of the mind. Today Neisser has turned against his own theory and is advocating a more social and ecological theory. His shift from a cognitive-information processing paradigm in psychology to an interpersonal and ecological "self"-psychology has come as a surprise.

It is of course dangerous to generalize about the developments in fields with many differentiated theories, but I do find evidence for a development in which modern psychology, linguistics, semiotics, compositional studies, and so on, are all looking at language and other cognitive processes in the context of socio-cultural development (rather than in an intrapsychological framework, in which linguistics is seen as part of cognitive psychology). The Russian psychologist L. S. Vygotsky, who died in 1934, is seen as one of the "classics" and is today very popular also in American psychology. His works (e.g., Vygotsky, 1962, 1978, 1982) represent in my view an important development from a very mechanistic and positivistic science toward a more social and realistic science. Vygotsky was predated by several decades by the American philosopher John Dewey, who described the manner in which socioeconomic relations influence psychology:

Occupations determine the fundamental modes of activity, and hence control the formation and use of habits. . . . The occupations determine the chief modes of satisfaction, the standards of success and failure. Hence they furnish the working classifications and definitions of value; they control the desire processes. Moreover, they decide the sets of objects and relations that are important, and thereby provide the content or material of attention, and the qualities that are interestingly significant. The directions given to mental life thereby extend to emotional and intellectual characteristics. So fundamental and pervasive is the group of occupational activities that it affords the scheme or pattern of the structural organization of mental traits. Occupations integrate special elements into a functional whole. (Dewey, 1902, pp. 219–220)

Modern activity theory is closely related to Dewey's theory (which is famous for its principle "learning by doing"). But as Bauersfeld (1992, p. 22) writes, there are also important differences. It is not the doing of the individual subject alone which has the developing power. It is the coordinated action in the form of participating in a functioning culture.

This also means that within psychology the trends have developed from more domain-general to more domain-specific theories. The development of children's thinking is not seen to follow as abstract patterns as earlier described by Jean Piaget, for example, but is closely related to the concrete knowledge base which the child possesses (cf. Chi, Hutchinson, & Robin, 1989; Keil, 1989; Siegler,

1989). The thinking of human beings is today viewed as much more domain-specific than the founders of cognitive science imagined.

The approach in psychology established by John Dewey is very rewarding. The approach named activity theory is also very fruitful to IS. Some authors emphasize the differences between these approaches, but I look upon Dewey as one of the founders of activity theory, and I find that my orientation is thus very much connected to recent reorientations in mainstream psychology and philosophy (cf. Putnam, 1990, 1992). But it is of course difficult to work on two fronts at one time: the basic problem both of psychology and of information science. It is, however, my feeling that the application of psychology and philosophy to such real-life problems as information retrieval is a rewarding enterprise.

Information seeking has mainly been studied in two large subareas of information science: user studies and information retrieval. It is this author's opinion that both areas are—and have always been—in a crisis and that they are relatively isolated from each other. User studies can take a rather holistic perspective over the users' relationships to the system of information sources. Information retrieval research typically adopts a very atomistic perspective in studying the "match" between a representation of a query and a representation of a document (e.g., a match based on statistical or linguistic analysis of questions and document representations).

In this work it is assumed that a study of information seeking which critically analyzes the positivistic and idealistic assumptions about knowledge and science in information science and which introduces an alternative view of knowledge can help to overcome the crisis in both user studies and in information retrieval research. In addition it can unite these areas. A nonidealistic view of knowledge and science inspired by a pragmatic philosophy understands knowledge as a tool shaped in order to increase man's adjustment to his physical, biological, and cultural environment, and sees knowledge as historically and culturally developed products organized in collective human organizations such as scientific disciplines. Such a view of knowledge is the opposite of a philosophical "idealistic" point of view. In short it can be called a "realistic" view, but it covers different traditions in psychology and philosophy: primarily pragmatism, scientific realism, and activity theory.

The users' behavior (and the subjective perceptions and assumptions behind that behavior) must be interpreted in the light of the scientific situation in a given area. In the same way, representation of knowledge in documents and databases must be interpreted on the basis of the scientific situation. It is meaningless to investigate the "micro events," the micro behavior of information searching and representation, if you have no indication whether this behavior contributes to human knowledge or not. Discussions of positivism, hermeneutics, pragmatism, social constructivism, and scientific realism are almost unknown in the subject literature of information science.

Knowledge of problems in the philosophy of science and in the theory of science makes researchers much better equipped to interpret information science problems like obsolescence, "overload," the cumulative nature of science, the structures of the information landscape, information use behavior, retrieval of information, and subject representation.[1] According to the empiricist point of view, knowledge grows in one way: fact being added to fact. From Thomas Kuhn's theory, knowledge does not accumulate in this way at all, but shifts with the "paradigm" in the field.

User studies are mostly made without any such relation to analyses of theories of knowledge. But how can you empirically examine the users' behavior when you do not have an adequate model of the users' role in the creation of knowledge or in the development of knowledge in a holistic perspective? How can information science deal with the problem of "match" if it has no knowledge of how a single paper fits into the structure of science? Words can match, as can sentences, but according to the view of semantic holism, concepts mean different things in different areas. Information science needs to establish how subject-specific terminology is generated. The problem of "match" is most often seen in IS as a simple mechanical question, not a humanistic/social scientific question of interpretation.

The study of user behavior is mostly made on the basis of a positivistic theory, and this is assumed to be "objective" research. But the users' behavior of course reflects their subjective knowledge and attitudes. These subjective attitudes must be interpreted in some way. It is of little help to know what information sources are used if you don't know whether the sources and strategies used are adequate and represent the optimum. How can you assist users by giving access to information sources without some knowledge of what is important and what is trivial?

It is therefore important that empirical studies give up their positivistic assumptions and begin to study user behavior from the perspective of history, sociology, theory of science, and so on. Kuhn's famous book (1970) is well-known within information science, but it has never really changed or influenced the methodology of the field. Of course, Kuhn's work is further developed and questioned in the modern debate between social constructivism and scientific realism, but as it stands it implies very important methodological implications for research in information seeking and IS. In this book I try to explicate the methodological consequences of nonpositivistic epistemologies such as Kuhn's. My basic methodological principles are that the point of view in information science should be seen as "methodological collectivism," as studies of knowledge domains (and, for example, paradigms), as study of language and of domain-specific cognition in individuals. Such an approach is an alternative to mechanical, formalist and "methodological individualistic" approaches that dominate in both physical and cognitivist approaches today. The problems are difficult theoretical ones, and we have to take a humble attitude toward them, contrary to the ideology of the technological fix, which has characterized information science since the days of Vannevar Bush.

ORGANIZATION OF THE BOOK

Chapter 2 analyzes the problems of subject retrieval and subject representation data. As a background, a typology of information searches are provided and the concepts of "document," "medium," and "work" are illuminated.

A well-reputed Danish dictionary (*Informationsordbogen*, 1991) defines subject retrieval as retrieval of information by use of subject representation data—which is defined in opposition to "descriptive data." I do not agree with this definition, and I show that the question of how to define it is not trivial: an adequate theory of information retrieval must be based on an adequate definition of subject retrieval.

My proposed definition is as follows: Subject retrieval is the search for unknown documents (as opposed to a "known item search") whose contents can contribute to the solution of a concrete problem or satisfy a need for information. All kinds of data which can give a clue (even a vague one) regarding the identification or evaluation of potentially relevant documents can be used in subject retrieval, including the document's own data (such as title, abstracts, list of references, author) or data different from the document itself (including classification codes, descriptors, book reviews, evaluations, and citations in other documents).

The chapter also takes a very short view of the large field of subject representation data or information retrieval languages and introduces some important distinctions and points of view. Among others, I differentiate between explicit subject representation data (which are data constructed explicitly in order to facilitate information retrieval) and implicit subject representation data (which are data constructed for other purposes, but that are sometimes useful in retrieval). If a publisher is called Danish Psychological Publishers, this name can sometimes be useful in searching for books about psychology. In the same way, for example, a journal's name can contribute valuable implicit subject representation data.

I also consider the difference between content-oriented subject description data and request-oriented subject data (introduced by Soergel, 1985, and others). I state that this work is an attempt at consequently applying the request-oriented or need-oriented line of thought. In this I find support in the philosophic hermeneutics of Gadamer, which states that it is meaningless to claim that a text has a meaning of its own independent of any interpretation. If it is meaningful at all to say that a text has a meaning in itself, "an objective meaning," this should be seen as the sum of all prior, contemporary, and future interpretations of that text.

Chapter 3 treats subject analysis and knowledge organization. Subject analysis is the interpretational process (made by man or eventually by machine) by which documents are analyzed and their explicit subject representation data are created.

It is stated that the classification system, the thesaurus, or, in general the knowledge organization system or the information retrieval language, which the subject analysis should be expressed in, works back on the subject analysis and functions as a decision support system for subject analysis. It is, however, very important to distinguish between the subject analysis itself and the following translation process or expression process, in which the result from the subject analysis is expressed in some retrieval language. If these two processes (of subject analysis and subject expression) are not separated analytically, we can never make adequate theories about either subject analysis or about retrieval languages. (This important principle is well pointed out in the works of Lancaster and Langridge).

The subject analysis could be more general or more specific. As pointed out in the literature by Lancaster, Soergel, and others, an analysis of a document in a pharmacological database like Ringdok would and should be more specific— better suited to the needs of the pharmacological industry—than an analysis of the same document in Chemical Abstracts. Subject analysis can have other dimensions too (not previously discussed in the literature). The analysis could be more abstract or more concrete. Concrete analysis is seen as a predominantly empirical/positivistic/nominalistic influence. An abstract analysis is seen as an important but underdeveloped alternative or supplementary analysis in line with realistic philosophies of knowledge.

This chapter ends by stating some basic principles of knowledge organization based mainly upon science studies.

Chapter 4 looks at the concept of subject or subject matter. The subject of a document is seen as that object, that "something," which the subject analysis focuses on and tries to identify. The discussions of the concepts of subject (and "aboutness") in the literature of library and information science are presented, analyzed, and criticized. Existing theories are interpreted, characterized, and criticized from four fundamental conceptions of knowledge and concepts:

1. Classical empiricism and subjective idealism (George Berkeley and empiricist epistemology), which sees knowledge and concepts as individual, subjective creations, which are best studied by empirical, psychological methods. The works on subject by Hutchins (and many other adherents to the concept of aboutness) and the cognitive viewpoint are interpreted as examples of this view.

2. Rationalism and objective idealism / conceptual realism (Plato, Descartes, and modern rationalism), which operates with permanent, inherent characteristics of knowledge. These permanent knowledge structures exist prior to the individual, subjective perception and are first and foremost studied by rationalistic methods. In IS, the works on subject by Ranganathan and Langridge, are interpreted as examples of this view.

3. Historism and pragmatism (Charles Sanders Peirce, William James, and John Dewey), which underlines the functionality and utility of knowledge and cognition and applies a teleological, goal-oriented viewpoint. However, there are internal conflicts in pragmatism, where William James has often popularized and debased the theory

by exemplifying basic issues by relating them to more immediate, short-term pragmatic purposes. The same conflict between long-term and short-term pragmatism is shown also to apply to information science problems, where short-term pragmatism has difficulties in explaining the more pure, scientific classification systems. Pragmatism thus is split between a kind of subjective idealism and scientific realism. Subject representation systems building on the concept of bibliographical coupling are analyzed as a special kind of systems building on pragmatic relations.

4. Activity theory and scientific realism (John Dewey, the cultural-historical school in Russian psychology, and others), which—like pragmatism—sees knowledge as biologically, culturally, and individually developed structures, suited to increase man's ability to accommodate to his physical, cultural, and psychological environment, and primarily organized in "epistemic communities." From this perspective, knowledge cannot be studied by either rationalistic or empiricist methods alone, but must be studied by rationalistic, empirical, and historical methods. The method must reflect the object under study.

Melvil Dewey's classification theory states: "No other feature of the DDC [Dewey Decimal Classification] is more basic than this: that it scatters subjects by discipline." This may be interpreted as an expression of a realistic philosophy of knowledge, because disciplines are historically developed structures which determine the way in which subjects are interpreted and organized. However, the only explicit theory of subject building on this realistic epistemology is my own theory: The subject of a document is the epistemological potential of that document. This realistic philosophy of knowledge appears essential not only in order to define the concept of subject matter, but to remove a fundamental theoretical block in information science as a whole.

Objective idealism will search subject matter in permanent, inherent characteristics of knowledge, or in permanent, inherent semantic relationships and try to establish standardized, permanent, fixed ways of analyzing documents (disregarding their potential use). Subjective idealism, on the other hand, will search for the subject matter of a document in either the author's or the users' subjective perception of the document and try to develop a theory of subject analysis based on either the author's psychological world (as in classical hermeneutics) or the users' psychological world (as is done in parts of modern cognitive viewpoint). None of these viewpoints are, however, developed or stated explicitly in the literature. A reason for this might be that these viewpoints—and especially subjective idealism—are in contradiction with reality, and therefore it is impossible to formulate the theory clearly without its quickly being contradicted by concrete examples from real life. In spite of this, the existing theories of subject analysis and subject matter tend to build on such idealistic philosophies of knowledge.

From the position of activity theory, we do not look on subject as either inherent characteristics or as something subjective in an individual way. The interpretation of a document's epistemological or informative potentials is theoretically a never-ending process (like Peirce's unlimited semiosis). This interpretative process is part of the same historical-cultural development as knowledge production itself. The discussion about the possibilities of an objective subject analysis is therefore intimately linked to the discussions about scientific objectivity. This is the philosophical debate concerning scientific realism. The conditions of subject analysis are linked to the conditions of scientific creation of knowledge. The state of scientific knowledge functions as the background against which the interpretation of the single document's subject matter is formed by individuals, on the basis of their subjective knowledge. The better this subjective knowledge "matches" the state of scientific knowledge, the more "objective" the analysis.

Chapter 5 analyzes some methodological problems in information science. The definition of information science, the concept of information and the basic problem of information retrieval (IR) theory are analyzed from the new methodological view presented in this book. IS is dominated by methodological individualism; that is, it studies knowledge by studying the individual subjects which are carriers of this knowledge. Collective knowledge is often seen as the sum of the knowledge of single persons. This point of view is related to the formerly described subjective idealism, most clearly to the reductionism of positivism.

The alternative point of view—methodological collectivism—is to see knowledge as a developed historical-cultural-social product. The alternative to studying individual subjects and individual information-seeking behavior is to study knowledge domains. That is to study their informational structures, their terminology, knowledge representation, communication patterns, all in connection with their theories of knowledge and theories of science. Individual subjects' behavior in relation to use and to representation of information should be interpreted in the light of a (sub)disciplinary context.

In information science you could say that bibliometrics represents a methodological collectivism. However, bibliometrics is itself a very positivistic and criticized methodology. Buckland (1991, pp. 22–23) says that in his opinion a reason for the crisis and pathology in the theory of IS is that an area such as bibliometrics—being easy to study quantitatively—has had such a big place in the field. Therefore, bibliometrics should not be seen as the main methodology for studying knowledge domains. It could be a supplement to other methods, including historical, sociological, and philosophical methods.

It is also important that the link between the psychological and the social levels is covered. Information seeking is mainly an individual act. Information science has lent itself to a psychology (cognitivism), which is based on methodological individualism (sometimes even methodological solipsism). In psychology, however, some researchers are working in order to overcome the methodological individualism. Information science should try to keep up with these collective tendencies in psychology. Important modern contributions in English include Forrester (1996); Middleton and Edwards (1990); Resnick, Levine, and Teasley (1991); Sinha (1988) and Tolman (1992). In the last mentioned work is an important discussion of the role of language as a methodological key to psychology and as a means of perceiving the objective world. This has never been grasped in the empiricist tradition from Aristotle to modern positivism and cognitivism, but it has been present in other lines of theories from Plato to modern interpretative tendencies in the humanities.

From these studies we must conclude that human concepts—human knowledge—do primarily emerge as a result of human cooperation and communication. The individual structures of knowledge can only be understood from a collective analysis of the language users. The knowledge of an individual person, his benefits from information systems, and the problems and barriers he meets in the utilization of knowledge are not primarily illuminated by psychological studies of the capacity and mechanics of the brain or by a differentiation between long-term memory and short-term memory, between semantic and episodic memory, and so on. Rather, they are illuminated by the knowledge of the social background of the person, his social roles and working commitments, his educational background, and his cooperative relationships, in addition to knowledge about the nature of the concrete domain of knowledge.

Chapter 6 is an analysis of information seeking from a methodological-collectivistic methodology. The principal uncertainty of information seeking (a concept introduced by Swanson) is discussed and supplanted by degrees of freedom determined by the scientific cooperation in a given field. Fields with a well-defined terminology and well-established standards of publishing (and a relatively small scattering of the literature) are giving the individual researcher fewer degrees of freedom than areas with a very loose terminology and without established standards for publication. In these latter areas there are greater possibilities of individual self-expression, but this increases the uncertainty of information seeking by others.

It is argued that the laws or regularities of information seeking are bound not by the process or technology of searching (such as the fixation on technology in information science would often like us to believe), but by scientific cooperation, the scientific organization, and the nature of the scientific object. The general conditions of information seeking can only be comprehended by going from a methodological individualism to a methodological collectivism.

Chapter 7 is about the concept of information needs and it contains a reinterpretation of R. S. Taylor's classic psychological study of the development of information need from the point of view of methodological collectivism. The basic thesis in this chapter is that the concept of information need must be understood in the light of both the individual user's cognitive development and of the collective status of knowledge in a given field of knowledge. "Information need" as traditionally understood is a "ghost in the machine."

NOTE

1. Philosophy of science and epistemology are well-established disciplines within philosophy. In Europe, theory of science (Danish "videnskabsteori") is becoming an

important interdisciplinary field, and many sciences, including economics, medicine, and psychology, are doing research and teaching in their respective theories of science. Epistemological studies in relation to behavioral science are still much underrepresented in English language literature as compared to Scandinavian, German, and other European language literatures. A book like Tolman (1992) is an important exception. Thus, science theory is mostly done by specialists in the respective disciplines. The terms *science studies* or *metasciences* are related but often more empirically understood. Tolman (1992) is an example of the theory of science in psychology. The present book is an example of theory of science in IS. Activity theory is an approach based on explicit analysis of epistemological questions.

2

Subject Searching
and Subject Representation Data

INTRODUCTION: TYPES OF INFORMATION SEARCHES

Information seeking and information retrieval are core concepts in information science (IS). The terms *information retrieval* (IR) and *information retrieval languages* were introduced in IS by Calvin Mooers (1951, p. 25). According to him, IR "embraces the intellectual aspects of the description of information and its specification for search, and also whatever system, technique, or machines that are employed to carry out the operation." This term today must be considered as a standard concept in IS, despite some unpleasant linguistic consequences. In reality, information retrieval is mostly meant document retrieval or text retrieval, not fact retrieval. Besides, the word *retrieval*, with the prefix "re," indicates that some items are found again.[1] At best, this expression presupposes some conscious coding of documents, but—as we shall see later—in actual retrieval many implicit subject access points are often used. It is therefore more precise to say that some items are identified (rather than retrieved) in IR.

Schwartz (1992, p. 129) calls the notion that there are scientific laws concerning information seeking waiting to be discovered the second myth of information science. He writes: "Many commentators have declared, rather elliptically, that the future of library and information science depends on theory building and, further, that the way people seek information for scholarly purposes is the main issue." This study is an attempt to clarify the general theory of information seeking. In contrast to Schwartz I believe that even if laws cannot be discovered, then at least general principles can.

The Behavioral Ecology of Finding Resources

From the point of view of pragmatism and activity theory, all information-seeking behavior shares a common purpose: the identification of resources of some kind. Foellesdal, Walløe, and Elster (1992, pp. 164–165) provide an analysis of the problem of information gathering from the point of view of rational decision theory. How much information is it rational to obtain before one forms one's opinion of the matter?

Suppose we are going mushrooming. Our goal is to gather mushrooms, and we do not know where the best place is. It would be rather stupid to select the first place where some mushrooms are found. Possibly, nearby, is a place with many more mushrooms. On the other hand, one should not use too much time to search for the best place, because then there may be too little time left for gathering. You should use the optimal time to collect information about where the best places are. The problem is that we are in no position to know what the optimal time for that purpose is. Surely, some solution to this problem exists, but we cannot find it, at least not without further information. And how much time should be used to get that information? The problem continues in this way in a never-ending manner.

Paradoxes exist in philosophy, but in real life, animals and humans succeed very often in getting food, mates, and resources without ending like Buridan's ass. How do they make a decision in situations where no rational argument can tell when to stop the gathering of information? And how do we develop a theory of optimal information gathering in libraries and databases given this logical paradox of rational decision?

As long as information science operates from a model of the abstract and generalized individual user facing the cumulation of the world's knowledge in electronic databases, there is no possible escape from the above cited paradox. It can never be decided what kind of information seeking is optimal or efficient. A new model is mandatory. This new model must be evolutionary, ecological, functionalistic, and collectivistic.

In nature, many "strategies" exist, and many more are tried in the course of biological development. Some birds specialize in finding insects in old trees, while others go fishing. The individual animal does not sit down and think about any theoretical possibility in order to make "a rational choice." Nature is rational in another way. The individual is locked into a certain biotope in what Maturana calls a "consensual domain," a mutual phylogenetic structural coupling between biological mechanisms.[2] Think of the flowers and the insects. As Charles Darwin wrote in *The Origin of Species*, without the insects, green would have been the only color in the vegetable kingdom. No individual or species can be understood without reference to its environment and to the developmental processes shaping the species as part of a niche in the ecosystem. This is valid both in regard to developments in anatomy and in relation to behavior. All parts of an individual, including its anatomy, instincts, learning mechanisms, and information-seeking behavior, are developed to adapt to an ecological niche. The understanding of an individual's optimal choice in information seeking is based on some conditions about the ecosystem in which that individual forms a part. There exists a division of labor both between arts and between individuals. The rationality of the behavior of the individual can only be understood from a systems view of the whole ecological and cultural system.

Document versus Nondocument-Based Information Searches

As seen in Table 2.1, a major distinction is between document and non-document searches. Nondocument searching covers both physical things (e.g., mushrooms) and theoretical concepts such as facts or ideas. The distinction between document and nondocument is a difficult one, but it is important for the identity of IS, and we shall therefore spend some time on it.

Information seeking in the broadest sense consists of more than one field of study. One example of the topic is from biology, where Bell's book (1991) is wholly devoted to animals' searching behavior. Even though such research may have some relevance for IS, biology is clearly not a part of IS. One relevant difference is that animals communicate and search by signals, not by documents. Another kind of information-seeking behavior is consumer behavior: how people select services, shops, and brands. Again, this is not document searching, although documents may represent one kind of article, among others. Two kinds of information searches which actually are based on documents are the use of mass media and information-seeking behavior in education. These forms of information searching fall somewhat outside the narrow scope of IS. In mass media research the purpose is not primarily to design information systems, which allow the user to identify "the best textual means to some end" (P. Wilson, 1968), but to study the psychological, cultural, commercial, and political effects of the media on individuals and groups.

Information seeking in education and learning processes approaches that in IS. If the learning process is an advanced university degree (e.g., a master's thesis), then the information search process can come very close to that of professional scientists. In my view, a normative model of professional information-seeking behavior must precede a theory of information seeking among students.

Another example is scientists' searching behavior. When scientists or scholars do research, they collect information about their objects, for example, atoms, planets, or ancient cultures. How scientists should do research is a question for the methodologies of the sciences, not primarily for IS—with the exception of some questions such as document retrieval, which should be seen as a special part of scientific methodology. Some special parts of science and scholarship do, however, have documents as their primary objects. This is the case in some of the human sciences, especially in the history of literature. But in general, scientists' direct study of their objects falls outside the domain of IS. However, as soon as scientists communicate their findings by means of documents, their search behavior is part of the focus of information science.

It follows that the concept of document might be decisive in defining the difference between information seeking as the object of IS and other kinds of information seeking. But what, then is a document?

Table 2.1
Typology of Information Searches

I. Nondocumentary searches

A. Individual information-seeking behavior [3]
(e.g., locating a restaurant or gathering mushrooms)

B. Collective organized information seeking
(e.g., finding new energy resources or
identifying ways to cure illness)

- Primary research activities
- Informal communications
- Fact retrieval

II. Document seeking and retrieval

A. Known item retrieval

- Verification of documents
- Searching for supplementary information about an item (e.g., abstracts, reviews, price or location data for making a decision about obtaining the item)
- Access to specific items in order to utilize the potential information in the document (reading or scanning)

B. Identification of unknown item(s)

- Identification of items corresponding to certain formal attributes in documents (e.g., documents in specific languages or by specific publishers)
- Subject retrieval: Identification of items with the potential of contributing to solve a problem or satisfy an information need
    a. searching for items with potentials for solving a concrete problem or a specific information need
    b. searching for items with potential for contributing to a general understanding of a problem field or a nonspecific information need
  In either case, subject retrieval may be disciplinary or interdisciplinary, local or global, current or retrospective, and so on.

In library and information science (LIS) the term *document* is used as a generic term. Typical kinds of documents in libraries and bibliographical databases are books, journal articles, manuscripts, pictures, films, videos, computer programs, and so on. The term is thus much broader than it is in everyday understanding, in which typical documents are, for example, official papers and have a connotation as a type of medium (typically paper, but sometimes microfilms). This meaning is not the one used in LIS, where you can speak of, for example, electronic documents. Both traditional paper-based catalogs and modern online catalogs can be examples of documents in the generic meaning used in LIS.

This, however, makes it very difficult to define what is *not* a document. The development in the electronic media makes it especially difficult to distinguish between documents and nondocuments. Everything carrying information can be described in databases for later retrieval, and can thus be seen as a document.

The *Shorter Oxford English Dictionary* defines document as "That which serves to show or prove something; evidence, proof. . . . Something written, inscribed, etc., which furnishes evidence or information upon any subject, as a manuscript, titledeed, coin, etc." This broad definition corresponds well to the way in which *document* is employed in LIS, as information carrier or "information-as-thing" as Buckland (1991) expresses it. Vickery and Vickery (1987, p. 36) define it in this way:

A document is a physical medium modified so as to carry marks that are signs in some agreed code. The marks can be images that we recognize or accept as representing some visual aspect of the world; they can be recordings of natural or man-made sound, similarly recognizable; or they can be conventional signs that are accepted as symbols for any mental concept or its referent in the world. The conventional signs can be the letters and words of a natural language, and thus be related to its spoken form, or they can be a special-purpose code. (for example, Morse code, Braille, codes for computers, chemical symbolism)

Buckland (1991, pp. 46–48) analyzes important aspects of the history of the concept. Early in the twentieth century, the documentalists felt that there existed a need for a generic term, an expression for the objects which the activity of documentation deat with. They included not only texts, but also natural objects, artifacts, models designed to represent ideas, and objects of art. The concept *document* (or unit of documentation) was applied in a special meaning as a designation for informative physical objects. A wild antelope was not a document, but a captured specimen which was studied, described, and incorporated in a zoo for the purpose of educational and scientific study was considered a document. Perhaps a person had to be a dedicated documentalist in order to look at an antelope as a document. But even so, as Buckland points out, the word is derived from the Latin *docere*, which means "to teach or to inform," with the suffix -ment, which means tool. That is, the word *document* originally meant a tool to teach or inform, no matter if it was a lecture, an experience, or a text. Limiting the meaning to objects carrying text came only at a later time.

Hjerppe (1994) presents an important theoretical argument for a broad concept of documents. He speaks about generalized documents. His concept of generalized documents builds on a concept of generalized texts, which again builds on a generalized concept of reading. Such generalized concepts of documents, texts, and reading have become necessary now that many kinds of knowledge and information have become coordinated, as, for example, in multimedia and hypertext systems. An important aspect of Hjerppe's theory is that the generalized concept of reading is something learned in a culture.

However, Hjerppe does not illuminate the limits of a single document. Where does one document end and the next begin? In traditional philosophical thinking, single things, such as one book, are conceived as concrete, whereas the communication processes that they serve, are seen as something abstract. Both the technological developments and important theories in communication, however, change this relationship. As texts are integrated, for example, in hypertext systems, the single text becomes difficult to delimit: it consists of parts, which are combined with other documents. The semiotician Julia Kristeva (1974, pp. 59–60) has formulated a theory about intertextuality. According to this theory a text cannot be regarded as something given, with a definite meaning. It is nothing but a mosaic which can be understood only through its absorption and transformation of the other writings to which it is related. No text can ever be free of other texts. Some kinds of relationships between texts are echo, allusion, acceptance, rejection, and so on. A particular text is a confluence of many writings: by the author, the historical contexts, and so on. The concept of text is applied by Kristeva—like other simioticans—to everything capable of signifying. Also, communication theorists like Nystrand, Greene, and Wiemelt (1993) point to the need to understand texts (and documents) as phenomena in "discourse communities." The documents cannot be analyzed in isolation; the single text becomes an abstraction in a fluent stream of communication.

To understand documents, we must therefore understand the communication processes they serve. It is very important to distinguish among, for example, primary communication, secondary communication, and tertiary communication (see Figure 5.2 in Chapter 5). Typically, there are different kinds of documents serving each of these forms of communication (e.g., primary journals, bibliographic databases, and handbooks). It is also important to distinguish between communication between scientists (peers) and communication to lay people and to students. Specific forms of documents are serving such purposes (e.g., magazines and textbooks).

The different types of documents can be linked to the different roles in the social division of labor. In the division of labor scientific objects like antelopes are not studied by documentalists or information scientists, but by zoologists. Nature is the primary sources of information for the natural scientist. Documents about antelopes are secondary sources for the zoologist, but they are primary sources of information for, for example, the historian of science and the information scientist. The concept of information sources is therefore broader than the concept of documents.

Unpublished documents in archives are the typical primary information sources of historians, who often see it as a purpose in itself to transfer the most important part of these information sources to published documents, whereby they are made visible and readable for much broader parts of society. For the lawyer and jurisprudent, laws and pronouncements of sentences are primary information sources.

The concept of documents is not identical with the concept of *media*. The medium is the physical material in itself (e.g., paper, film, radio waves), whereas the document is a unit in a communication process: a medium coded with a specific content. That content often corresponds with the concept of a work (by some author). The concept of work is used in copyright law and elsewhere. A work need not be fixed in a document. It can be fixed in different documents, and a work can be translated and fixed in a new document.

Documents contain "texts" (in a generalized meaning, including, e.g., pictures) written by other people. The study of them must build on some kind of theory of communication and signs (semiotics).[4]

It is well known from many user studies that informal communication plays an important role in information gathering in science. Normally, we would say that such informal communication is one kind of nondocumentary information searching, but the limits are extremely difficult to draw. Clearly a letter, a fax, and an Internet message are both documents and informal communication channels. If scientists (like antelopes above) are described in databases according to research qualifications and interests—as in project registrations—they are in fact "indexed" and treated as documents.

We can conclude that documents are prepared by humans to serve special communicative functions. The understanding of documents presumes an understanding of whom they are serving as primary, secondary, or tertiary information channels, what other communication channels they compete with, and how the social communication system is designed.

Document Retrieval versus Fact Retrieval

Another important distinction between document-based and non-document-based searches is the difference between document retrieval and fact retrieval. If a librarian answers a question by phone by using an encyclopedia as the source of information, then the service which he or she is offering is *fact retrieval*. If, on the other hand, he sends by fax a copy of the relevant article in the same encyclopedia, then the service is *document retrieval*.[5] At first glance the distinction between fact retrieval and document retrieval is a superficial and unimportant one. Because it is of interest to know the source (in order to compare it with other sources and to evaluate its authority), document retrieval is more scientific in the meaning of source criticism: it is perhaps less user-friendly, but much more scholarly. What is fact is often debatable, and empirical facts may—as Henning Spang-Hanssen (1970) has formulated it—not have an all too safe future. Fact retrieval systems could be seen as systems which hide their information sources and keep them exclusively for themselves and only communicate some of the content from these.

However, the distinction is not without relevance because libraries try to build reference collections which enable them to offer quick reference services. They also evaluate information sources from their functions as ready-at-hand answering tools. Also, computer scientists have shown some interest in programs that enable them to answer specific questions from a database. As a contrast, document retrieval systems do not attempt to answer concrete questions, but to produce a list of references which within a reasonable degree of certainty provide the answer as this is currently known by science or mankind.[6] Some very distinguished researchers in IS have regarded the creation of fact retrieval systems as the ultimate goal of IS. Karen Sparck Jones (1987, p. 9) claims that "we are concerned with access and, more materially, indirect access to the information the user wants: he wants the information in the documents, but the system only gives him the documents." This statement represents a very ordinary view with roots back to the foundation of documentation and information science. This view is related to a positivist view of science. I shall try to analyze the consequences of this view and to present an alternative view. In positivism, facts are seen as the units of science.

Some of Paul Otlet's basic ideas—still visible in much contemporary research—are described by Rayward (1994) as the outmoded paradigm of nineteenth-century positivism:

Otlet's concern was for the objective knowledge that was both contained in and hidden by documents. His view of knowledge was authoritarian, reductionist, positivist, simplistic—and optimistic! . . . It is merely a question of institutionalizing certain processes for analyzing and organizing the content of documents. For him that aspect of the content of documents with which we must be concerned is facts. He speaks almost everywhere of *facts*. . . .

At first sight there is a startling contrast between what Otlet was writing about and what Landow and others who are interested in understanding hypertext in terms of modern critical theory are describing. But when posed in this way, the difference makes us look a little more closely at what some of the accounts of modern hypertext systems, especially in their grandiose, theoretical, "macrotext" manifestations, are actually saying. Is it possible that, despite the rhetorical flourishes, there is, deeply embedded in the accounts of some of these systems, what might be described as a "remainder" of nineteenth-century positivism? . . .

In describing the Xanadu Project, Nelson (1987) for example, in capital letters, says that it is "just one thing: a new form of interconnection for computer files—CORRE-SPONDING TO THE TRUE INTERCONNECTION OF IDEAS which can be refined and elaborated into a shared network" (p. 143). These words and the sentiments that they both express and seem to imply could be, except for the term "computer files," Otlet's own. They suggest an atavistic positivist perspective that takes one by surprise. (Rayward, 1994, pp. 247–248)

Of course, many people want the information contained in the documents, not the documents for their own sake. But, if you look around, fact retrieval systems as opposed to document retrieval systems are often rather primitive or constructed to a rather nonscholarly purpose. A researcher does not just ask for the facts (e.g., about cancer). He is asking for the documentation behind the facts, for the cognitive authority behind scientific claims, and so on. In short, he is not primarily asking for postulates about the truth about some matter, but he is asking about the truth—the worthiness or the substantiating—about some facts or, more common, about some strategies to cope with a certain problem area.

In the above point of view is hidden the importance of document retrieval. From this point of view, fact retrieval systems are just a kind of information system, one that is holding back or hiding information about the source of the claims about some facts or information. Fact retrieval systems do not allow dialog between the users and the producers of information; neither do they allow the user to question the methodology, basic theoretical assumptions, and so on.

This point of view is connected to modern changes in the concept of knowledge. According to the classical view, knowledge was an accumulation of something true, derived from either the senses (empiricism) or thinking (rationalism). According to modern comprehension (developed from the pragmatic philosophers among others), knowledge is more a collection of theories fulfilling some purpose for the living organisms. These theories are shaped in some contexts and from some assumptions. The production and evaluation of knowledge cannot be done by empiricism or rationalism alone, but by a combination, in addition to historical knowledge of the origin of the theories. Among other important modern views of knowledge is Kuhn's theory of science and its paradigms.

All this brings the documents and their content, not disconnected information, into focus. In fact, information systems, data archives, and so on, are themselves kinds of documents, metadocuments, or collections of documents; that is, they are containers of information (or rather, potential information) that have been designed to fulfill certain functions and that are created on given theoretical, economical, political, and cultural conditions.

A document does have a history, one or more authors or producers, a connection to other documents, and so on. All this is very well known and understood in many areas in the humanities, where there are disciplines such as the history of literature, criticism of documents (including films), and source criticism in history, but often less well understood in the technological fields.

It would be misleading to say that this difference is just due to the difference between the sciences and the arts, or between "hard" and "soft" disciplines. Of course there are important differences: The humanities are more "subjective," and the systems of documentation reflect these differences between knowledge domains. But to regard science as a cumulative process of collecting objective facts represents a positivistic/rationalistic ideal of science, which has had a dominating influence, but which has now been rejected by most serious philosophers of science.

Searching for Known Items versus Searching for Unknown Items

Another important distinction is between a known item search on the one side and on the other side identification of unknown documents, which have the potential of contributing to satisfy some kind of information need.

In order to facilitate the search for known items, databases describe documents according to so called descriptive bibliographical data. If you already have some data about a document, for example, author, title, publisher, or series, the descriptive cataloging allows you to use this information to identify the document in an unambiguous way. Fine and detailed standards such as the Anglo-American Cataloging Rules (AACR2) exist in order to make the input to databases well suited to such known item searching. The development and application of such descriptive expertise constitute an important part of the professional skills of librarians and information specialists.

Subject Retrieval

Most of the information-seeking tasks in libraries and databases can be called subject searches. In fact, most of the literature on information seeking and the concept of IR is concerned with subject searching. If what we call library and information science can be said to have a basic research problem at all, it is connected with information seeking and the possibilities for optimizing retrieval in databases—in other words, problems connected with subject searching.

But what do we mean by the concept of *subject searching*? *Informationsord-bogen* [*The Information Dictionary*] (1991) defines the concept in the follo-wing—rather traditional—way: "Subject searching (subject retrieval): Information seeking by means of subject data." *The Information Dictionary* views explicit descriptive data and subject data as opposites, which I do not—although they are traditionally viewed as such in library administration practices. There may be separate departments for descriptive cataloging and systematic cataloging. In my view these two types of data are overlapping categories. I do not agree with the dictionary's definition of subject searching, since descriptive data, for instance, titles and title words, are also often used in subject searches. Modern computer-based retrieval techniques make it possible to utilize every piece of information in a bibliographical record, in full-text records or links between records in information retrieval. The generic term for the kinds of information used in information retrieval is *subject access points*.

Typical subject access points in bibliographical databases include:

- words from titles[7]
- words from abstracts
- descriptors
- identifiers
- classification codes

- subject headings

- cited references (in citation searching)

- words from the text itself (in full-text searching)

For example, when a librarian or a user performs a subject search, say for literature on anorexia nervosa, many different types of data are used in the process. In a public library one can do the following: browse the shelves under the call numbers 61.642 and 13.7,[8] search an online catalog and look for titles under "anorexia" or "eating disorders," look for a familiar author's name in a database, look in the reference lists in the books one already has, check citation indexes to find out who is citing the authors one is already aware of, or use informal information channels. All of this represents various strategies of the same subject-searching task.

It is, of course, reasonable—although fairly formal—to claim that what we are talking about here are different types of searches: subject searching, title searching, author searching, citation searching, and so on, but it would be unnatural to say that what are described above are not different strategies in a subject search. The question can be clarified by defining the concept of *subject*, which will be discussed in Chapter 4. However, I will here anticipate the subject definition and claim that on the one hand, in a subject search we use classification codes and index terms, that is, explicit subject representations added to the bibliographic records by the library. On the other hand, in a subject search we also use title words, author names, literature references, and much more, some of which is traditionally called descriptive data, in contrast to subject data. Only if the different types of data are viewed in relation to their role in the same function (subject searching) will it be possible to develop theories and knowledge of the relative strengths and weaknesses of the various types of data in subject searching.

It is therefore necessary to define subject searching differently from the definition that, for instance, *The Information Dictionary* uses. It is central to the concept of subject searching that we are (1) dealing with searching for unknown documents or information sources, using content-related criteria and (2) searching for documents which will contribute to clarifying a certain problem or satisfying a certain information need.

Subject searching is a kind of information seeking but one in contrast to searching for documents that are known to the user (known item search) or documents for which he or she already has some information, for instance, author, title, publisher, or series, which has nothing to do with the content of the document. We can claim that looking for information about the books published by Greenwood Press or the books written by a particular author represents an information-seeking task, but we cannot claim that it is a subject-searching task.

If a user wants to find a book in a catalog and remembers only certain things about it, for instance, that it was published by Danish Psychological Publishers (DPP), the publisher's name is used as a kind of verification, not as a subject search. But if a user wants to review the psychological literature published in Denmark, or wants to examine all the publications from DPP and uses the field for publisher as a search argument in the database search, the name of the publisher becomes a part of the search argument in a subject search.[9]

Subject searching is thus not limited to the particular data that are produced exclusively for subject searching. But subject searching and other types of searches use overlapping data categories. Document titles are used a great deal, for instance, in automated catalogs (title words in free-text searching) for subject-searching tasks, but the same data are also frequently used for searching for a particular document where the title is known.

One important conclusion is the following: There is no sharp borderline between subject access points (or subject access data) and other kinds of access data. What are the most relevant access points depends on the nature of the question at hand. The core problem of IS is to help searchers optimize the given information and to help system designers to optimize the amount of work put into database building. The core problem is a theory about explicit and implicit subject representation.

Theories in IS should not build on restrictions imposed by either the paper-based publication system or by databases with limited amounts of data, such as typical bibliographical databases, citation indexes, and so on. The existence of full-text databases, the possibility of making hypermedia links to other records in other databases, and possible value-added information to full-text records should be regarded as the preconditions for scientific and theoretical studies in modern IS.

In this ocean of electronic texts, links, and value-added information, what is then the basic problem of information retrieval? This is broadly recognized—I think—as being to facilitate information transfer to the users (cf. Ingwersen, 1992). Traditional areas of IS include classification, indexing, knowledge representation, information seeking, search logic, and relevance judgments. All these traditional problems must of course be reconsidered in the new reality consisting of full-text retrieval, the World Wide Web, and so on. From our perspective, the basic problem of IS must be reformulated as: How do we measure the informational value of different subject access points in databases (or in systems of connected databases)? This is closely related to theories of meaning and semantics and could be termed *database semantics*.

A full-text record consists of elements such as title, abstracts, introduction, methodology, results, conclusion, and references. When is it fruitful to use words from titles as subject access points? When is it fruitful to use the words in abstracts or the words in some section of the complete text record? When is it fruitful to use descriptors and classifications? (That is value-added information added by information professionals). When do references represent a useful access point, as utilized in citation indexes? How can the name of the journal in which the paper is published be used in IR? How are single papers connected implicitly or explicitly and how can knowledge about these connections be utilized in information seeking? Table 2.2 shows some of the possible subject access points for a typical scientific article. According to the basic view formulated in this book, there exist different epistemological views (presented in Chapter 4), and each view implies different standards or ideals regarding the structure of documents. Thus a typical empiricist article reflects the development of the empiricist research tradition.[10]

Of course, real-life information seeking always involves a combination of many different subject access points. Online IR is really an art, where trained information specialists use a lot of skills and talent.[11] A major problem for IS is to formulate more explicit theories and knowledge about how different access points are utilized and combined by competent searchers—and how competent subject analysts can produce value-added information to representations of documents.

In bibliographic databases documents are represented as records in files. A typical bibliographic database, such as PsycINFO, provides, among others, the following fields and subject access points in each record: Title (/TI); Descriptor (/DE); Identifier (/ID) and Abstracts (/AB). Other databases provide other fields and access points, where full text and citations are theoretically the most important. Each field contains a different meaning and has a different informational value. Together they extend the search possibilities. An example:

Table 2.2
Structure and Elements in a Typical Scientific Article

Norms of scientific method and philosophy of science external to the article	Elements contained in the article	Value-added information (Subject access points, access and evaluation information)
	Bibliographical identification (journal name, volume number, pages) Title Author(s) with corporate affiliation and address Author abstract (Author keywords) Introduction Apparatus and materials Method Results Discussion Conclusion (Acknowledgments) References	Bibliographical description Relations to other editions Identifier Biographical information Institutional information Indexer abstracts Indexer descriptors Classification codes Language codes Document type codes Editorial comments Links to citing papers, reviews, and criticism Information about availability of document
Observation and description Problem statement Hypothesis Experiment Theory building		

S1	2130	ANOREXIA/TI
S2	2455	ANOREXIA/ID
S3	2758	ANOREXIA/DE
S4	3155	ANOREXIA/AB
S5	3909	ANOREXIA
S6	3909	S1 OR S2 OR S3 OR S4

The general heuristic lesson from this example is that you can increase recall by moving down among these possibilities, and you can increase precision by moving up among them.[12] Such heuristics is not, however, without problems. It is not just a question of getting more or less, but what kinds of studies are selected. Other words have different meanings and can have different distributions. The differences are, for example, much more important and exaggerated if we search the word "female":

S7	128336	FEMALE?
S8	10800	FEMALE?/TI
S9	23483	FEMALE?/DE
S10	73029	FEMALE?/ID
S11	87693	FEMALE?/AB

Female has another distribution because sex is a formal research variable often mentioned in abstracts and identifiers, even if this question is not the central issue in other respects. It is important to know the conventions used by the people producing the respective fields. For example, methods and experimental variables are often mentioned in the ID field, but not as often in the title. When a term, for example, "burnout" is not official, but a kind of slang, it is often used in titles, but never in descriptors (the adequate descriptor in this database is "occupational stress"):

S12	1148	BURNOUT/TI
S13	1261	BURNOUT/ID
S14	0	BURNOUT/DE
S15	996	BURNOUT/AB

Trained human searchers can interpret meanings in search terms and use them in IR in ways which algorithms cannot. Information retrieval has to develop a theory which takes content, meaning, and semantics into account. Universal quantitative relations among kinds of terms or codes are not sufficient.

One basic principle in database semantics is that no kind of subject access point can be evaluated in isolation, but should be evaluated in the context of the full range of existing access points. For example, there is no need to add descriptors to records if they do not contribute to increasing retrieval effectiveness. Another basic principle is that the measurement or evaluation of single subject access points in naturalistic surroundings must precede any systems development. You cannot formulate design priorities for information systems if you do not know the informational value of, say, abstracts or references. The relative value of such elements as abstracts, titles, references, and so on, forms part of a much broader area than the artificial elements such as descriptors and classification symbols created by information professionals. The foundation of IS therefore lies in types of documents and structures in and between documents, where documents are regarded in their functionality as information sources to user groups.

The question whether a text is an optimal representation of itself raises new questions such as What are we using subject access points for? What are we trying to identify? Who are the users? What is the "subject" of a document? Is it something objective and inherent in the document? Or is it something subjective, seen in the documents by the individual user? These questions imply deep philosophical problems. But if we have no answer to these questions, our judgment of relevance and hence our measurement of recall and precision are unsupported.

This brief discussion has shown that clarifying the basic concepts is not a trivial task. Furthermore, it shows that these basic concepts have great theoretical consequences for the theory of information seeking. Even if information seeking is a key problem in the library, documentation, and information field, the theoretical literature on this problem seems to have inadequate links to central theoretical foundations in science studies, philosophy, and psychology. This is why the basic concepts and theories of information seeking often remain formalistic, atheoretical, and technology-fixated.

SUBJECT REPRESENTATION DATA

At this point I will define *subject data* as data whose intended or unintended function is to aid information searchers in identifying relevant documents using content-related criteria. I will call subject data *explicit subject data* when they were produced for the purpose of subject searching. If the data were not directly produced for the purpose of subject searching, the data will be called *implicit subject data*. In other words, subject data is a broader concept than, for example, call numbers, descriptors, index terms, subject words, title words, abstract words, full-text words, and so on. My conception of subject data is thus broader than *The Information Dictionary*'s in that I include both data that directly (explicitly) aim at subject searching and data that in fact aid in subject-searching tasks, even if they might have been produced for other purposes. In my opinion types or categories of subject data are synonymous with the concept of information retrieval language, which was introduced to information science by Calvin Mooers in 1951. This concept emphasizes that types of subject data should be evaluated in relation to their function in the search process.

Next I will discuss *the functions of subject data*. These functions should be viewed against the background of the development of information technology. Back when libraries used printed catalog cards, subject data were often in practice limited to, for instance, Dewey Decimal call numbers, perhaps supplemented by a subject index system that made it possible to create cross-references to groups of call numbers or to individual documents. In the era of automated systems these possibilities have expanded considerably. On the one hand, several data categories function as subject data (e.g., title words in online systems); on the other hand, libraries and other information systems often exchange subject data. An example is the Royal Library in Copenhagen, which receives bibliographic records with Dewey and LC call numbers, PRECIS-subject strings, and so on, from abroad to supplement its own subject data.

Library subject data have never been able to meet all user needs, nor will they ever do so. First, libraries rarely analyze articles in journals or collected works (which is taken care of by so-called document databases). Second, their subject data level is much lower than in, for instance, disciplinary document databases. Only lately have we—thanks to the fact that full-text databases have entered the scene—begun to guess how far we must go in order to reach a level of subject representation that is satisfactory on the disciplinary level and that matches what a well-developed electronic communication system can offer.

There are several concurrent tendencies in this technological development. The most important one is that the automated systems are developing extremely rapidly. This has direct, multidimensional consequences for our subject data problems:

1. The potential size of a bibliographic record in a bibliographic database is growing.

2. More documents will become available in full-text databases.

3. Different types of databases, for example, bibliographic databases, full-text databases, review databases, citation databases, and dictionary databases, can be found within the same information system, and they can be made searchable and linked through registers, references, and so on.

4. Retrieval techniques will be improved. Hypertext is one such important development.

The fact that the content of the records can grow, and that full-text records are becoming more common, does not mean that intellectual subject analysis of documents is made redundant. Experiments performed in, for example, full-text medical databases (McKinin et al., 1991) show that fulltext databases significantly increase retrieval rates, but precision is not as great when searching full-text databases as when searching databases containing descriptor fields with, for example, thesaurus-based indexing. In addition, it is important to remember that a considerable number of documents can be identified only through indexed databases. Such results show—along with theoretical analyses—that the subjects of documents are not only "semantic condensations"[13] of those documents (as is often claimed in the literature). A document does not necessarily contain explicit information about its own subject, and it may be necessary to add this by performing an intellectual subject analysis. But it is of course imperative to evaluate the function of subject data in light of the new situation: explicit subject data should—in order to be worthwhile—*supplement* the information in the document data, which are (or become) searchable (either as title, abstract, SAP indexing,[14] or full text).

Subject data that do not keep up with the technical development or the environment in which it exists may hurt more than help. Larson (1991) reveals that the use of the LCSH (Library of Congress subject headings) is decreasing in some settings, while at the same time the use of title word searching is increasing in the same online catalogs. It is assumed that two circumstances contribute to this tendency: the users' problems formulating queries using LCSH and problems with overload. This example shows that it is absolutely necessary to reevaluate the quality and functionality of given subject data in light of the technological development: subject data may be wasted effort and an unnecessary cost, bringing more noise than information to the retrieval process.

A natural evolution would be to improve monograph records with tables of contents, introductions, cover texts, and so on. SAP indexing is such an example. This kind of information does not have to be added by several different institutions (e.g., if every library were to add this information to the records). Rather, it would be more appropriate if such data found in the document itself were to be viewed as a form of document data and be edited or registered by the descriptive cataloging performed by the national libraries. It would, in other words, be extracted by the authority that performs the subject analysis, which could then focus on the real subject analysis.

In the literature on this topic, subject data are often viewed as document surrogates or condensations (see, e.g., Hutchins, 1978). I would like to argue against this position. I acknowledge that subject data sometimes function as document surrogates. A user who stands in front of a card catalog or looks in a bibliography does not have immediate access to the document itself, and subject data serve the function of providing some information about the contents of the document. Such a function is justified in some (especially manual) circumstances, but if the function of the subject data is limited to this, it will be redundant when we have electronic communication between scientists, full-text databases, and so on. When a journal editor receives a scientist's manuscript, the editing and acceptance process adds value-added information, and later information workers add more value-added information, among other things subject data. None of these processes will (or should) be made redundant by the technological development. I therefore conclude in respect to the functions of subject data that:

1. the real (deepest) function of subject data is to give the information seeker information about the document that might aid in the retrieval process (and which may not necessarily be present in the document itself or in the way it has been registered descriptively). Often subject data are identical with the concepts in the document, but that may be coincidence or selection. Such selection ("extraction") is also an expression of the fact that information has been added to the record!

2. subject data sometimes have the (additional) function of being document surrogates or condensations; that is, for practical reasons the subject data simply repeat document information, because it is practical to duplicate the same information.

This division corresponds to a division made by Soergel (1985) into need-oriented versus content-oriented indexing, which has been an important source of inspiration for my theory. It is of course not a question of clearly delimited categories, but of overlapping functions that can be isolated only on the theoretical level. The content-oriented school of thought has dominated so far. One of the main goals of this book is to thoroughly reconsider the need-oriented school of thought.

Technological development will lead to more information about a given document becoming available in electronically searchable format, for example, introductions, reference lists, tables of contents, subtitles, and cover texts, and eventually full text. This information can be linked to reviews, notes, citing papers, and so on in a hypertext-based system. We can easily imagine that in the future parts of this information will be found in the descriptive part of the records in, for example, the national bibliography. This would be a rational approach that would take care of the problem once and for all, whereas SAP indexing (see Wormell, 1985 and Poulsen, 1987) presupposes that each library includes this information.

If we suppose that bibliographic records are being "born" with information like tables of contents and cover texts, the explicit subject data function is cleared of presenting data that serve other than the real purpose: to identify documents that meet potential user needs through content-oriented criteria, unless these are already clear from the record.[15] The fact that subject data in practice serve the function of semantic condensations (the importance of which will be reduced by the new information technology) has, in my opinion, contributed to a theoretical blockage within the discipline. Therefore, subject data are often perceived as semantic condensations of documents.

In printed bibliographies and abstract publications, subject data are often limited to the tables of contents (classification schemes) and indexes based on subject words or descriptors. In online abstract publications many of the data elements are subject data; the most important ones are—besides descriptors and classification codes—title words and abstract words (used, for example, for Boolean searches, searches using proximity operators, or string searching).

In citation indexes the document reference lists are included and made searchable. That is, the explicit references (and in the Arts and Humanities Citation Index partly also the implicit ones) in the indexed documents are potential subject data.

Gradually more documents will become available in full-text, machine-readable form. Examples of already existing documents are the Bible, encyclopedias and dictionaries, chemical books, many newspapers, and selected journals in some disciplines. In such full-text databases the whole document text constitutes potential subject data.

It is of course a very important task for library and information science to examine how this wide range of subject data can be optimized. The relative strengths and weaknesses of individual subject data need to be examined, as well as their levels of mutual overlapping and supplementing, economy and user-friendliness,[16] suitability within various disciplines, and so on. This is not the place to delve any deeper into these questions, but I will briefly examine some broader theoretical aspects.

Many library debates start with the question Should we have "classification" or "verbal subject words?" and "Which system should we use?" I think it is important that these questions are viewed within the framework of a more coherent theory on subject, subject analysis, and subject representation: we should of course have the systems or "languages" that are most efficient in terms of retrieval. I will later show that the most important factor in making retrieval an efficient process is adequate subject analysis. The most important characteristic of an IR language is its ability to express the results of the subject analysis. It seems that the debate more often deals with formal than with substantial questions regarding IR languages, as if we cannot disregard the concrete, existing system when thinking about these problems.

The subject of a document can be expressed in various ways, in various information retrieval languages, for instance, in the title, through classification schemes, via controlled or uncontrolled subject words, and so on. These languages have distinct characteristics, which library and information professionals need to be familiar with. An example of this is the well-known fact that classification schemes may consist of smaller or larger numbers of classes, and this might limit how precisely the subject(s) of a document can be expressed.

IR languages also have other characteristics. Verbal subject data are more user-friendly because they are easier to remember than codes. In contrast, they do not display structure, and the similarity between everyday language and subject words can lead the user to believe that the system uses the concepts in the way that he is used to. Verbal subject data are popular and considered user-friendly because most users do not aim for complete searches, and perhaps because of certain ideological tendencies.

Indexing systems are often considered "open," while classification systems are "closed." It is true that it is possible to construct more or less open indexing systems (it is a question of control, for example, how the conceptual content of the indexing terms is defined). The more open a system is, the less consistency there will be in the indexing.

I do not consider the most profound difference in IR languages to be the traditional division into classification and indexing. Every classification can be viewed as indexing, and each indexing can be viewed as classification, which is also emphasized by the fact that under certain conditions a classification system can be made into a thesaurus and the other way around. This type of work has been carried out in connection with, for instance, the Bliss system (Aitchison, 1986) and with the Universal Decimal Classification (UDC) (Riesthuis, 1991). This does not mean that what traditionally is called classification is the same as verbal indexing. Traditional classification is characterized by a top-down analysis of a knowledge domain, while most of the verbal systems build upon document terms, and they are bottom-up analyses. I do not claim that the differences are completely insignificant, but the differences are subordinate when compared to other aspects of subject data.

An important feature of the traditional classification systems that has been partly lost in the descriptor-based systems is the possibility of illustrating concepts in a general way. A classification system is traditionally divided in the following way:

Subject X in general
Aspect 1 of X
Aspect 2 of X
:
:
Aspect n of X
Other aspects of X

If one is not interested in aspects 2, 3, and n of X, these can be left out of the search, whereas in a descriptor-based system it is difficult to enumerate all the descriptors that cover the aspects that one has no interest in, since they are not included as being related to X, and one cannot get an overview of them. For instance, it is difficult to find literature on "Developing countries in general" in a descriptor-based system, for example, literature that not only provides information on a variety of problems in developing countries—such as, corruption, inflation, drought—but also gives general knowledge of developing countries.

Kaae (1990, pp. 45–46) discusses the use of the subject word "Denmark" in connection with all Danish localities in order to be able to search under a concept. He writes that "By using 'Denmark' it would not be possible to limit the literature that only treats the topic in/for the whole of Denmark." In this example a solution might be to operate with two descriptors: "Denmark in general" and "Places in Denmark." The last mentioned would always be supplemented by a more specific place descriptor. Such an option implies searches on the general as well as on the specific level. This last type of descriptor is rarely used, even if it means that some of the advantages of classification could be transferred to the verbal format.

The most profound difference is, in my opinion, between controlled and uncontrolled subject data systems. In a controlled system the document subject is expressed by a choice among a finite number of categories. In an uncontrolled system the document subject is expressed as a choice among a—practically speaking—nonfinite number of categories (all combinations of all the words in the language). In a controlled system the user has to choose among the given categories. The task is to familiarize oneself with all the categories and choose the one that comes closest to the epistemological interest. This advantage is, however, counteracted by the drawback that all documents are placed under existing categories, which cannot cope with the special aspects in the documents in hand. For example, a document about "burnout" has to be indexed under "occupational stress." The content of this category might therefore have low specificity. In an uncontrolled system there is no way for the user to obtain a general grasp of the categories that have been used, and it is impossible to systematically identify the most relevant categories. This is, of course, first of all a problem for the searcher, but it is reinforced by the fact that not even the indexers who are choosing the categories have an overview of the system, and thus there are no guidelines. The categories are used differently from case to case. If, for instance, a controlled system contains one class called "psychology" and another class called "psychiatry," the system will offer a definition that the indexers can choose among when determining the categories (it does not matter whether it is called "61.642" or "psychiatry," that is, if it is expressed verbally or in code). But in an uncontrolled system it is up to the individual indexer and his or her more or less incidental interpretations of the concepts. The categories will therefore not be scientifically exact, but will reflect the ambiguousness of everyday language. But there are two advantages. First, the user does not have to be familiar with any specific codes or specified prescribed meanings, and he can express himself spontaneously. Second, we avoid some of the overcrowding that is the result of having to squeeze a document into a category when a choice has to be made among a limited number of categories. Both theory and practical search experience tell us that controlled and uncontrolled IR languages supplement each other and that both are needed. The controlled languages are a rigid filter that ensures basic classification, while the uncontrolled are a more flexible form of expression. But it is necessary to study more closely how they supplement each other and whether both types are as important within all knowledge domains.

In up-to-date automated systems several subject descriptions of the same document can be found side by side in the same record. Both theory and experience tell us that there is no upper limit as to how many subject data can be added: more new subject data will allow better recall and precision (the latter on the condition that they can be deselected). But there are of course practical and economical limits for how much is worth doing. The boundaries keep shifting as the existing technology and the possibilities for data capture improve. But the crucial point is not the number of different subject descriptions, but the quality of the subject data. Later I will explore how the quality of the subject data depends on the subject analysis, on implicit or explicit epistemological interests, and on how well the IR language expresses the results of the subject analysis. We can easily imagine records (and encounter them in real life) that contain a mass of low-quality subject data that do more harm than good.

The context plays an important role for subject data in databases. When articles that were written in a particular context are included in a database with other articles, the original context is moved back and information is lost. If an article about dreams was published in a psychoanalytically oriented journal, the word *psychoanalysis* is probably not used in the title of the article, and this implicit information disappears when a title search is performed in the database (in practice the journal title is rarely included in a search, even if there is no technical obstacle to doing it). The same thing happens when subject data are transferred from special libraries to big shared databases: special libraries often utilize implicit information that cannot be transferred directly to the shared systems. However, if one is aware of it, one can do something to find this implicit information. If a psychology library uses a class called "stress," this implies that this category probably contains documents on stress seen from a psychological, not a physiological or engineering, point of view.

A technical library does not have the same need to differentiate the social science literature as does a social science library. It will tend to use very unspecified terms (e.g., sociology). This is a problem if the records are pooled in a shared database.

Today we are at a crossroads in terms of subject data. Many large research libraries do not know which path to choose (disregarding the fact that the tendency is toward verbal subject data). The theory of information science has been marked by theoretical difficulties, among other things the fact that much of the research has focused on cognitivistic theories that attach importance to subjective and individual analysis of information needs, rather than on analysis of epistemological interests based on theory of science. This will be discussed later in more depth.

As to the discipline-specific IR languages, their quality varies a great deal. Quite often there are serious deficiencies in the dominating thesauri, but since they are being developed by large organizations, it is impossible to compete with them. These systems, therefore, in reality offer a de facto standard that cannot be neglected. This does not mean that one cannot develop other systems outside the dominating organizations. But what it does mean is that all development needs to be based on and take into account this reality.

Before I leave subject data and move on to subject analysis, I will briefly formulate some important distinctions among types of subject data.

Subject data may be in the document itself or may be found outside of it. Title words, abstract words, reference lists, and full-text words are examples of subject data that are contained in the document itself. If it were true that these document data always provide 100 percent satisfaction as subject data, there would be no need for library subject analysis and subject descriptions of individual documents.

Many printed bibliographies (e.g., ERIC) use the title of the documents in their subject index, so that under a given subject word you find both the document title and a number that refers to the main entry of the bibliography. In other bibliographies (e.g., in Psychological Abstracts) document titles are considered too vague and meaningless, and instead of them specially developed index phrases are used, which are a kind of title surrogate. Such index phrases are an example of how the indexer has added to the index such information that cannot be found in the document itself (so-called value-added service).

It is obviously important to clarify to what extent—if at all—document enrichment as to subject is going to be necessary in the electronic communication environment of the future. Earlier I referred to Hutchins's perception that subject description is simply a form of semantic condensation of a document text. If this is true, there will be no need for library-based subject enrichment of bibliographic records. If subject description is going to serve a purpose, it needs to add such information to the record that does not already exist in the document or in the bibliographic records issued by other authorities.

Subject data can be either explicit or implicit. Classification codes and descriptors are examples of explicit subject data. If, on the other hand, a publisher is called the Danish Psychology Press, the field for publisher in the bibliographic record will contain implicit subject data. Similarly, journal titles can be used as implicit subject data. The document text itself—if viewed as subject data—may vary from the explicit to the implicit. A document text typically contains data that can be regarded as explicit subject data, and other data that can be regarded as implicit subject data. The more implicit something is, the more interpretation is required by the information searcher or the indexer, and the more difficult it is to automate the search function. (For a further analysis of this dimension, see Nystrand & Wiemelt, 1991.)

Subject data can be either verbal or symbolic. Title words, abstract words, document words, subject words, and descriptors are examples of verbal subject data. Classification symbols (codes) are examples of symbolic subject data. There is no sharp boundary between verbal and coded subject data, since professional language can be said to be a kind of a code, and language in general has "symbolic" meaning. Nevertheless, the distinction is of importance for the construction of information systems. Verbal and symbolic subject data have different qualities as to retrieval performance as well as to user-friendliness.

Subject data may be either predominantly content-oriented or need-oriented, a distinction developed by Soergel (1985).[17] Later we will see that this distinction has extremely important consequences for the perception of subject data, subject analysis, and the concept of subject itself. A document should not only be analyzed in and of itself, but should be analyzed from the point of view of what questions it might answer. Foskett formulates it in the following way:

At the indexing stage we are trying to foresee ways in which users may later wish to find a document; at the searching stage we are trying to achieve a better match between our formulation of the query and that used by the indexer or author to define his approach. It should be remembered that every document is in effect the answer to a question that may—or may not—be posed in the future. The librarian is in the strange but fortunate position of being able to say: We have all the answers—what are the questions? (Foskett, 1982, p. 84)

The notion that a text always should be understood in terms of its own interpretative possibilities has been well illustrated in modern hermeneutics, for instance by Gadamer.[18] But Gadamers ideas have, as far as I know, never been discussed in association with subject data problems.

Subject data may be more or less normative/critical or nonevaluative. This item is closely connected with the need-oriented indexing that was discussed above. To the extent that subject data only reflect the point of view of the document itself and its concepts, it is difficult to meet the needs of the users. This point is central in a theory concerning the possibilities and boundaries of automated subject analysis of documents.

Last, subject descriptions may be more or less "objective" (intersubjective) or "subjective." Since literature often requires very specific qualifications before its epistemological potential can be understood, attempts to describe the features of a document that most easily can be understood by many people (i.e., the "objective" features) often lead to a focus on the more trivial features of the document than on the more important ones. Such a search for facts at the expense of interpretation is associated with positivism.

For some of the logical positivists the ideal was to be able to perform scientific descriptions using space-time coordinates. Positivists have a tendency to break up general concepts, because of a desire to verify the concepts by concretizing them. What I earlier called "objective" subject descriptions correspond to the positivist tendency to give priority to the factual at the expense of theoretical considerations, the generalized, and the intellectualized. Elsewhere (Hjørland, 1990a, p. 64) I have criticized the fairly widespread use of the concepts of "subjective" and "objective." I prefer—in the tradition of Habermas and many others (e.g., Hortsmann, 1990)—to call the fact-fixation of positivism "objectivism," and I make a sharp distinction between objectivity and objectivism. When one is performing a subject description there might be good reasons for looking for the factual, the concrete, the objectivist, but there might also be good—and perhaps better—reasons for trying to see its limitations.

CONCLUSION

Above I have presented a new conceptual apparatus and a new way of thinking about subject data, and I have connected subject data with philosophical epistemology and the theory of science.

The ideal subject data optimize the performance of retrieval systems. When we attempt to measure this we call it the evaluation of information retrieval. An important objective for information science is to be able to measure or estimate the information value of various subject data in the search process. One of the central issues in terms of evaluating subject data and retrieval systems is the concept of relevance. The concept of relevance is difficult, and we shall return to it later. However, it can be fruitful to look at its opposition: nonrelevance. It is relatively easy in a given search set to determine different kinds of non-relevance; for example, "false drops," wrong word meanings, too specific investigations, problematic research methods, lack of perspective or horizon, implications that are politically problematic, documents which are too time-demanding to use for different reasons, lack of confidence in some authors, and so on. In this way, research in the concept of relevance is related to research in the citing behavior of authors (discussed in Chapter 6) and the theory of database semantics is connected to how information is used and ultimately to epistemological theories about the sources of knowledge.

I have now briefly discussed the concepts of subject searching and subject data and called attention to some fundamental distinctions of subject data. The quality of subject data determines the quality of the subject search. The quality of explicit subject data is determined by how they are created. I will now move on to look at how explicit subject data are created in the process that is called subject analysis.

NOTES

1. Retrieve is derived from the French verb *retrouver*, "to find again," according to *Webster's Ninth Collegiate Dictionary* (1987).

2. Maturana's theory is introduced in Winograd & Flores (1987).

3. Pure individual information-seeking behavior is an abstraction. All kinds of information seeking is, more or less, formed by sociohistorical conditions. Locating a restaurant or gathering mushrooms implies a knowledge about what restaurants or mushrooms are, where to expect to find them, and so on.

4. Semiotics (or semiology) is the study of signs. Among the founders of this discipline—or rather of this cross-disciplinary area—we must highlight the Swiss linguist Ferdinand de Saussure (1857–1913) and the American philosophers Charles S. Peirce (1839–1914) and Charles Morris (1901–1979). Semiotics is a multidisciplinary area grounded in linguistics, philosophy, psychology, and sociology. Within it you can find the same basic assumptions as in the founding disciplines: for example, positivism, behaviorism, structuralism, cognitivism, pragmatism, and historical materialism. Saussure defined semiology as "the study of the social life of the sign in society," but in reality, semiotics has seldom provided such a social analysis. (For a critique of a cognitivist semiotics, see Petrilli, 1993).

A few textbooks and expositions of information science are built on a theoretical framework imported from semiotics, for example, Liebenau and Backhouse (1990). A kind of related work is Bøgh Andersen (1990). A very valuable semiotic dictionary (covering many concepts of relevance for information science) is Sebeok (1994).

5. A third possibility is that the librarian delivers a bibliographical reference to the text, leaving it to the user to decide, how and when to get the document. This is what most modern information retrieval systems do. For this discussion, the second and third possibilities are both regarded as document retrieval.

6. The demand that retrieval systems should provide answers as they are currently known by science or mankind implies that they face the problems of information authority, of evaluation, and of selection. Information retrieval is thus not just a technical problem, but an intellectual problem.

7. Since titles are very fundamental and important subject access points, research on the informativity of titles is important. Yitzhaki (1996) represents an example of research on this issue. He includes analysis of applications of significant title words in different domains and their developments in time. More research of this kind is fundamental if we

are to develop a knowledge base for information seeking. It should contain information that provides the information seeker with relevant information in his or her decision-making process during searching.

8. These call numbers refer to the Danish Dewey Decimal System (DK5).

9. However, it would not be possible to use Greenwood as a search argument in a subject search, since the name does not limit the subject: this publisher does not specialize in a subject area.

10. An example of an important charter document for the writing of scientific documents is *Publication Manual of the American Psychological Association* (1994). This manual reflects one particular epistemological point of view. It is not universally accepted as the only correct way to compose psychological documents. Vipond (1993, pp. 55–76) is a discussion of this manual and the philosophy behind it. Further debate can be found in Madigan, Johnson, & Linton (1995); Josselson & Lieblich (1996); Brand (1996); Vipond (1996), and Madigan, Linton, & Johnson (1996).

A more detailed discussion of the structure of scientific literature is given in the literature about genre analysis (e.g., Malmkjær, 1995c, pp. 176–181) and about composition studies (see the bibliography in Nystrand, Greene, & Wiemelt, 1993).

11. A recommended textbook on online retrieval is Harter (1986).

12. Recall is the number of relevant documents retrieved in relation to the total number of relevant records in a database. Recall = a : (a+c) x 100%, where a is the number of retrieved relevant documents, and c is the number of nonretrieved relevant documents (sometimes c is called "silence"). Precision is the number of relevant documents retrieved in relation to all retrieved records. Precision = a : (a+b) x 100%, where b is the number of retrieved nonrelevant documents (sometimes b is called "noise"). These measures were first introduced in information science by C. W. Cleverdon et al. (1966) in the Cranfield II experiments.

13. I argue that subject data are more than semantic condensations of documents. The concepts of *semantics* and *meaning* are controversial, deeply philosophical concepts. The meaning of a text and a word varies by the interpreters of the text and the word. In a way one can say that subject data represent a certain semantic interpretation and condensation. I am opposed to the notion of subject data as a concentration of the document itself on its own premises, since this means that the author's interpretation of the document forms the basis for it. This problem will be discussed in detail in Chapter 4.

14. SAP indexing (the initials come from Subject Access Project) is a new kind of indexing developed at Syracuse University in New York (Atherton, 1978).

15. Subject data should add information to the record. It may be necessary to repeat in another field data that already exist in the record. It is nevertheless a question of adding new information to the record. This is the case especially when metaphorical language is used. A book on psychotherapy is called, for example, *A Return Ticket to the Garbage Can*. It is not about garbage cans. An article is called "The Conflict Between Egypt and Israel: A Nightmare in Modern Politics," but it is not about the psychological concept of nightmares. If one is looking for literature on garbage cans or nightmares such titles are noise. The information seeker needs to consider whether it would be better not to search in the title field in order to improve the precision of the search. But if the search is not performed in the title field, it is necessary that the words *garbage can* and *nightmare* be repeated as subject words, if the words in the title are used in the literal sense. Otherwise they would not be found through searches that exclude title searching. Repetition of information from a document in another field represents an addition of

information to the record (that is, if it is done as a result of interpretation, and not mechanically). This principle is correctly understood and described in Kaae (1990), but not always evident in the subject data debate.

16. Information systems should of course be user-friendly. To claim the opposite would be absurd. A lack of user-friendliness may be the same as a lack of functionality and performance; it may result from a lack of documentation, low accessibility both physically and intellectually, incorrect ideas about the users and their needs, and so on.

The degree of user-friendliness often means weighing cost versus performance. But user-friendliness may also be an expression of a real dilemma between various alternatives, which separately are desirable. There is a widespread ideological desire that information systems should be so easy to use that one does not need to invest very much time in the learning process. This often happens at the expense of long-term and efficient solutions.

17. The distinction that Soergel makes between content and need orientation can, according to Lancaster (1991, p. 8), be traced to Dabney (1986) and is also implicit in Cooper's (1978) "gedanken" approach.

18. The German philosopher Hans-Georg Gadamer (b. 1900) has—most importantly in his main work *Wahrheit und Methode* (*Truth and Method*) from 1960—presented a significant theory of texts and their interpretation. Gadamer is known as one of the leading hermeneutic philosophers. According to him a text can never be said to be interpreted in a definitive way. Every new culture, community, or generation has to start over and interpret anew. The text or sign reveals itself again and again through new aspects of meaning, that is, as increasingly new answers to new questions, which are born when increasingly new fusions of horizons are created through the historical process of which our interpretation is a part. However, *it is the same text* that the author, earlier interpreters, we, and future interpreters are reading.

Gadamer is on the one hand opposed to the notion that a text has a meaning "in itself," regardless of any interpretation. It is therefore an illusion to talk about an "ideal" interpretation of the text, such as it is "in itself." Even if one perceives this ideal as something we can only approach, but never quite reach, we are talking about an illusion. On the other hand, however, Gadamer also wants to avoid ending up in relativistic subjectivism. Relativism is, according to Gadamer, objectivism turned upside down, on the principle that if there is no objectivity which exists independently of the interpretations, then every interpretation is equally good and everything is relative. Hence we can say anything about anything.

A text only "exists" because it can be a part of possible interpretations. Or if we absolutely want to talk about what the text is "in itself," then we have to say that in itself the text is identical to the whole spectrum of meanings that all earlier, current, and future interpreters can find in the text.

The text, like everything else, must be experienced within a horizon (a set of problems, a worldview, an understanding) that gives itself through the truth processes (*Wahrheitsgeschehen*) of the interpretations. Outside these frameworks it is meaningless to speak of the text being something in itself.

This hermeneutical view of interpretation shares important qualities with the ideas of the pragmatic philosopher John Dewey. Hilary Putnam—following Quine's concept of semantic holism—has also argued that there are no facts about the meaning of a text.

3

Subject Analysis
and Knowledge Organization

TERMINOLOGICAL INTRODUCTION

The concept of *subject analysis* is well established to denote the analysis of documents in indexing and classification, but other terminology has also been used in the library and information science (LIS) literature. The famous Cranfield Project (1966) used *content analysis*, and the same terminology is used in the earliest volumes of *Annual Review of Information Science and Technology*, or ARIST (cf. Fairthorne, 1969). Lancaster (1991, p. 10) remarks that he prefers to call it *conceptual analysis* (but the same author also uses subject analysis, e.g., in Lancaster, Elliker, & Connell, 1989). The thesaurus to the INSPEC database applies the expression *information analysis* to denote indexing and classification of documents. The expression *aboutness analysis* has been used rather widely. Particularly within the field of linguistics (and computational linguistics), the concept of *text analysis* is being used, while *content analysis* is used, for example, in the social sciences. Subject analysis, however, seems to be the commonly agreed upon terminology within the LIS field.

In my opinion, text analysis and content analysis can be undertaken for different purposes, but the purpose of subject analysis is always retrieval; that is, it implies some kind of relevance evaluation in relation to a more or less specific objective. Examples of content analyses are ideology analyses in mass media and textbooks (e.g., gender role stereotypes). Text analysis that is performed in linguistics typically includes analyses of text structures. Subject analysis is a form of content analysis and therefore a subgroup of it. As I define it, subject analysis is the intellectual or automated process of analyzing the subjects of a document (or an information source) and the subsequent expression of this analysis as subject representation data.

THEORETICAL OUTLINE

A theory of subject analysis clearly needs a theory of subject. At present, there is no consensus regarding this matter in LIS, but I will discuss it in more detail in the next chapter of this book. One of the few books discussing subject analysis is Langridge (1989). However, he does not treat the concept of subject very extensively. Langridge writes (pp. 5–6) that *content analysis* would be a more inclusive designation, but he prefers the more established term *subject analysis*. Langridge apparently views the subject(s) of a document as a content-related correspondence between the document and some preestablished knowledge categories, which are characterized as "permanent, inherent characteristics of knowledge." Langridge apparently did not contemplate the difference between content-oriented and need-oriented indexing, which I claim to be of central importance.

The fact that Langridge does not take the potential use of the document into account is in my opinion due to the lack of a pragmatic dimension in subject analysis (Hjørland, 1992a). I regard it as an example of rationalism/objective idealism, referring to both Langridge's view of knowledge categories as "permanent, inherent characteristics of knowledge" as well as the fact that he does not advocate continual updating of these categories as science evolves. According to my epistemological framework, there are no permanent knowledge categories, only relatively stable forms of knowledge, for example, scientific generalizations.

Theories of automated indexing (and systems based on artificial intelligence) are predisposed toward objective idealism, as they are based upon the assumption that the surface of a document hides a knowledge category that can be determined. Rather than being dependent on the potential use of the document, it is related to some "permanent, inherent characteristics of knowledge."

Other theories, for example, many of the aboutness theoreticians' ideas, as well as those offered by representatives of the cognitive paradigm, suggest that subject analyses are best performed by the matching of a document with subjective knowledge structures. It is common to view the subject as something the author has intended and as a reflection of the author's subjective views or knowledge structures. This method is used by representatives of classical hermeneutics, and it is also championed by the cognitive viewpoint in information science. Other researchers try to find the key to subject analysis and the concept of subject in the users' subjective, individual needs and knowledge structures.

According to my subject theory (first formulated in Hjørland, 1992a, and elaborated in this book), the subject of a document is its *informative potential*. First of all, this potential is not acknowledged and described through a study of "permanent, inherent characteristics of knowledge" or by the individual and subjective interests, knowledge, and needs of the authors or users, but by a domain analysis that includes an analysis of the knowledge domain based on philosophy of science and the sociology and history of discourse communities.

A subject analysis implies an interpretation of the potential of the document (or other information entity) in relation to the knowledge interests[1] of a given information system, and this analysis is undertaken in a given historical, cultural, professional, and pragmatic context.

Subject analysis can be more or less goal-oriented or general. A discipline- or task-specific information service probably analyzes potentials more narrowly in relation to the needs of the discipline or of the activities in, for instance, a specific company. The database Ringdok (see Soergel, 1985), for instance, describes documents from the point of view of the pharmacological industry. A general information service would, on the other hand, tend to use a more general description. Chemical Abstracts, for instance, describes documents in a more general way than does Ringdok. We can see how the pragmatic and economic context plays an important role in practical subject analysis. Another example of this is the Royal Library in Copenhagen, which describes music according to the instrumentation (the number of different instruments, their types, and combinations). Such a description can be done in a fairly economical, consistent and objective way, but, on the other hand, it is perhaps less informative for many users than a real musical analysis might be. A real musical analysis should make it possible for a user to choose from his needs and preferences. Of course, this is a utopian goal, but many different selection criteria would help to fulfill this goal. The most basic analysis would probably be genre and style analysis, including a cultural-historical classification. The principle of subject analysis as interpretation of the document's potential is modified by pragmatic factors. This modification is often so specific that it might be difficult to see that an interpretation of the document's potential has been performed. The connection between user needs and document analysis is very indirect: the user himself has to identify the relevant documents based on, for instance, the instrumentation, and this might not always be possible.

Subject analysis implies conceptual construction of the contents and the potential of a document. Conceptual construction regarding, for instance, an article on Watergate or the Tamil case in Denmark may of course be connected with concrete facts, time periods, persons, places, and so on. Such conceptual construction tends to be positivist. It is perhaps relevant for some types of information needs, perhaps especially those of the tabloid press. Another form of conceptual construction might, for instance, be "concrete examples of ethical problems in political systems" (or maybe just "ethics in politics"). Such a concept assignation is not positivist, but implies generalization based upon theoretical analysis and abstraction. In practice there is nothing to prevent one from assigning several subject descriptions to the same document, both positivist and generalized. The generalized subject descriptions serve more esoteric knowledge needs, either of a scholarly or more penetratingly journalistic nature.

A subject analysis cannot be viewed in isolation from the culture, the environment, and the context in which the analysis is performed, including the individual and collective knowledge interests that the analysis is based upon. But the aim of the analysis should not be subjective, for instance, influenced by the person who is performing the analysis. Rather, it should be as precise and objective as possible and should conform as much as possible to its object (pragmatic realism).

In the theory that I propose, there is no "correct" subject analysis of a document in the sense that there are no "correct" answers (just as semantic holists like Putnam maintain that there are no facts about the meaning of a text). Document analysis is not a question of finding a correspondence or certain equivalents between the document and its subject assignations. The decisive quality criterion in the subject analysis of documents is that this analysis results in subject data, which reflect the essential rather than the incidental character-istics of the document. Such an evaluation of the essential characteristics assumes that there is an independent analysis in relation to the document's self-description such as it is expressed in title, headings, and so on. There are no standard rules for analyzing the essential characteristics of documents. Sometimes the research methodology of a document is an essential characteristic, but at other times it is a less important feature.

We can also say that subject analysis assumes impartiality, an ability to see through possible commercial self-promoting aspects of a document. It is, for instance, common that a document claims to treat a far broader topic than it in reality does.

Another point is that subject analysis as far as possible should be undertaken from the point of view of professional knowledge interests, that is, from the point of view of one or several scientific disciplines or subdisciplines. In a universal system, the idea is to place a document in just one disciplinary context. This causes irresolvable problems in terms of determining whether a document representing, for example, social psychology is more psychology or more sociology. If a system of (sub)disciplinary thesauri and/or a classification system is used, this problem will become a pseudo-problem and disappear: every discipline will come to a decision as to the disciplinary relevance of the document and assign it a place within the disciplinary context. A document has not just one true subject. It has several epistemological potentialities that are given priority based on disciplinary viewpoints. Bibliographic records may contain various disciplinary priorities, but it should be possible to distinguish them. Descriptors that have been assigned by, for example, medical librarians using National Library of Medicine's subject headings are placed in one of the fields in the record and are therefore not experienced as noise by a person who is looking for literature with a psychological bias.[2]

SUBJECT ANALYSIS AND IR LANGUAGES

In practice, subject analysis is often performed by library personnel using a given classification scheme, thesaurus, or IR language to express the result of the subject analysis. Classification systems and thesauri represent kinds of IR languages, and documents analyzed using such systems represent "organized knowledge." This IR language can affect the subject analysis, and the worldview of the librarian may be colored by a specific classification scheme. An IR language is in fact itself a decision support system for the subject analysis. As such this system may of course be more or less adequate. The fact that the IR language affects the subject analysis may have both positive and negative effects.

The fact that an IR language is being used often has a positive effect in that the subject analysis that is undertaken is neither more in-depth nor more time-consuming than the system can use or express. Furthermore, the IR language often has a built-in knowledge interest, which the subject analysis takes as its starting point.

The negative effect of the IR system may be that the theoretical assumptions of the IR language (which perhaps has become the librarian's/information specialist's socialized worldview) are forced upon the theoretical assumptions of the document instead of resulting in an attempt to update or modify the assumption of the IR language. If an IR system gives priority to a particular viewpoint or knowledge interest which perhaps was adequate in the context where the system was developed, but not in concrete usage, then the IR system not only leads to difficulty in expressing the result of a given subject analysis, but also risks causing misinterpretations for the subject analysis itself. The information specialist is perhaps not even able to acknowledge the limitations of the IR system nor work toward redressing these within or outside the framework of the IR system.

If the information specialist assumes that the subject world can be expressed in an objective system, the structure of which in one way or another is taken for granted in relation to scientific knowledge, which continually is reflected in the professional literature, then he or she applies a rationalistic, objective idealistic mode of thinking, which may not be optimal. I will later discuss why some of the classification theoreticians (e.g., Ranganathan and Langridge) can be said to belong to this category.

It is important to make a fundamental distinction between on the one hand the subject analysis, the interpretation of a document's potential, and on the other hand the subsequent translation process, where an attempt is made to express the subject of the document by using a concrete IR language. If these two things are confused—which of course is understandable since the IR language may affect the subject analysis—it is impossible to analyze and evaluate the subject analysis and the IR language separately from each other, and one might end up viewing classification and indexing as fundamentally different analysis methods, and in other ways reach an incorrect view of the theoretical and practical problems. Experience shows—as Langridge (1989, p. 6) also emphasizes—that in practice the subject analysis creates far more troubles than the translation problems.

STANDARDS FOR SUBJECT ANALYSIS

There is an international International Standard Organization (ISO) standard 5963 (1985) called "Methods for Examining Documents, Determining Their

Subjects, and Selecting Indexing Terms." According to this standard, indexing consists of three stages, which are not clearly separated:

1. Examining the document and determining its subject content.

2. Determining the subject's most important concepts.

3. Expressing the concepts using the language in a given vocabulary.

In the ideal case, the document should be read through, but this is often neither possible nor necessary. In practice, subject analysis varies from a few seconds to hours. The indexer should, however, make sure that no useful information is left out and should never base the subject analysis on title and abstract alone.

The ISO standard contains a summary of the elements to which particular attention should be paid, including title, table of contents, introduction, and so on, but fails to mention that, for example, the reference list may be a part of the subject analysis—it can serve as a guide to identifying the (sub)discipline or discourse community to which a document belongs.

As to determining the concepts, the standard recommends a check list, which enumerates the object of action; an active concept, that is, an action, an operation, or a process; that which is affected by the action; agent, instruments, techniques, and methods for accomplishing an action; place; dependent and independent variables; special viewpoints. The indexer does not need to use all the concepts that were identified: the selection depends on the purpose of the indexing. The selection of concepts should be made on the basis of the potential value of a concept as an element in the determination of the subject of a document, as well as in the retrieval process. The indexer should (1) select the concepts that are considered suitable for a given user group, in that the purpose of the indexing should be kept in mind, and (2) if it is deemed necessary, change both indexing tools and methods as a result of feedback through inquiries.

No arbitrary limits should be set for how many indexing words and phrases are allowed to be added to the subject description. Such limits cause a loss of objectivity and exclusion of information that has potential value in the search process. The selection of indexing terms and phrases should be made based on knowledge of the field, the vocabulary, and its possibilities and limitations.

Even though the ISO standard can in many ways be reasonable and useful, it can be noted that the prescribed guidelines for subject analysis are fairly document-centered and almost assume a "unified science" approach. The standard does not offer any specific insights into how disciplines or user groups differ or explain the fact that they require particular domain-specific analyses. The document could, for instance, have mentioned that where social science and humanities disciplines are concerned, the indexers need to pay special attention to worldviews and theoretical orientation; that is, it could have emphasized the importance of the subject-object relation in these disciplines. The fact that this was not done shows the danger in publishing international standards in this area: paying attention to inconsequential external features in the analysis gives a false impression of general, objective criteria that in reality cannot be described in a standard, since subject analysis is a theoretical and intellectual process that is dependent on the concrete situation within the knowledge domain in question.[3]

SOME PRINCIPLES OF KNOWLEDGE ORGANIZATION

From the librarian's point of view, knowledge organization typically means classification schemes, thesauri, structured bibliographies and datafiles, and so on. LIS looks upon itself—and sometimes upon cognitive science—as the profession(s) about knowledge organization. Anderson (1996) writes that organization of knowledge is:

the description of documents, their content, features and purpose, and the organization of these descriptions so as to make these documents and their parts accessible to persons seeking them or the messages that they contain. Knowledge organization encompasses every type and method of indexing, abstracting, cataloguing, classification, records management, bibliography and the creation of textual or bibliographic databases for information retrieval.

Messages are represented through the creation of texts—organized sets of symbols using systems devised to represent language, music, images, scientific and mathematical phenomena, dance, and many other forms of art and communication. Texts are formatted in various genres and are recorded in a wide variety of media. The combination of text (representing a message) and its medium constitutes a document. Thus it is the document (message represented in a text recorded in a medium) which is at the focus of most systems of knowledge organization for information retrieval.

Knowledge resides in the human mind. Humans have learned how to represent knowledge in messages recorded in documents, through which we endeavor to convey parts and aspects of our knowledge to others—to inform them by providing potential information. In the context of library and information science, the organization of knowledge (often called the organization of information) is the organization of documented messages in which knowledge or information is represented. The organization of knowledge within the mind, or brain, is a primary focus of cognitive psychology and cognitive science. (1996, p. 336)

The social dimension, however, is almost absent in Anderson's presentation. From this point of view, knowledge is organized in learned institutions, in professionals, in journals, in libraries, and so on. Knowledge is produced as a part of human activities and tied to the division of labor in society. From the point of view of activity theory, this is the primary organization of knowledge. The organization of knowledge in IS is secondary or derived, and so is, in certain ways, the cognitive organization of knowledge in individual minds. The organization of knowledge is determined by evolution of different kinds of functional forms and principles which vary according to specific needs, contents, and conditions.

In an earlier work (Hjørland, 1994), I have discussed some principles of knowledge organization.[4] Here I shall present some of the most important principles.

From studying the literature of LIS, one could get the impression that the only consensus is that disciplinary principles should be avoided in the organization of knowledge. The attitude of Eric de Grolier is typical in this respect:

At least one general tendency, however, can be discerned: need to bypass the procrustean bed of traditional "disciplines." Correlatively, it is clear that one must begin with an analysis of what we could call the "deep structure" of concepts and their interrelationships. (Grolier, 1992, p. 227)

The relationships between concepts is an epistemological question. Chapter 4 discusses the main epistemological theories about this issue. While it is sufficient to say that de Grolier's view about knowledge organization is related to the view of classical rationalism,[5] this is not the position taken by activity theory. In my view there is a deep wisdom in classification systems such as Dewey (which states the opposite of Grolier, cf. the citation from Dewey in Chapter 4), which implies that the concept of disciplines is very important to information science.[6]

Knowledge organization always serves pragmatic purposes and should reflect this. For practical purposes, knowledge can be organized in different ways and with different levels of ambition:

- *Ad hoc classification* (or *categorization*, if you prefer) reflects a very low level of ambition in knowledge organization. Every time you arrange flowers in your private home, you use a kind of ad hoc classification determined by your private taste, the colors of your rooms, what other things they are going to match with, and so on. Much classification or categorization or ordering is based on ad hoc principles. Scientific principles, for example, botanical taxonomies seem unfruitful for most such purposes.

- *Pragmatic classification* reflects a middle level of ambition in knowledge organization. It is a compromise between ad hoc classification and scientific classification. Jacob's (1994) examples—that the amateur gardener or the horticulturist have other criteria for categorizing rhododendrons and azaleas than the biologist—imply that the words and concepts in horticulture diverge (more or less) from those in biology (in my terminology: they have different knowledge interests).

- *Scientific classification* reflects a very high level of ambition in knowledge organization. It is a highly abstract and generalized way of organizing knowledge (e.g., classification of animals and plants according to biological taxonomies).

In all three cases, categorizations/classifications serve human action. From a pragmatic-philosophical perspective, the purpose of science is to serve human action.[7] Any given categorization should reflect the purpose of that categorization. It is very important to teach information science students to make careful assessments and apply ad hoc classifications, pragmatic classifications, or scientific classifications whenever each kind of classification is most appropriate. (In LIS, there are many examples of librarians advocating classification schemes such as Dewey's in situations where they are not appropriate at all.) It is very important that you teach how to exploit subject information already at hand, how to use the most modern information technology, and how to be aware of the great costs of establishing new high-quality subject analysis.

However, if you are going to teach principles of knowledge classification to information specialists, it is difficult to teach ad hoc principles because they contain very little knowledge that can be generalized from one situation to another. On the contrary, principles of scientific classification contain much knowledge that can be generalized from one situation to another. This is simply a consequence of the nature of scientific research as generalized work. If scientific classifications have a high degree of consensus, they will in many situations also represent the most pragmatic choice in knowledge organization. It is much easier in many cases to employ an existing geographical, botanical, or chemical system (possibly in a customized form) than to establish local principles from scratch.

We must consciously choose the purpose of our classification. In doing so, we can choose between very general purposes (like the fundamental sciences) or more immediate purposes like the applied sciences, or we can choose ad hoc categorizations. In the first two cases, it implies principles developed in some kind of science, not some kind of extrascientific principles. A search for such extrascientific principles is meaningless, because it implies the same sort of difficulties as the sciences are trying to solve in their knowledge organization. In the last case, we are faced with the problem of generalizing principles for ad hoc purposes (which to some degree seems contradictory).[8]

The Concept of Polyrepresentation

Ingwersen (1994, 1996) introduces the concept of *polyrepresentation*. In typical information-seeking situations, some categorizations are useful to some degree and others to some other degree. Sometimes it is very important to limit the meaning of a term to a particular scientific discipline or tradition; at other times, it is very important to compare across disciplinary borders. In spite of the obvious problems of, for example, homonymy with free-text searching, it is a fact that such a search strategy is very valuable to many purposes. To some extent, this principle is a consequence of an uncertainty principle in science.

The attitude that scientific classifications are too restrictive because of the special perspectives in the sciences is right to the degree that there exist many needs and that there is a great amount of uncertainty and unpredictability in most information needs. One kind of uncertainty is which disciplines have contributed the most to a given problem and how the contributions are scattered across disciplinary borders. This implies that it is too limited an approach to design an information system based on only one kind of subject representation reflecting only one kind of knowledge interest. Many different subject access points should be available to the searcher based on titles, abstracts, full-text, descriptors, classification codes, identifiers, authors, citations, reviews, and so on. These should supplement each other providing polyrepresentation of subject analysis.

Also, the concept of *interdisciplinary search* (Klein, 1990; Bartolo & Smith, 1993) shows the need for polyrepresentation, for not limiting the analysis to one narrow scientific analysis only. But this is not identical to the attitude that a narrow scientific analysis is not necessary and therefore should be replaced by some alternative categorization. In my view the scientific, discipline-oriented subject analysis is still the most central point of departure (presuming that you can agree with the discipline's theoretical and methodological principles. If you cannot agree, an argument about those principles is needed).

Different human activities—including different sciences—could be understood as different ways of organizing the same phenomena—a kind of poly-representation. Economics, history, sociology, psychology, and so on, are all studying the same "things" (e.g., family life or unemployment), but from different theoretical viewpoints, and they integrate the phenomena in different conceptual structures. In addition, there exist paradigms of an intradisciplinary or interdisciplinary nature, such as structuralism, behaviorism, cognitivism, and so on. Often such paradigms reflect different perceptions of human beings, of human society, of science, and thereby of political and ideological matters.

Knowledge Organization and Kinds of Disciplines

The nature of disciplines varies. The distinction between "hard sciences" and "soft sciences" is well known, but perhaps not very fruitful. One alternative classification is presented by Whitley (1984). Also, in the opinion of the present author, a difference between, for example, "mature sciences" versus "immature" sciences is better than hard versus soft.

In information science, Mote (1962) represents an attempt to analyze different kinds of research areas from the point of view of information needs. He distinguishes three kinds of areas:

1. Areas in which the underlying principles are well developed, the literature is well organized, and the subject area is relatively well defined.

2. Broader areas where the information is less well organized and defined.

3. Areas with many overlapping disciplines and an almost nonexistent knowledge organization. Much literature exists in this third category, but the existing organization is useless for existing purposes—to put it mildly.

Of time-consuming questions in an information service, Mote found that the number of questions in each category was 18, 32, and 50. In the first category, there might in his opinion be a greater need for a library in which researchers can serve themselves than for a regular information service.

From Mote's investigation one can get the impression that there is a greater need for information services (and professionals) in the humanities as compared to the sciences. This is, however, in contradiction to the well-documented fact (see, e.g., Stone, 1982, pp. 294–295) that humanists do not have the same tendency to delegate literature searching, which may have a connection with problems of formulating their needs to others and with problems in interpreting the relevance of the identified information.

The consequence of the different nature of disciplines might very well be that information specialists and information science should apply different strategies in different knowledge fields. But very little research has been done which can illuminate this important problem.

Many authors, including Jaenecke (1994), have pointed toward the important problem, that the quality of the knowledge production in many disciplines is in great trouble. It seems as if the priorities get more and more short-term, that fewer efforts are made to develop long-term, well-organized, and well-maintained bodies of knowledge and literature. This means that the integrity of scientific knowledge as well as other forms of knowledge is threatened.

In the traditional view, knowledge organization is concerned only with subject matter, not with quality issues. But if knowledge organization should be helpful for users identifying the "best textual means to some ends" (P. Wilson, 1968), then those distinctions (e.g., of the methodological kind) which can help users distinguish relevant from nonrelevant documents become part of the subject analysis, and the distinction between analysis of subject matter and analysis of quality becomes blurred.

Like Jaenecke, I am convinced that the problems with quality in knowledge production are very important not only for the disciplines involved and for the larger society, but also for the issues facing IS, for what role is left to our discipline.

It is a fact that some transdisciplinary tendencies in research can be described and discussed, for example, the connection of a view on a theory of knowledge (positivism) and quality problems (production of trivialism) (cf. Olaisen, 1991). Theories of knowledge do have implications for the possibilities of establishing fruitful categorizations. It is this condition that can establish a platform for information scientists.

Therefore, information scientists should join the philosophers and sociologists of science; engage in interdisciplinary research (Klein, 1990); criticize ways of thinking based on fundamentalist epistemologies; and analyze the role of values, goals, and perspectives in research and scientific categorizations/classifications.

CONCLUSION

In this chapter I have discussed how explicit subject data are produced from the process called subject analysis. I have shown that IS must give up its illusory goals of establishing fundamental principles of knowledge organization external to scientific criteria. Instead, IS must have a much more limited and humble scope: to help facilitate the fruitful principles of knowledge organization and avoid the unfruitful by analyzing the different criteria for knowledge organization developing in all kinds of human activities, as well as their implicit or explicit goals, functions, and consequences.

In Chapter 4 I will examine more closely what one is looking to identify in a subject analysis; that is, which object, which "something," the subject analysis is directed toward and is attempting to capture: the concept of subject. This analysis will take us to the most fundamental theories of knowledge, cognition, and meaning. The next chapter will conclude by providing two concrete examples of the subject analyses of books.

NOTES

1. The concept of *knowledge interest* or *epistemological interest* is used throughout the book and is elaborated in Chapter 7 on information needs. The concept is important in the pragmatic theory of knowledge, but in classical epistemology knowledge was conceived as being independent of human interests. Today, this concept is mostly known from the works of Jürgen Habermas (e.g., 1968).

2. At the Royal Library in Copenhagen subject analysis is performed in such a way that the books circulate among the relevant subject librarians. The individual subject librarian (e.g., the psychology librarian) makes decisions about (1) whether he should perform a subject analysis, if the book is relevant to the discipline in question and (2) where in the system the book should be placed. The leading principle is that subject analysis is subordinate to disciplinary relevance criteria. The book may thus be placed in several disciplinary contexts and be analyzed several times from the point of view of different disciplines (or knowledge interests). I suggest that this principle be expanded such that every document in principle would be circulated and analyzed from the point of view of all disciplines, for example, through interlibrary cooperation.

3. A standard should not state what is necessarily the truth, but what might be otherwise. It would be hard to imagine another universal standard about subject analysis with different principles.

4. In Hjørland (1994), nine principles of knowledge organization were proposed: (1) naive-realistic subject analysis is not possible; (2) categorizations and classifications should unite related subjects and separate unrelated subjects; (3) different levels of ambition in knowledge organization exist; (4) any given categorization should reflect the purpose of that categorization; (5) concrete scientific categorizations and classifications can always be questioned; (6) the concept of polyrepresentation is important; (7) different sciences could be understood as different ways of organizing the same phenomena; (8) the nature of disciplines varies; (9) the quality of the knowledge production should be analyzed.

5. Grolier's quotation continues:

> The rejection of a "disciplinary" basis for a new system is now rather clear: with one exception (Wåhlin's "Field system") all post 1970 schemes have abandoned this feature, still present—as seen above—in BC2. But this leaves open the question: where to place "disciplines" themselves, as it is obvious that they are still represented in the literature, university programs and structural charts of governmental science policy administrations? (Grolier, 1992, p. 230)

I cannot find support for this view in modern philosophy of science (e.g., Shapere, 1984). In the view of scientific realism, the "epistemic community," with its theories, concepts, and so on, is a reflection of its object. From the view of social constructivism, the objects, their properties, and their relations are constructed by the discipline. It is not clear whether social constructivism and scientific realism can be united. In both cases, however, it follows that the objects should be organized by discipline. I have elsewhere (Hjørland, 1993a) defended the view that a thing is always either shaped by or perceived by some knowledge interests, typically represented by scientific disciplines. Objects, properties, and relations should be organized from the point of view of a scientific field.

Grolier (and with him almost all contemporary researchers in IS) seems to believe that we can disregard the discoveries of science in our search for principles about knowledge organization, that the concept of discipline should be avoided, and that we can have "more fundamental principles," "deeper semantic structures," "permanent inherent characteristics of knowledge," or the like. In Chapter 4 in this book—and earlier in Hjørland, 1992a and Hjørland, 1993a—I have analyzed the theoretical view of knowledge behind this view. In my opinion the search for such principles represents a search for illusionary goals based on a kind of rationalism close to the "immortal ideas" of Platonic idealism. One of the very few researchers who regard the philosophy of science as important for knowledge organization is Ingetraut Dahlberg (e.g., 1992a).

Categorizations and classifications should unite related subjects and separate unrelated subjects. In naive realism, subject relationships are based on similarity or resemblance. Two things or subjects are seen as related if they are alike, that is, if they have common properties (descriptive terms) ascribed.

But, as Shapere (1989, pp. 427f.) shows, the properties ascribed to some phenomena (e.g., electrons) will change with the changing theoretical context in the field. For example, first the properties ABCD are ascribed, then perhaps ABC, then ABCF, and finally HKGF. There need not be any essential common properties between the thing as first and last understood in this scientific development. There is no similarity.

At one point in history, astronomy and astrology were regarded as related subjects. In modern science they are obviously not. Astronomy and astrology both study planets and stars, and some of the same words may therefore occur in texts from astronomy and astrology. But this kind of resemblance or similarity does not make the two fields related. Such a view of relatedness is superficial and naive. Real subject-relatedness does not depend on perceptions of similarity but on theoretical analysis!

No advanced indexing, subject analysis, categorization, or classification can therefore be based on common properties or similarities; rather, subjects should be interpreted in the light of the theoretical context. Similarity is therefore an unfruitful concept. What should be grouped together for the purpose of the subject analysis are documents with identical or related functions. This is one of the reasons for the success of citation indexing, where related documents can be identified without any form of linguistic similarity. The concept of similarity should therefore be replaced by the concept of *functional equivalence* (or *isomorphism*). This insight also has important implications with regard to algorithmic retrieval, since a match between query and text representation can only be based on some kind of similarity.

6. The concepts of *disciplines, subdisciplines, discourse communities,* and *epistemic communities* are used interchangeably throughout this book. The ideals about scientific communication stated are mostly met on the subdisciplinary level where the problems are most precise and the communication most effective. Disciplines are perhaps often too big to serve as epistemic communities, but to a lesser degree the same principles also prevail

on this level. Most formal planning of information systems and databases are done at the disciplinary level.

7. As we shall elaborate in Chapter 6, science is part of the division of labor in society. Science is general labor. What constitutes "good" science is, according to pragmatic philosophy, eventually determined by the utility for human practice. The more fundamental a science is, the more general and perhaps abstract a form of labor it represents. Applied science represents a middle ground between basic science on one end and ordinary human action on the other end. This is the rationale behind the secret powers of scientific classifications: to the degree that a public need for establishing and organizing knowledge in one or another field exists, a scientific discipline is likely to be formed to perform this task. This new discipline will establish its identity in relation to other sciences, and "as science proceeds, the connection between knowledge-claims, domain groupings, and descriptions (and often naming) tend to become tighter and tighter" (Shapere, 1984). Jacob (1994) takes the stand that scientific classification is too restrictive, too constrained because of the special perspectives in the sciences, and that less domain-specific, less rigid categorizations are needed. In my view this depends on the purpose of the classification.

8. It can happen that the scientific community does not serve the kind of human actions that you would like your categorization/classification to serve. In economics, Robert B. Reich (1993) criticizes the standard way to classify jobs as being unfruitful in helping to solve the problems of unemployment. He then makes a new categorization of types of work: (1) routine production services, (2) in-person services, and (3) symbol analytics.

Reich's classification is an alternative to the traditional, "scientific" classifications of jobs in economics. However, it is not an unscientific classification, but rather one that contains a critique of the traditional science of economics and its classification (Reich uses the expression "the perils of vestigial thought"). In a classical theory on the sociology of science (Merton, 1968, pp. 614–615), science is understood as organized scepticism. The problem is that science—as also shown by R. B. Reich—often has built into itself a conservative way of looking at reality. Science is not only a reflection of reality, but also a social institution with its own ideology, which can have some difficulties in its self-image and in open dialog about its self-image. Unfruitful principles of methodology or classification can be a part of such an ideology.

I am not sure that sciences always apply very formal, restrictive classifications as Jacob (1994) maintains. In psychology and psychiatry, for example, some researchers work with rather formal classifications of intelligence (e.g., Guilford's well-known model), of mental disorders, and so on. But to my judgment, this kind of research is not regarded as being the most prominent. Eminent contributors such as Sigmund Freud have been very sceptical about applying rigid definitions and formal classifications. In a field like psychology, there is, or should be, a dialog and debate concerning many issues, including the value of different forms of classification—or when to classify at all. The opinion that scientific classification is too restrictive and too constrained because of the special perspectives in the sciences represents, therefore, a critique of the sciences for not serving human practice. If the sciences use classifications that are too restrictive, then they should use the classifications that are appropriate for their special purposes (fundamental sciences like biology therefore use classifications different from more applied sciences such as horticulture). If a kind of human practice needs organized knowledge, a form of applied science is likely to be established, attempting to organize that knowledge in the best way it can. In the humanities, for example, art and literature, a historical principle of organization often represents the best compromise between pragmatic and scientific criteria.

Science should be seen as a dialog in a discipline or a "discourse community" working to solve some problems for the larger society. This dialog also comprises the fruitfulness of classification and different ways of categorizing knowledge. Different approaches or paradigms have different implications for categorization. There are no a priori scientific methods of classification/categorization. The criticism of a scientific categorization normally implies a critique of the science which has developed that categorization.

The deepest criteria of meanings, semantic relations, and scientific categorization and classification rest upon scientific principles, which are negotiated in the disciplines, not upon isolated users' subjective perception. Users can have more or less informed perceptions about meanings, semantic relations, and classifications. (Even the majority of a discipline or the entire discipline itself can be wrong.) Methodological criteria for deciding the appropriateness of views are formulated and discussed in the theory of knowledge and theory of science.

Some sciences (e.g., biology) are more fundamental than others (e.g., horticulture). The fundamental sciences work with more abstract and general problems than the more applied sciences do. The knowledge, concepts, theories, categories, and so on, of fundamental sciences have less direct applicability, but are in the larger perspective very useful because they can be generalized to many different situations. The basic sciences reflect a kind of economic principle in knowledge organization (the knowledge of the biologist is more useful to the horticulturist than inversely).

While the arts and sciences are collective ways of establishing knowledge in the social division of labor, knowledge organizations in arts and sciences reflect important human values, goals, and influences of power (or lack of power). Disciplines (and intra- or interdisciplinary paradigms) could be seen as (part of) different human projects serving various (more or less conscious) goals. Sometimes such human projects have effects that are contrary to the goals that initiated them.

4

The Concept of Subject
or Subject Matter
and Basic Epistemological Positions

HISTORICAL INTRODUCTION TO THE CONCEPT OF SUBJECT

The central part of information seeking and IR theory concerns subject searching. The most central part of value-added information provided by information specialists concerns subject representation data. One of the most central topics in information science seems to be subject access points in electronic databases. The concept of *subject* or *subject matter* seems to be a very essential concept. But what does it mean?

The concept of subject is used both in library and information science as well as in other fields, including philosophy, linguistics, and phenomenological psychology. In ancient and medieval philosophy, the meanings of *subject* and *substance* were the same: it is something actually existing as a stone. The stone as a mental concept, was called the *object*. In modern usage, the meanings of this pair have become reversed, where subject also mean an individual mind. In linguistics, the subject term in a sentence denotes the bearer of a property, and the predicate denotes the property. The subject is that about which something is said. Togeby (1977, page 28–30) states that in every transfer of information something is presupposed while other things are new. The concept of subject (e.g., the subject of a conversation) is connected with what is presumed to be known by the receiver. Linguistics studies how language is used to organize subjects in speech and writing—for instance, how a conversation "keeps on track," meaning, how it concentrates on one or more specific subjects. In modern cognitive psychology, subject per se is not a concept, but the notion plays an important role in phenomenology, where it is mostly used with the meaning of "intentional object."[1]

In spite of its very important role in library and information science, and in spite of the fact that different conceptions have very important implications for the theory of information science, the concept of subject has been extremely neglected in the literature. Metcalfe (1973) is one of the few exceptions. He reviews the use of this concept in LIS for nearly one hundred years. However, his conclusion is that the concept is so vague that it is almost useless.

Miksa (1983a, 1983b) discusses Charles A. Cutter's concept of subject. According to his two definitions of this concept subject is "the theme or themes of the book, whether stated in the title or not" (Cutter, 1904, p. 23), or "the matter on which the author is seeking to give or the reader to obtain information" (Cutter, 1904, p. 16). For Cutter the stability of subjects depends on a social process in which their meanings are stabilized in a name or a designation. A subject "referred . . . to those intellections . . . that had received a name that itself represented a distinct consensus in usage" (Miksa, 1983a, p. 60). The "systematic structure of established subjects" is "resident in the public realm" (Miksa, 1983a, p. 69), while "subjects are by their very nature locations in a classificatory structure of publicly accumulated knowledge" (Miksa, 1983a, p. 61).

Miksa (1983b) shows that Cutter's conception of subject was closely related to and dependent on a particular view of psychology and epistemology. His illumination of this is indeed very valuable and scholarly. Miksa also demonstrates how the limitations of Cutter's view are related to the limitations in the philosophical assumptions, and he provides an alternative view on the concept of subject under the label "the modern idea of a subject" (pp. 56–57). This "modern" view is discussed below (in the section about empiricism and subjectivism). However, even if Miksa has a clear understanding that Cutter's concept of subject is closely related to certain philosophical views, he makes no attempt to anchor his own alternative in an epistemological theory, and in my view does not reach a satisfactory determination of this concept.

Frohmann (1994, pp. 112–113) continues the discussion of Cutter's view:

The stability of the public realm in turn relies upon natural and objective mental structures which, with proper education, govern a natural progression from particular to general concepts. Since for Cutter, mind, society, and SKO [systems of knowledge organization] stand one behind the other, each supporting each, all manifesting the same structure, his discursive construction of subjects invites connections with discourses of mind, education, and society. The DDC [Dewey Decimal Classification, founded by Melvil Dewey], by contrast, severs those connections. [Melvil] Dewey emphasized more than once that his system maps no structure beyond its own; there is neither a "transcendental deduction" of its categories nor any reference to Cutter's objective structure of social consensus. It is content-free: Dewey disdained any philosophical excogitation of the meaning of his class symbols, leaving the job of finding verbal equivalents to others. His innovation and the essence of the system lay in the notation. The DDC is a purely semiotic system of expanding nests of ten digits, lacking any referent beyond itself. In it, a subject is wholly constituted in terms of its position in the system. The essential characteristic of a subject is a class symbol which refers only to other symbols. Its verbal equivalent is accidental, a merely pragmatic characteristic. . . .

The conflict of interpretations over "subjects" became explicit in the battles between "bibliography" (an approach to subjects having much in common with Cutter's) and Melvil Dewey's "close classification." William Fletcher spoke for the scholarly biblio-grapher. . . . Fletcher's "subjects," like Cutter's, referred to the categories of a fantasized, stable social order, whereas [Melvil] Dewey's subjects were elements of a semiological system of standardized, techno-bureaucratic administrative software for the library in its corporate, rather than high culture, incarnation.

From Frohmann's discussion it becomes clear that the concept of subject played a role in the debate of library and information science late in the nineteenth century and that different conceptions do have implications that are not trivial.

A leading philosopher of information science, Patrick Wilson (1968), illuminates different ways to analyze the subject of a document. Wilson investigates—especially via thought experiments—the suitability of these different methods of determining the subject of a document:

1. identifing the author's purpose in writing the document

2. weighing the relative dominance and subordination of different elements in the picture given by reading the document

3. grouping or counting the document's use of concepts and references

4. inventing a set of rules of selection for what are the essential elements (in contrast to the inessential) of the document in its entirety

Patrick Wilson demonstrates convincingly that each of these methods by itself is insufficient to determine the subject of a document, and he concludes (p. 89): *"The notion of the subject of a writing is indeterminate"* (emphasis added).

He also says, in a section on what a user can expect to find under a particular position in a library's classification system: "For nothing definite *can* be expected of the things found at any given position." (p. 92). In connection with this last remark Wilson includes an interesting footnote, in which he directs attention to the often imprecise use made of concepts by the authors of documents ("hostility" is mentioned as an example). Even though the librarian personally might attain a very precise grasp of a concept, he will be unable to make use of it in his classification since none of the documents use the concept in the same precise way. Therefore, Wilson concludes, "If people write on what are for them ill-defined phenomena, a correct description of their subjects must reflect the ill-definedness."

Insofar as no subjective instance in its role relative to the document can guarantee a correct analysis of subject matter (that analysis always is subjective), this can lead to an agnostic conception of subject: it is impossible to say what a subject is and how it is to be determined. Renouncing an exact determination of one of the basic concepts of information science is a questionable matter. Such agnosticism as Patrick Wilson expresses in the above citations is hardly a necessary solution. As we shall see later, it *is* possible to define subjects (which, however, is *not* the same as to give an objective statement concerning the subject of a document).

Attempts to move beyond an agnostic conception raise these questions: What are the criteria for the subject of a document? Are subjects perceptions or "ideas" in some people's minds, or what else can they be? What is to be understood by the statement "document (or statement) A belongs to subject category X"?

Wilson's methods reveal the character of this problem. His first method (to identify the author's purpose in writing the document) is connected with the theory put forward by classical hermeneutics, which primarily analyzed writings by studying the author's intentionality, personality, and biography. His second method (to weigh the relative dominance and subordination of different elements in the picture given by reading the document) is related to modern psychological, cognitive, and user-oriented approaches. The third method (to group or count the document's use of terms and references) is related to positivistic, bibliometric, and statistical ways of analyzing documents. The fourth method (to invent a set of rules of selection for what are the essential elements, in contrast to the inessential of the document in its entirety) is related to text linguistics and compositional methods for analyzing documents.

Methods for determining the subject of a document (or some piece of oral or written language as well as informational objects) are thus closely related to theories of meaning and interpretation. This is an interdisciplinary field which includes among other fields linguistics, psychology, sociology, philosophy, and semiotics. Many approaches and theories exist in all these disciplines, and the overall picture today is confusing.

However, crossing these disciplinary boundaries are fundamental epistemologies such as classical empiricism, classical rationalism, pragmatism, and scientific realism. Some epistemologies concentrate on the subjective side, others on the objective side of knowledge. Some epistemologies search for the meaning and subject of a message in the mind of the author, others in the mind of the reader. And still others search for the meaning and subject in social interaction, outside the minds of any particular person.

THE NAIVE CONCEPTION OF SUBJECT

From a naive point of view the concept of subject or subject matter poses no problem: it is rather obvious what subjects are. The book *General Psychology* has quite naturally the subject of psychology, and the *Cambridge History of England* has history as its subject, which can be further subdivided if one wishes to do so into world history and the history of England.

A slightly less naive viewpoint would recognize that there need not be a correspondence between, for example, the title of a book and its actual subject. Not all handbooks (e.g., *Handbook of Psychology*) use this term in their titles, nor do all such titles necessarily correspond to the user's view of the content of the book. Authors with a background in one particular discipline (e.g., psychology, psychiatry, or sociology) may have a tendency to give their works titles which name their own discipline, even though the contents of the works might just as easily justify mention of another field. *A History of Dynamic Psychiatry* could also properly be titled *A History of Dynamic Psychology*. So what is its actual subject? The naive viewpoint has run into difficulties!

To return to the naive point of view, it corresponds in part to a child's lack of differentiation between linguistic forms and meanings. It is apparently typical of a primitive perception of language that a word and its phonetic construction are viewed as an attribute of the thing itself which cannot be separated from its other characteristics (cf. Vygotsky, 1982, pp. 358–359). The naive person typically views a subject as a part of, for example, a book's attributes, a concentration as it were of what is stated in its title and which cannot be separated from the other attributes of the book. This attitude is in a way related to the philosophical concept of *naive realism*, according to which the experience of the senses provides direct access to reality. For example, the naive realist sees that the stars are smaller than the moon, and therefore assumes that they are smaller.

The naive conception cannot differentiate between such concepts as subject, theme, topic, aboutness, content, discipline, object, reference or representation of documents.

A more detailed characterization, scrutiny, or investigation of the naive conception of the concept of subject requires that we ourselves have attained a solid conception of subject, which is the purpose of this chapter.

CLASSICAL EMPIRICISM AND SUBJECTIVISM

Empiricism is one of the classic epistemologies. Together with rationalism it represents a classical system, where logical knowledge is given a priori, while experience is given a posteriori. In both views perception is based on information from the physical-chemical stimuli alone (reductionism). Empiricism is built—contrary to rationalism—on the basic assumption that all knowledge (except logical knowledge) is derived from the senses (*Nihil est in intellectu quod non prius fuerit in sensu*). To assure the truth and objectivity of knowledge, all collection of knowledge is reduced to "facts" of a sensory nature.

The most famous philosophers in this tradition are John Locke (1632–1704), George Berkeley (1685–1753), David Hume (1711–1776) and J. S. Mill (1806–1873). In modern times empiricism is especially developed further in classical positivism and neopositivism. Connectionism and neural networks are modern concepts in cognitive science directly related to the philosophy of classical empiricism. The most basic assumptions of classical empiricism are listed in Table 4.1.

Table 4.1
Basic Principles in Classical Empiricism[2]

- It is possible to formulate the basic principles on how to obtain knowledge.

- Knowledge is infallible.

- Knowledge consists of elements (facts or modules) of infallible knowledge. The elements can be combined to larger units. Therefore, in principle, knowledge is modular.

- All knowledge which is not pure logical knowledge originates from experiences (from the senses).

- Knowledge of universal and necessary relations is given a priori.

- Knowledge of particularities and of contingent relations are only given a posteriori.

- All knowledge based on experience concerns something particular (isolated); empirical knowledge is therefore fragmented.

- The sensations of the individual human being are the basis for obtaining knowledge (Individualism; methodological individualism).

- Concepts which are employed to describe and explain factual circumstances, come from sensory attributes/experiences.

- Sensory experiences are private. Knowledge must therefore be subjective (subjective idealism).

- There is no point in speaking about some reality behind senseimpressions. Science must keep to the observed (the phenomena) and to observable connecions between the phenomena (phenomenalism).

- Complex concepts must be defined from simple concepts, which refer to sense-impressions (associationism).

- Direct experiences must not rely on deductions, and the knowledge obtained from the senses shall be absolutely certain.

- Deduction from the knowledgebase is allowed either as falsification or complete verification.

- Inductive conclusions are allowed under certain conditions. For example, one is not allowed to operate with invisible or theoretical quantities.

- Generalizations are problematic, according to the arguments put forward by Hume. This results in scepticism. Classical empiricism "does not carry enough luggage."

The important issue is that empiricism and positivism represent a paradox. In their search for objective knowledge, they accept only sensory data, not conceptual knowledge from other sources. But sensory knowledge is private knowledge and thus subjective. In their effort to build an absolutely sure foundation for true knowledge and to avoid metaphysical and traditional knowledge, they end up with a purely subjective knowledge. Classical empiricism thus is strongly connected to phenomenalism and subjective idealism: the only things that really exist are our sense impressions; the world is purely subjective.

Of course there exist other opinions inside empiricism and positivism. Some philosophers and scientists try to base empiricism on physicalism and forms of materialism. But one widely held view in the philosophy of science—shared by the present author—is that a basic characteristic of empiricism and positivism is reduction of knowledge to sensory experience and that this view implies subjectivity, phenomenalism and subjective idealism. If these characteristics are not present, we are no longer speaking of empiricism or positivism but of some other position (e.g. pragmatism or scientific realism). The basic tendency in empiricism is to search for objectivity in research by securing intersubjective, transferable facts or data.

Idealism is a fundamental conception in philosophy, of which the main characteristic is that the mental process or consciousness is viewed as primary, or determining, in relation to reality or the material world. In opposition to idealism are the different varieties of realistic or materialistic philosophy,[3] in which the mental is conceived of as something secondary, or derived, in relation to reality or the material world.

Some researchers and philosophers are proclaimed idealists, but it is far more common that researchers do not consider themselves to be idealists, nor do they assume a consciously idealistic point of departure (and, e.g., view the clash between idealism and realism as an irrelevant issue), but in their thinking they inadvertently fall into idealistic modes of thought.

Subjects as Perceived "Aboutness"

An idealistic concept of subject matter holds that a subject is an idea, either in an objective (e.g., Platonic) sense or in a more subjective sense. The implication of an objective idealistic view is that different people should arrive at the same subject—that consistency is the ideal in indexing and classification. The implication of a subjective idealistic view is that different persons may arrive at different subjects (subjects are individual judgments). A scientific realist conception of subject does not look upon subjects as ideas, but as properties. They are objective in some sense, but not in the same sense as that of objective idealism. In this section we will look more closely at subjective idealistic concepts of subject, in the next sections, the objective idealistic, the pragmatic, and the realistic views will be considered.

Subjective idealism takes concepts and subjects to be the expression of the perceptions or views of one or more individuals (subjects). Concepts and subjects are those which are subjectively comprehended or understood by them. The key to the concept of subject therefore lies in the study of the minds of some people, for example, the authors or users of documents. From the point of view of epistemology, subjective idealism is characterized by making perception and thinking independent in a subjectivistic manner.

In the field of library and information science, the application of mentalistic, intrapsychological approaches (as in the cognitive paradigm) seems to imply that the information system should reflect the users' subjective perception of knowledge and information, not some objective reality (which could contribute to the development of the users' knowledge). This view seems problematic with regard to philosophical realism. For example, if you are going to design an information system for, say, Scandinavian geography, the obvious approach would be to design it according to a scientific realistic theory, using geographers as cognitive authorities, not to design it the way the users think it is (for example, misplacing Copenhagen in Sweden). How can cognitive studies of users contribute to such a design task?

Possibly, mentalistic approaches would defend themselves by saying that the objective content of the information systems should be taken for granted. What the cognitivist approach cares about is just to make the systems user-friendly. The cognitivist position would then imply that the principles that it can supply to IS do not relate to the content of the database or to the primary classification of its objects. They are only related to the user interface of the information system.

But if this is the case, the cognitive paradigm cannot deliver a definition of subject matter, but must rely on conceptions developed by some other approach. But this has never been the case. On the contrary, the cognitive paradigm seems to maintain a user-based conception of subject matter or, as cognitivists often prefer to name it, "aboutness."

The concept of *aboutness* was introduced in information science in the early 1970s. Fairthorne (1969) was one of the first who tried to define the concept. He made a distinction between "extensional aboutness" (a kind of inherent subject) and "intentional aboutness" (a kind of user-oriented subject).

One reason to prefer the term aboutness is given by Hutchins (1975, p. 115):

From this account of indexing one thing should now be clear, namely, that the notion of the "subject" of a document is peculiarly vague. We may mean the "extensional aboutness" or the "intentional aboutness," as given by the author in his title or as given by the abstractor or by the indexer; we may mean the NL [natural language] phrase expressing the Topic or we may mean the DL [documentary language] expression denoting the document content. There are clearly so many variables involved that whenever we talk of the "subject" of a document we ought always to say what *kind* of subject we are intending.

These questions of definition are, of course, a quite separate issue from the point stressed at the beginning of this chapter, namely that we should never talk of *the* subject of a document. As we have seen, judgments of subject content (by authors, readers and indexers) are influenced by so many factors that any particular statement of a document's content should never be regarded as anything other than just one of many possible such statements. In other contexts and from other perspectives the same document may have other, quite different "subjects."

Through the concept of the thematic organization of a text, Hutchins distinguishes between the new knowledge in a text and—as a prerequisite for introducing this—the text's connection between the existing (old) knowledge and the new knowledge. Here is the connection to the potential reader's basis for understanding the text. In other words, Hutchins introduces the concept of the user's level of presupposition.

Traditional indexers do not—according to Hutchins—distinguish between what is new and what is presupposed in a text. This kind of indexing may be satisfactory for users who are experts in the field, because experts are interested in following the development in the field and can use all texts which contain new knowledge. On the contrary such indexing lets the novice down. A novice needs a text aimed at his own level. Therefore—according to Hutchins and adherents to the cognitive approach—a new theory and praxis of indexing should be developed which takes into account the user's level of presupposition.

But in my opinion, this has not brought us any closer to a clarification of the concept of subject or the fundamental problems of representing documents for retrieval. We need a concept that can be useful for all kinds of indexing, for both experts and novices. In my opinion, the theory of aboutness, as summarized here, is caught in the mentalistic (and idealistic) trap, also described by Frohmann (1990).

The argument for introducing the concept of aboutness in information science was thus difficulties with the concept of subject. This means that if we succeed in providing a satisfactory definition of subject, then most of the justification for using the term aboutness disappears. In my view, the introduction of the concept of aboutness did not solve the problem, but just gave it a new name.

Clearly, the subjectivistic point of view is of greatest relevance in systems functioning as intermediaries toward some specific kinds of users, for example, children. If the mentalistic and cognitivistic approaches take this stand, they clearly must admit that some other, more basic approaches are needed, from which they can take over. For instance, you have to know to what degree the objectivity of knowledge can be taken for granted. It follows that problems in the theory of knowledge are more fundamental than knowledge about the users of information systems: the users cannot express needs that they have no ideas about.

If the issue is the aboutness or subject matter of a book, there are many different agents, each representing its own aboutness or version of subjectivism:

- the author's version (often expressed in the title or the text, either implicitly or explicitly)

- the reader's version (great variation is possible here)

- the publisher's version, as often indicated in a series title (e.g., European Monographs in Social Psychology)

- the librarian's version, which may well be expressed in a library's classification practices

Sometimes, there are agreements between different subject analysts. Most often such agreements are seen as an ideal ("indexing consistency").[4] But agreements can represent a subject analysis of low quality. If a document has a misleading title, the indexer may choose an unsuitable descriptor because he is misguided by the title. This gives high consistency, but bad indexing. Subject analysis should never be built on the title or the self-understanding of the document (which would allow high consistency), but on the optimal representation in the perspective of the potential users and their questions and requirements.

A theory of subject matter must accept and build upon the existence of these different versions of the aboutness/subject matter of a document. But it is not enough to accept these different views in a relativistic way without developing criteria for what represents an optimal subject analysis of a document for a given purpose. This means that a theory of meanings and subjects must be able to explain why different people arrive at different solutions. The subjectivity should not just be taken for granted, but should itself be explained. Information science needs a theory of subjects which can be used to differentiate good from bad subject analyses of documents and makes it possible for information services to produce optimal document representations. In the section on activity theory below, I introduce a view of these agents as members of discourse communities.

Bente Ahlers Moeller (1979/1981) published a paper in which she compares classification of the same books in the system used at the State and University Library in Aarhus, Denmark, with the Dewey Decimal Classifications. She demonstrates that there can be amazing differences between subjective perceptions of what the subjects of the books are. But this subjectivity may well be extremely well-founded: subjectivity is not noise or error; it is a consistent and thoroughly underpinned analytical tendency. We are not merely speaking of the different structures which different classification systems give to subjects (e.g., more or less subdivision), but unequivocal differences in the conception of the subject of a book, where one view places a book discussing the book trade under the subject "books," and another view places the same book under the subject "trade."

With regard to the subjective idealistic theory of subject matter we will demonstrate that neither the author's, the reader's, the librarian's or information specialist's nor any other person's (e.g., the publisher's) point of view or subjective understanding can have any certain or objective knowledge about the subject of a document, nor define the concept of subject. Each of these viewpoints can contribute something to a determination of the subject, but the subjective idealistic conception of subject overemphasizes certain aspects of the document either from the author's, the reader's, or an interpreter's point of view.

A book can—but need not—contain an assertion of what its subject is. The *author* can explicitly discuss the subject of his work, e.g., in the introduction, and he may note its relation to other subjects. If a book is called *General Psychology*, it may contain a discussion of what general psychology is. Since the basis of psychology is a complex theoretical problem, the author's views need naturally not be true, but may be merely the expression of his more or less well-founded (subjective) ideas. That which is psychology for some may—after theoretical considerations—prove rather to be sociology or physiology. The book may not at all deal with that which the author thinks it does, nor with what the title indicates.

Just as often, however, a work does not contain any explicit discussion of its subject. *The History of Dynamic Psychiatry* assumes implicitly that psycho-analysis is part of medical science (psychiatry) and not of psychology. Much can be said about this, but the given label of a given book need not be correct. A book need not treat the subject of psychiatry because it says it does. A truly scientific analysis of the subjects of documents for databases would have to assume certain consistent definitions, which would sometimes, but by no means always, be in agreement with the version of the subject given in the document itself.

With regard to the *user*, a document can be ordered with the user's conceptual structures and subject perceptions in mind. The user may well have his subjective grasp of what the subject of the book is.

Some information retrieval theorists appear to work from the premise that an information retrieval system ought to order subjects according to each user's subjective reading. They are inclined to build on psychological investigations of the users' perceptions of the subject, their knowledge structures. There are also examples of investigations carried out on such a basis (e.g., Mark Pejtersen, 1979, & 1980). A related mode of consideration is, for example, Belkin, Oddy, and Brooks's "ASK model" (1982).

We claim that there are types of information systems which clearly ought to aim to tailor the description of the subjects to the user's subjective perceptions. Examples of this are library systems for children or pedagogical systems in which a point of departure and a goal can be described for both a learning process and for advising students. Both types express a certain paternalism, that is, someone assumes the responsibility for the direction of others' information searches. This is done by presuming to create the connections between given documents and the user's subject universe, that is, undertaking to interpret the subjects or information content of the documents from a psychological or pedagogical evaluation of needs and goals.

Aside from such paternalistic approaches, should subject descriptions then take the psychology of the user into account? Yes, in a certain way this is indeed desirable. Information retrieval systems should be made user-friendly, and this can be done by having knowledge of the users' language and subjective perceptions and use this knowledge, for example, in cross-references to the preferred terms. So it is even the ideal that all systems in a certain way relate to the users. But this does not mean that one interprets the subject content of documents based on knowledge of the users' subjective perceptions, but that these perceptions are employed to create the necessary references and instructions, that is, to make the system user-friendly. In my opinion the question of user-friendliness is not *the* central theoretical issue in information retrieval. The central issue is knowledge representation, how to represent the knowledge in documents. The question of user-friendliness is a cognitive-ergonomic question that must be implemented in a system, but is of secondary interest compared to the adequate representation of knowledge in databases.

Scientific information systems must in my opinion presuppose that the user acquires the categories, terminology, and classifications of science, scholarship, and information systems, rather than the reverse. The adoption of the user's categories and terminology by science and its information systems is a job for popularization, not primarily for information science. Reference is often made to using the principles of psychology and linguistics for system design, but such principles often present dilemmas or contradictions in contrast to purely disciplinary considerations. My conclusion here is that he who seeks the key to the concept of subject in the mind of the user commits an error of psychologism.

A third subjective conception can be expressed by the *librarian or information specialist* in a subject description of documents in a database. In the best instances a system is used (of classification, a thesaurus, or something else) which makes possible a highly explicit and consistent basis for analysis. As demonstrated (e.g., in Ahlers Moeller, 1979/1981), different systems employ different (subjective) principles of analysis and thereby determinations of subjects. This situation will not be further documented here, since it makes up a significant part of the argument in the section on the activity theoretical view on subject matter. I will here merely establish that both the individual information worker and the different IR systems display considerable variations in their descriptions of the subjects of given documents. To the extent that this subjectivity is made a quality of the subject concept itself, we are talking about a subjective idealistic conception.

A worthwhile critique of mentalistic (and thereby idealistic) tendencies in information retrieval theory has recently been published by Frohmann (1990). My own attempts at clarification of information science are in definitive ways identical to Frohmann's point of departure.

As mentioned in the historical introduction to this chapter, Miksa confronts Cutter's view with "the modern idea of a subject," which he formulates in this way:

To speak of subjects in relation to books is simply to identify particular subjects that have been written about. To speak of subjects in relation to a classification scheme is simply to place those particular subjects in the context of their relationships with other subjects. The essential likeness remains. Subjects in either case are singular mental loci of thought. They are, for all practical purposes, named intellections that have their own separate identities. They are the mental particles that make up the intellectual universe, much in the same manner that atomic particles make up the physical universe. They may be broad or narrow, simple or complex in denotation and connotation, abstract or concrete in their reference as the case may be, easily named with a single word or named only with great difficulty by the precoordination of several words, and so on through a variety of characterizations. The factor common to all subjects is not their location—that is, whether found in a book, in a portion of a book, in the form of a spoken address or other communication, or as a location signified by a symbol in a classification scheme—but rather that they are the thoughts of people expressed in some way. Moreover, given all thinking beings at all times, their named thoughts constitute a total set of such subjects. With this in mind, the arrangement of subjects in some classificatory order would appear to be posterior or extraneous to their existence. (Miksa, 1983b, p. 57)

Miksa is very profound in establishing the connection between Cutter's concept of subject and his epistemological position. However, in introducing his own modern understanding of subject, Miksa makes no attempt to anchor it in epistemology. In my perception, his view is related to classical empiricism. To speak of mental atoms, to accept their subjective nature, to assume no given connections between them, and to relate them only to minds of single individuals (or the sum thereof) are characteristic of the empirical and subjective idealistic view.

Nominalism

Empiricism/positivism is closely related to a nominalistic view of meaning. Nominalism is a philosophical position which maintains that universals do not exist, that the world consists of single phenomena, which are labeled by individual terms. There is no deeper reality, no "essence": all that exists, is open and directly given. Wittgenstein in the *Tractatus Logico-Philosophicus* put forward his picture theory of meaning. According to this theory, a sentence or proposition is a picture of a (possible) state of affairs. Terms correspond to nonlinguistic elements, and those terms' arrangements in sentences have the same form as arrangements of elements in the states of affairs the sentences stand for. Nominalism is characterized by the assumption that cognition in relation to language and tradition can stand on its own feet. Some positivistic ideals which try to describe everything in physicalist languages, referring to objects in time and space, represent a kind of nominalism. Positivism tends to dissolve general concepts because it wants to verify them by making them concrete. In some information retrieval languages (e.g., the PsycINFO thesaurus) this ideal clearly prevails by giving priority to concrete terms such as anatomical terms, drugs, countries, and so on, at the expense of more theoretical, psychological concepts.

The pragmatic philosopher John Dewey is one of the most important critics of nominalism:

It was the way in which nominalism obscures the importance of the interactions between organic beings, more than the issue of whether the uses of words (regarded as instruments) reveal universal characters in things, which formed the basis of [John] Dewey's criticism of nominalism. Nominalism invites us to consider the context in which humans use language in abstraction from all social interaction, to regard a linguistic act or its vehicle purely as a particular existence. (Tiles, 1988, p. 86)

In *Reconstruction in Philosophy*, John Dewey writes about knowledge organization:

The pragmatic value of organization is so conspicuously enforced in contemporary life that it hardly seems necessary to dwell upon the instrumental significance of classification and systematization. When the existence of qualitative and fixed species was denied to be the supreme object of knowledge, classification was often regarded, especially by the empirical school, as merely a linguistic device. It was convenient for memory and communication to have words that sum up a number of particulars. Classes were supposed to exist only in speech. Later, ideas were recognized as a kind of *tertium quid* between things and words. Classes were allowed to exist in the mind as purely mental things. The critical disposition of empiricism is well exemplified here. To assign any objectivity to classes was to encourage a belief in eternal species and occult essences and to strengthen the arms of a decadent and obnoxious science—a point of view well illustrated in Locke. General *ideas* are useful in economizing effort, enabling us to condense particular experiences into simpler and more easily carried bunches and making it easier to identify new observations.

So far nominalism and conceptualism—the theory that kinds exist only in words or in ideas—was on the right track. It emphasized the teleological character of systems and classifications, that they exist for the sake of economy and efficiency in reaching ends. But this truth was perverted into a false notion, because the active and doing side of experience was denied or ignored. (Dewey, 1948, p. 151, emphasis in original)

It is thus typical of the nominalistic viewpoint that it is based on individual and concrete (reductionistic) perception and that it disregards larger interpretative "horizons." The empiricist approach therefore typically sees subject analysis as something straightforward, as something simple, that can easily be extracted from users or texts.

At this point the conclusion is that it is typical of the subjective idealistic conception of subject that it over emphasizes certain aspects of the document either from the author's, the reader's, or an interpreter's point of view.

RATIONALISM AND OBJECTIVISM

Rationalism is an epistemological theory which stresses the role of reason in cognition (see Table 4.2). Sense experiences are seen as fragmented and therefore unable to provide general knowledge; they presuppose concepts and categories to classify them. Rationalism tends to perceive reality as governed by general rules, principles, and ideas (objective idealism). Classical rationalists are Plato, Descartes, Spinoza, Leibniz, and Kant. Euclidean geometry is often seen as the model science (and the development of non-Euclidean geometry in the nineteenth century was a heavy blow to rationalism). In modern cognitive science rationalism is represented by the classical paradigm of artificial intelligence: cognition as symbol manipulation according to general rules (programs). The linguist Noam Chomsky is one of the leading figures in modern rationalism.[5]

It is important to state that the opposite of rationalism is not necessarily irrationalism or antirationalism. Different epistemologies try to develop a rational basis for cognition and science. The classical opposition to rationalism was empiricism, which tried to develop an epistemology based on rational grounds. Today empiricism and rationalism are perceived as more related, and the big difference is between fundamentalistic and atomistic theories on the one hand, and relativistic and holistic theories on the other hand. All camps build on rational arguments.

The subjective idealistic subject theory viewed subjects as subjective categories, for which person X and person Y each had his own subjective grasp of the subject of a given document.[6] Objective idealism does not consider a subject as subjective in this way: persons X and Y will—if they perform correct analysis—arrive at the same subject for a given document, the subject of which can then be termed objective.

Whereas subjective idealism in general is characterized by overemphasis on the perceptions of the senses, rationalism tends to over emphasize certain aspects of theoretical analysis and make them absolute.

The idealistic conception indicates that a subject is a designation of an *idea*. In Ranganathan's system this is made explicit: "Subject—an organized body of ideas, whose extension and intension are likely to fall coherently within the field of interests and comfortably within the intellectual competence and the field of inevitable specialization of a normal person." (Ranganathan, 1967, p. 82). One of his students (Gopinath, 1976, p. 51) defines it in this way: "A subject is an organized and systematized body of ideas. It may consist of one idea or a combination of several."[7] This comes very close to Ranganathan's own conception, even though he sometimes avoids the problem, as in *Documentation and Its Facets* (1963, p. 27), where he declares subject to mean "assumed term."

The British classification researcher D. W. Langridge works in the tradition of Ranganathan. In his monograph on subject analysis (1989), the concept of subject is analyzed in two major components:

1. Central to his book is the thesis that fundamental categories of knowledge exist. These are the philosophical categories, which go back to Plato and Aristotle and which were introduced to LIS especially by S. R. Ranganathan. Langridge prefers the expression "forms of knowledge" for these fundamental categories. There are relatively few forms of knowledge; Langridge lists twelve, including philosophy, natural science, technology, human (behavioral or social) science, history, religion, art, criticism, and personal experience.

2. Besides these forms of knowledge Langridge operates with "topics," which are "the phenomena that we perceive." Where human science is a form of knowledge, human behavior is a topic.

Besides these two fundamental components, Langridge (1989, p. 31) discusses a third one:

3. The concept of discipline (or "field of learning"): "Unfortunately, this extremely important distinction has been blurred in many people's minds by the existence of a third kind of term which combines both form of knowledge and topic. For example, ethics is the philosophy (form) of morals (topic); zoology is the science (form) of animals (topic); psychology is the science (form) of human behavior (topic)."

Langridge does not favor the concept of scientific disciplines as a concept in subject analysis because they are unstable: "the disciplines that constitute specializations may be unstable, but the fundamental disciplines, or forms of knowledge, are not. The specializations are a practical convenience for sharing the world's intellectual labours: the forms are permanent, inherent characteristics of knowledge" (p. 32). Langridge's concept of subject takes the above mentioned fundamental components as points of departure for subject analysis. It does *not* make reference to the user context, to the pragmatic viewpoint of subject analysis.

To elucidate more closely the view which rationalism takes of the concept of the subject, we will start by looking at its view of concepts in general. Objective idealism (as represented, e.g., by Plato or scholastic realism) considers a concept to be an abstract psychic or mental entity (an idea) which exists in and of itself, and the relationship of this to concrete things is such that these things share in the mental entities which represent them via the concept. Realism (in the above meaning) considers, in other words, that general concepts represent something universal, which exists outside of and independent of the human consciousness, and which at the same time exists prior to separate things (originally with reference to God, but today rather a form of a priori cognition in a Kantian sense).

Translated into the terms of the problem of subject, this means that the concrete documents share ideas expressed in a given subject. These ideas exist outside the human consciousness (or within it as a priori perceptions) and are also prior to the individual concepts expressed in the individual documents. These ideas or subjects have universal or fixed properties: they can be analyzed

Table 4.2
Basic Principles in Classical Rationalism

- It is possible to formulate the basic principles on how to obtain knowledge. Knowledge is infallible. It consists of elements (facts or modules) of infallible knowledge, which can be combined into larger units. Therefore, in principle, knowledge is modular.

- Besides the pure logical principles, other general principles exist.

- Pure and isolated experience provides no knowledge. You have to have hypotheses or other fundamental assumptions as well.

- In every domain of knowledge, it is possible to organize the knowledge in axioms, definitions, and theorems.

- It is the thinking of the individual human being and the sense of evidence which forms the basis for the attainment of knowledge (methodological individualism).

- Simple (nondefined) concepts are concepts which cannot be defined from other concepts in interesting ways. Fundamental concepts are concepts which are indispensable to describe or explain a topic.

- Simple and fundamental concepts enter into some necessary relations to each other. These relations reflect basic principles of reason.

- The analysis of an arbitrary topic leads to a number of simple and fundamental concepts.

- Every concept can be organized in an all-embracing structure of concepts.

- The difference between simple and compound concepts is absolute. It is not just the case that something is simple and something is compound when seen from a certain point of view (knowledge interest) or in a certain respect.

- Empirical experience can be used to check ideas on general connections. However, it is never decisive for insight into these.

- You can never determine the content of a concept by the presentation of examples of that concept. On the contrary: every sensory recognition presupposes that the perceiving person already has certain concepts ("carries something in the luggage").

- An analytical statement is a statement whose truth-value is logically established. To a rationalist, there exist necessary statements which are not analytical. However, to an empiricist there is no necessity in the world; everything that happens is contingent.

- The predisposition to realize basic concepts that do not originate from experience must be inborn. It is our way to form concepts, which determine the essential connections between the things we can learn.

once and for all in a universal system and, for instance, be decomposed or separated into individual facets.

This theoretical point of departure continues to have far-reaching influence on today's theories about subjects. It can be traced to the views of Ranganathan (Gopinath, 1976), Thomas Johansen (1975, 1985, 1987a, 1987b, 1989), and others who treat the subject as an idea which can be analyzed in its individual parts.

Ranganathan's "colon classification" is discussed in an article by Gopinath, in which he states (1976, p. 60):

a subject is largely the product of human thinking. It presents an organized pattern of *ideas* created by the specialists in any field of inquiry. Working at the near-seminal level and postulating about helpful sequence among the facets and isolates *has led to the conjecture that there may be an "absolute syntax" among the constituents of the subjects within a basic subject, perhaps parallel to the sequence of thought process itself, irrespective of the language in which the ideas may be expressed, irrespective of the cultural background or other differences in the environments in which the specialists, as creators as well as the users of the subject, may be placed.* (emphasis added)

This view—that human thought, human language, human consciousness, the human subject universe has an "absolute syntax," that is, that it is fundamentally independent of the functional context of the mental processes—is a pattern of the rationalistic and idealistic conception, a direct contrast to the view that the mental processes are tools, formed by and suited to the tasks and conditions in which they function. Since there is no question of person X and person Y having different syntax, this is an objective, not a subjective, idealism.

Objective idealism manifests itself in its methodological framework for classification of knowledge with the view that classification of documents can be done independent of the context in which classification is being used. The syntax in Ranganathan's system is the PMEST formula (personality, matter, energy, space, time). Gopinath (1976, p. 60) gives an example of the analysis of a document. The subject "exercise of franchise by the Indian citizen in the 1960s" is analyzed as follows in the colon system:

History	[Basic subject]
Indian community	[Personality round 1, level 1]
Citizen	[Personality round 1, level 2]
Franchise	[Matter round 1, level 2]
Exercise	[Energy round 1]
1960s	[Time level 1]

It is my claim that this type of analysis, which determines the priorities of the viewpoints to be taken on a subject, is not optimal in every situation. One can imagine researchers working on the technical aspects of the election process who wish to compare them in several countries. For such a person the election would be the central subject, and it would be inconvenient if this were a sub-topic of history and India. (Computer searching has to a large degree made fixed sequences among facets superfluous; the problem only remains for printed catalogs and other one-dimensional ordering systems, but that is another issue.)

It is indeed my claim that an objective idealistic concept of subject matter tend towards subject descriptions which only have an abstract relationship to the needs for subject description and the contexts in which they are used, because such descriptions are based on the a priori given properties of ideas. In other words, subjects are viewed as innate properties in things or documents. This is a consequence of the theory's concept of objective ideas, separated from the individual items of reality. In other words, this is also an expression of objective idealism's special conception of the relationship between the general and the particular: that the general exists outside of and independent of the particular. This is in contrast to the concept that a subject only exists in the specific documents and that every subject description contains an analysis with its point of departure within the very contexts of its use, which is to be examined more closely below. The idealistic concept of subject has furthermore the consequence that neither the worldviews nor the academic disciplinary and political priorities expressed in information systems are recognized, which has been criticized by Steiger (1973), among others.

To sum up: The rationalistic point of view does not—as did the subjective idealistic viewpoint—seek the concept of subject in the minds of some people. Instead it presumes that some kind of abstract analysis or fixed procedure could be used to penetrate the surface of documents, thereby revealing their true subjects. As we shall see later, no such fixed procedure can guarantee a correct subject analysis. Among other things, this approach lacks consideration of the pragmatic aspects of subjects: the potential use of the documents.

HISTORISM AND PRAGMATISM

There exist many alternatives to classical empiricism and rationalism. Many of these have some common assumptions, which can be labeled epistemological historism. One of the most influential philosophers on this view has been George Wilhelm Friedrich Hegel (1770–1831). Some of the main principles are listed in Table 4.3.

Epistemological historism covers several traditions which are mutually very different. Among others, they include hermeneutics, pragmatism, historical materialism, critical theory, and social constructivism.

In information science discourse analysis and social constructivism as applied by Frohmann (1994) and others, are closely related to epistemological historism. This research represents a renewal and a much needed historical orientation in information science. However, it seems more adequate for analyzing biases in existing systems than for developing criteria for designing new ones. As Frohmann concludes: "The social constructivist approach to knowledge organization does not, therefore, offer alternatives to specific systems, but shows the social character of any SKO [system of knowledge organization]."

Table 4.3
Basic Principles in Epistemological Historism

- Knowledge is historically, socially, and culturally determined; also the criteria of true knowledge are determined by historical and social conditions.

- It is not possible to formulate exhaustive and fundamental principles on how to obtain knowledge. These principles are themselves developed historically.

- Concepts are not primarily defined from individual sensations or by eternal criteria, but from cultural learning and influence.

- The function of knowledge is studied not only by focusing on the isolated and abstract human being and his or her ability to sense, remember, and form concepts, but in addition by involving the whole person's developmental history, both individually and collectively. Attention should also be given to the study of what knowledge actually performs and has earlier performed—to the history of culture and ideas.

- Knowledge or learning is searching for a unified whole (holism).

- All experiences, even the most simple, happen only on the basis of an understanding of the coherence in which the phenomena form a part.

- The mastering of a common concept implies the ability to use that concept on a multitude of phenomena in many different connections.

- Knowledge is not modular and does not consist of a sum of knowledge about single things, but about relevant connections.

- All experience happens from a certain perspective and in a certain historical and social context.

- Experience is self-correcting (adjusting) based upon knowledge about its own history.

- Knowledge is best studied by giving a historical account for how relevant concepts, theories, and interpretations have been developed in connection with the circumstances under which they have been developed.

- Development of knowledge is connected with recognition (epistemical authority).

- The individualistic account for the cognitive system provided by both empiricism and rationalism is seen as narrow-mindedness because they do not include the signification of the role of tradition and social communities for learning and conceptual development.

- Abduction (conclusion to the most probable) is seen as more important than the inductive and deductive conclusions preferred by empiricism and rationalism.

Cornelius (1996a, 1996b) has provided a sharp analysis of interpretation and hermeneutics in relation to information studies. His conclusion is:

It may seem from this that the interpretative approach is incommensurate with other approaches to the concept of information. If this is so, we cannot dismiss the interpretative approach merly because it resists any tests of integretion with other approaches: interpretation introduces a broadening of the problem of information. This is a gloomy conclusion for the technical processes of out field, but I am optimistic that application of this approach, the interpretative approach, to information will generate a clearer understanding of information, and that in time it will lead to a clearer and better practice. (Cornelius, 1996a, p. 20)

Cornelius' interpretative approach is related to the use of documents and thus to practice and to pragmatism. Pragmatism is a philosophy developed by the American philosophers Charles Sanders Peirce (1839–1914), William James (1842–1940), and John Dewey (1859–1952). Pragmatism stresses the instrumentality of human knowledge and concepts, and the relation of theory to praxis and directed action as the starting point for reflection. It is inspired by Darwinism and could be labeled an evolutionary epistemology. In addition, the Marxist tradition (including neo-Marxist viewpoints such as Jürgen Habermas's, Vygotsky's, and Leontiev's) has a strong practice orientation and are related to pragmatism.

There are, however, some contradictions in pragmatic philosophy. Where the pragmatism of Charles Sanders Peirce and John Dewey was mostly from a long-term perspective, William James popularized—and vulgarized—pragmatism.[8] In the examples provided by James, truth was often connected to utility from a short-term perspective. My own thinking is mostly related to that of activity theory (Dewey, Vygotsky, and Leontiev among others). Important principles in the pragmatic theory of knowledge are outlined by Sarvimäki in Table 4.4.

Pragmatic Conception of Subject Matter

Subject representation data clearly have a pragmatic purpose: A user has a particular (specific) need for information, a problem to be solved for which information is required. This information is searched for in libraries or databases in which documents (carriers or conveyors of information) are indexed by subject. The indexing of subjects by librarians or information specialists must—for the process to be meaningful—anticipate the needs of the user: it must make it possible for the user to find that for which he is searching. Subject data in libraries and information systems have an instrumental or pragmatic function. As Bookstein and Swanson (1975) write: "Documents are indexed for the purpose of retrieval, and one can arrive at a theoretically well-founded procedure for indexing by being true to that purpose."

Table 4.4
Basic Principles in the Pragmatic Theory of Knowledge

- Man is primarily an actor, living and acting in a biophysical, a sociocultural, and a subjective world.

- Living and acting in the three worlds constitutes the a priori of human knowledge.

- Since living and acting constitutes the a priori of knowledge, knowledge is constructed in such a way that an application of well constructed knowledge will directly or indirectly serve living and acting.

- When knowledge becomes part of an acting system, it functions as an internal action determinant.

- There is a continuous interaction between knowledge and action so that knowledge is created in and through action and so that experiences that the actor acquires through action influence subsequent action.

- Value-knowledge, factual knowledge, and procedural knowledge are three types of knowledge connected to the three types of internal action determinants. Having value-knowledge means knowing what fulfills the criteria of good values. Having factual knowledge means having true beliefs about the three worlds in which one is living. Having procedural knowledge means knowing how to carry out a specific act or act sequence.

- Knowledge can be unarticulated or articulated. Unarticulated knowledge is, for instance, tacit knowledge, familiarity, knowledge by acquaintance. Knowledge can be articulated in everyday language, science, and art.

Source: Sarvimäki, 1988, pp. 58–59.

Dagobert Soergel (1985) has introduced a distinction between "content oriented indexing" and "request oriented indexing" which has proved most stimulating in my philosophizing on the concept of subject. Whether Soergel really invented request oriented indexing or just the name is not investigated here. He points out that it is only the first of these which is described in the library and information science literature and that the second is hardly known in theory, though examples do exist in practice (e.g., the database Ringdok, which describes the chemical literature in another way than in Chemical Abstracts, because Ringdok pays special attention to the needs of the pharmaceutical industry).

A *content-oriented indexing* is a description of subjects which has to be conceived as purely a function of the attributes of the document—as in the observation that "this document contains the chemical formula for sulphuric acid" (and the consequent categorization as, e.g., "inorganic chemistry"). It is my view that such content-oriented indexing is related to a rationalistic and nominalistic view of knowledge.

User-oriented or *need-oriented indexing* is a description of a subject which must be perceived as the relation between the properties of a document and a real or anticipated user need. For example, one may say, "this document deals with sulphuric acid. Sulphuric acid corrodes. Signmakers need corrosive agents" (and thus follow with a categorization such as "literature on chemicals for use in signmaking"). Need-oriented indexing is an instrumental (means-goals) relation between a document and a user need.

Bibliometric Linking as Pragmatic Relationships

Within information science, aids such as Science Citation Index, Social Science Citation Index, and Atlas of Science (all published by the Institute of Scientific Information in Philadelphia) provide links between subjects or categorizing of documents on the basis of a prior purely instrumental or means-goal relationship: the documents cited by the same document are assumed to be related in subject, since they have all contributed to the results of the document in question. In other words, these atlases (or the concepts of *bibliometric linking* and *co-citation*) are implicit expressions of a concept of subject in which a prior factual, instrumental relationship (as reflected in citation practice) provides the basis of definition.

Bibliometric linking or co-citation makes up one method of searching for literature which has taken its place in the system, and which has its advantages and disadvantages. It occupies a niche: it is not a question of merely mapping such prior instrumental connections and thereby producing a patent medicine for literature searching, or reducing the concept of the subject to these empirical relationships.

Several reasons play a role in this. First, a potential instrumental relationship cannot be extracted from a prior instrumental relation. In information science, the literature about telecommunications may be linked (co-cited) with the literature of information retrieval, because telecommunications in a certain stage of development was a crucial problem for information retrieval. But at a later time, the problems of telecommunications may be regarded as trivial, and this bibliographic linking may be a bad expression of present subject-relatedness. Second, certain conditions, either cultural or sociological, within the research environment skew the picture, insofar as the most epistemologically fertile documents are often not cited as much as those documents which easily lead to concrete investigations (i.e., there is an overemphasis on empiricism). A third and final reason is that a particular document most often contains essentially different types of information which it is useful to categorize in other ways than that to which a purely user-oriented practice would lead. For example, many psychological investigations cite statistical and methodological literature as well as literature of psychological substance (e.g., factor analysis and intelligence). It would be expedient to operate with these as different subjects, even though they appear together (through bibliometric links) within the psychological literature of a given period.

Further Problems in the Pragmatic Conception of Subject Matter

In the bibliometric section above, some major problems with the pragmatic conception of subject matter were analyzed. Pragmatic subject theory runs into other difficulties: if it is assumed that a given document is to be included in relation to all its possible uses, then this would give rise to all too numerous repetitions or multiple classifications. In the above example with sulphuric acid it would be impossible for a univeral library to classify sulphuric acid under all its potential uses. Therefore, Soergel's concept of request-oriented indexing is indeed significant, and for specialized information services it is important to classify according to the need of the target group.

Sometimes an interpretation of pragmatic indexing suggests "the strategy of unlimited aliasing" (e.g., Blair, 1990), which is a suggestion that implies that so many different subject descriptions as possible are put into the document representations. This theory can be disproved both theoretically and empirically (cf. Brooks, 1993).

Of course, the problem with a pragmatic concept of the subject lies in the most basic sense in the condition it shares with pragmatic philosophy: even though the goal is to develop human practice, a narrow practice-orientation is too short-sighted and superficial in its truth criteria. Short-term pragmatism contains no profound criteria for significance that can give direction to indicating the priority of the properties of a document.

For example, a cow can be described both zoologically as a mammal and pragmatically as a domestic animal or livestock. Dahlberg (1974, p. 194) designates the last relation as the relation between man and object, but assigns to the first another type—ontological. However, according to pragmatism all cognition is fundamentally instrumental for man. The concept of domestic animal has a more *immediate* connection to human practice, whereas the concept of mammal is an abstraction with a *less immediate* relation to human practice. Classification of a book on cows in the subject category "mammals" or in "domestic animals" is not dependent on the most significant property of the book (the central object is a cow in both cases). It depends basically on the evaluation of whether the book is of most use to people looking for literature under zoology or agriculture, that is, whether the book is of most use to a biologist or a farmer. This is a judgment based on the properties of the book in relation to perception of interests in an epistemological sense. This judgment is perhaps made primarily on the basis of the content of the book, but when subject description is intended for another target group, other decisions would be made (cf. the above example with Chemical Abstracts and Ringdok).

The abstract and general knowledge of biology and the other sciences has clearly demonstrated its significance for man, even though a designation of useful functions is less immediate than "domestic animal." Scientific systematization and terminology provide a topical organization of knowledge which on a superior level assures the most effective communication in the development of human knowledge. Such an organization of knowledge is difficult to justify from short-term pragmatic philosophy (as expressed by William James and in the commonsense understanding of this concept).

A danger of the pragmatic viewpoint is a relativistic "anything goes" or a narrow targeted analysis neglecting pure or autonomous inquiry. Even though short-term pragmatic subject theory has its limitations, it makes, however, an important contribution to perception of central properties of the concept of the subject by pointing out its means-goal nature (and thus repudiating the view of subjects as inherent qualities; subjects are no more inherent qualities than is the value of a thing).

This is supported by the etymology of *subject* (especially in the Scandinavian languages, but also in English and German).[9] *Subject* (Scandinavian *emne*) means "raw material," among other things. "Iron" is a subject for the smith. A "cow" is a subject for the zoologist and the farmer. "Epistemology" is a subject for the philosopher and the information researcher. A subject thus is always a subject for someone or for something. This is also supported by the meaning "intentional object" which it is given in the phenomenological tradition.

Pragmatic philosophy has, however, more to offer. This will be demonstrated below.

ACTIVITY THEORY AND REALISM

Activity theory is a psychological and anthropological theory mostly connected with the Russian psychologists Lev Vygotsky, Alexander Luria and A. N. Leontiev. It is also sometimes referred to as "the cultural-historical school in psychology."[10] Vygotsky and Leontiev were dedicated Marxists and developed their theory upon the epistemology of historical or dialectical materialism. It is my view, however, that there is a close connection between the pragmatic view of, among others, John Dewey and this Russian activity theory. It is also my view that central parts of dialectical materialism are simply wrong[11] but that other parts of the theory of materialism (as used by Vygotsky and Leontiev) are fruitful and are today regarded as forerunners of an understanding related to that of semiotics. While the young Vygotsky was not far from the behavioristic stimulus-response thinking which dominated American psychology at that time, his later approach represents a radical departure from that framework. For the later Vygotsky, the key to the nature of higher psychological functioning lies in the mediating role of the systems of signs. These systems, which form the fundamental basis of human mental functioning, are cultural creations. They are products of social history and are preserved in human activity, in the interpretative practices of the community. Thus for psychology to be scientific it must employ, not a reductionist method, but one adequate to the specific character of semiotic mediation. Psychology must become a sociohistorical discipline. David Bakhurst (1990, pp. 208–209) writes:

As Vygotsky explored this role, so he became fascinated with the notion of *meaning* and, with this, his account of mediation underwent an important change. While earlier he had portrayed signs as a class of special, artificial stimuli, operating alongside other "natural" stimuli, he now came to focus on our ability to create elaborate symbolic systems, such as natural language and mathematics, which mediate our relation to the world through the power of representation. For the later Vygotsky, the introduction of such semiotic systems of mediation completely transforms our psychological relation with reality. We now stand in relation not just to a brute, physical world, but to an *interpreted* environment, an environment conceived as being *of a certain kind*. This being so, our behaviour can never be simply "called forth" by the world in itself. Rather, we act in the light of some reading of reality, a reading that renders our behaviour an appropriate response to the perceived situation. On this view, our actions are more like conclusions to arguments than effects of physical causes. Such a position places the semiotic at the very heart of the relation between psychological subject and reality; the world is an environment endowed with significance, and the trajectory of the subject's behaviour is determined by the meaning he or she takes from the world. (emphasis in original)[12]

Activity theory stresses the development of cognition as a unity of biological development, cultural development, and individual development. It has a strong ecological and functional-historical orientation. It also stresses the activity of the subject and the object orientation of this activity.

Some general introductions to activity theory include Bedney and Meister (1997); Leontiev (1981); Martin, Nelson, and Tobach (1995); Nardi (1992); Vygotsky (1978); and Wertsch (1981). Activity theory is well known in information science with regard to the design of user interfaces[13] (and is an identifier in the INSPEC database), and it has also been applied to a kind of domain analysis,[14] but it has not yet been applied as a major paradigm for information science regarding problems of classification or subject analysis.

The Danish linguist and information scientist Peter Bøgh Andersen discusses what he labels "a materialistic view of language":

To adopt a materialistic view of language means to see the structure and development of language as an answer to demands caused by the practical situations in the daily life of the language users, to explain linguistic features by the culture and society in which the language exists, and to prefer historical explanations over ontological ones. . . .

The materialistic point of view may also contribute to our general understanding of language. Why is language as it is? If there are universals of language, what are the reasons for them? Chomsky (1968, section 3) believes that our cognitive apparatus determines the limits on possible language, and that, conversely, a study of language universals may be used to characterize the cognitive faculties of man. True as it may be, there are other explanations of language universals, namely that anything that functions as a human language must be able to perform certain functions (See e.g., Halliday 1978). Thus, universals of language do not necessarily express biological properties of the human brain, but may simply reflect basic constraints on human societies. (Bøgh Andersen, 1990, p. 63)

In my opinion, there is no difference between the use of the concept of materialism above and a pragmatic understanding of language as represented, for
example, in John Dewey's work. Thus, in my opinion both the term
"pragmatism" and the term "materialism" have some unfruitful connotations,
which is why I prefer the label "activity theory" to span important parts of both
traditions. In my understanding, John Dewey should be seen as one of the
founders of activity theory along with the Russian psychologists (predating them
by several decades). With the advent of the behavioristic and later the cognitivist
tradition in psychology and the analytic tradition in philosophy, Dewey's thought
fell out of favor for a long time. Today, however, we have an important
neopragmatic trend, emphasizing holism, antifoundationalism, contextualism,
functionalism and interest in philosophy and science studies. It is my
opinion—and hope—that information science can profit by becoming a part of
this new trend.

Activity theory regards the organism in relation to its environment. It is not
foundationalistic like classical empiricism and rationalism, but instead related to
historicism and holism. *Meaning holism* (or *semantic holism*) denotes the
following thesis about the nature of representation: the meanings of a symbol or
a term are relative to the entire system of representations containing it. This
concept was first formulated as a thesis against the positivist understanding by
the American philosopher W. V. O. Quine. Meaning holism implies that there
may be no fact of the matter about the meaning of texts (a view put forword by
Putnam, 1990) and that scientific theories that differ in their basic postulates are
empirically incommensurable (a view put forword by Thomas Kuhn, 1970).
Meaning holism is the opposite of *meaning atomism*: that the meaning of any
representation is not determined by the meaning of any other representation. The
classical resemblance theory stated that the idea of an object had an aboutness of
the object in virtue of its physical resemblance to the object. Some modern
philosophers are semantic atomists, but the resemblance theories are no longer
thought viable.

Activity theory also stresses the ecological and social nature of meaning.
Meaning is linked to the division of linguistic labor in society. For example, the
meaning of a term (say "gold") is set for the rest of us by chemical and other
specialists (Hilary Putnam). A person's use of a term may be determined not by
his individual usage, but by the usage of some social group to which he
semantically defers. Therefore, the content of a person's thoughts are themselves
in part a matter of social facts.

Activity theory represents a kind of realism. We are here faced with a kind
of realism and objectivity which could be called *pragmatical realism* (cf.
Mammen, 1994, p. 53). According to the realistic viewpoint, things exist objectively and encompass objective properties. This is a crucial point of departure
which is not always taken for granted.[15]

Meanings, classifications, subject representation data, and subjects are neither
subjective or objective in the positivist or rationalist meaning of these words:

They are not neutral with regard to the consequences of analysis and determination. Meaning analysis and subject analysis are goal-directed, teleological activities and hence also political activities: they are supporting some kinds of activities at the expense of other.[16] Both John Dewey's philosophy and the Russian activity theory therefore represent another concept of objectivity, building upon a theory of man as an active agent in the world.

John Dewey's above cited opinion about knowledge organization continues in this way:

Concrete things have *ways* [emphasis in original] of acting, as many ways of acting as they have points of interaction with other things. One thing is callous, unresponsive, inert in the presence of some other things; it is alert, eager, and on the aggressive with respect to other things; in a third case, it is receptive, docile. Now different ways of behaving, in spite of their endless diversity, may be classed together in view of common relationship to an end. No sensible person tries to do everything. He has certain main interests and leading aims by which he makes his behavior coherent and effective. To have an aim is to limit, select, concentrate, group. Thus a basis is furnished for selecting and organizing things according as their ways of acting are related to carrying forward pursuit. Cherry trees will be differently grouped by woodworkers, orchardists, artists, scientists and merry-makers. To the execution of different purposes different ways of acting and re-acting on the part of trees are important. Each classification may be equally sound when the difference of ends is borne in mind.

Nevertheless there is a genuine objective standard for the goodness of special classifications. [emphasis added]. One will further the cabinetmaker in reaching his end while another will hamper him. One classification will assist the botanist in carrying on fruitfully his work of inquiry, and another will retard and confuse him. The teleological theory of classification does not therefore commit us to the notion that classes are purely verbal or purely mental. Organization is no more merely nominal or mental in any art, including the art of inquiry, than it is in a department store or railway system. The necessity of execution supplies objective criteria. Things have to be sorted out and arranged so that their grouping will promote successful action for ends. Convenience, economy and efficiency are the bases of classification, but these things are not restricted to verbal communication with others nor to inner consciousness; they concern objective action. They must take effect in the world.

At the same time, a classification is not a bare transcript or duplicate of some finished and done-for arrangement pre-existing in nature. It is rather a repertory of weapons for attack upon the future and the unknown. For success, the details of past knowledge must be reduced from bare facts to meanings, the fewer, simpler and more extensive the better. (Dewey, 1948, pp. 151–154)

In this quotation, John Dewey only mentions *special classifications*. But the objectivity of classifications and subject analysis is valid both with regard to special classifications and with regard to *universal classifications*: they are also tools, which can be evaluated with regard to their utility. However, because universal classifications represent compromises between different goals and views of many disciplines, their "objectivity" is, however, much more difficult to establish.

The main problem with short-term pragmatism (or pragmatism as understood in ordinary language) is its inability to deal with pure inquiry, the pursuit of truth for its own sake. But in John Dewey's view, autonomous inquiry had an important function. Scientists are free to develop their own problematics and to pursue solutions to problems thus generated (cf. Tiles, 1988, p. 111). In the same way, information science should not only allow for short-term pragmatism in subject analysis and representation, but should also allow subject analysis with regard to pure inquiry, for example, biological taxonomies. Such a kind of abstract ordering and classification with only a very indirect connection to human practice is—in the long run—far the most pragmatic order for knowledge utilization. Short-term pragmatism is an unhealthy thing for science and knowledge production. Knowledge becomes fragmented, disorganized, and unclear (cf. Hjørland, 1996a).

THE ACTIVITY-THEORETICAL CONCEPTION OF SUBJECT MATTER

The activity-theoretical conception of subject is pragmatic in that it views cognition, knowledge, knowledge representation, and subject analysis in their functionality, their teleological and goal-oriented nature, and their consequences for human practice. It is opposed to short-term pragmatism that only tries to determine the use of documents in direct relation to some human practice. It is not only concerned with the actual practice and its immediate or proximal determinants in a narrow perspective, but also with the whole ecological and cultural system in which the concrete activity takes place and which forms the distal determinants of the actual activity. Therefore, a central aspect of this view is opposed to narrow pragmatism, but gives priority to the need for pure inquiry, which includes basic scientific classifications (e.g., biological taxonomies).

It is more in line with ordinary language to call this view "realism" (scientific realism) than to call it "pragmatism," but as pointed out above, the pragmatic philosophers have had an important influence on the development of this view, and "realistic" positions are often blurred with positivism.

The first important issue to consider is the object of classification. Activity theory is not atomistic, and it does not seek the concept of subject in either the mind of individuals or in rationalistic ideas, but in social practice. Classical empiricism focused on the individual and had no explanation of why aboutness is different when represented in different kinds of agents such as producers, users, and intermediaries (but viewed this difference as noice and sought the ideal as consistency in indexing). In contrast, activity theory looks upon these agents as members of discourse communities or disciplines with varying degrees of synchronized needs, knowledge, and criteria of relevance and subject analysis.

As cited in the section on rationalism above, Langridge (1989) did not like the concept of scientific disciplines as a concept in subject analysis because they are unstable. The view of pragmatism and activity theory differs from Langridge in fundamental ways. The philosophical categories are seen as important, but epistemologically they should be understood as generalizations of scientific research. Scientific research, by the way, is not only empirical research but also theoretical research. No sharp border exists between science and philosophy. These philosophical categories may be relatively stable, but they are not "permanent, inherent characteristics of knowledge."

Both the rationalistic and the empiricist points of view contain part of the truth; it is the absolutism of these viewpoints which leads to either subjective idealism or objective idealism. Science starts with such perceived phenomena as flowers (botany), stones (geology), stars (astronomy), chemicals (chemistry), and so on, but in the development of science, the perceivable objects are turned to more unperceivable objects. Plants are, for example, defined as living organisms with a chlorophyll granule, and microbiology knows living organisms which are both plants and animals (having both mouths and chlorophyll granules). That is, the perceived things influence sciences and forms of knowledge, and the theoretical knowledge thus obtained changes our perceptions and lets us see new things.[17]

What constitutes a subject according to activity theory is not independent of purpose, viewpoint, or theoretical influences. What constitutes a subject for one discipline or theory need not constitute a subject for another. This is in direct contradiction to classical rationalism. One approach in classification research is to construct independent structures, "modules," or standards which can be imported by different systems or locations in systems. One can imagine one system for human anatomy used by many different disciplinary thesauri (e.g. MEDLINE and PsycINFO). This would be a rationalist approach. The alternative is to consider each concept (e.g., anatomy) from the point of view of the specific discipline (e.g., psychology) and to modify its structure in order to fulfill its purpose in that context. To consider anatomy in psychology is to ask Why should anatomical terms be represented? Many different answers could be given, for example, neuropsychological, psychosomatic, perceptual, and social psychological. The requirements of these fields in psychology are not to have a copy of MEDLINE's anatomical system, but to have the human body described according to the specific questions asked in these fields, perhaps in a kind of polyrepresentational structure.

The scientific disciplines represent or reflect the world as it has been an object for collective human concerns. It is the same world we perceive. But many sciences are having difficulties saying what their objects are; this is not an evident or a neutral question. Sometimes different disciplines represent different theories about the same phenomena. This is illuminated in philosophy and in the disciplines themselves. It is not sensible for library and information science to ignore this problem, to take its own way, to try to go alone, and to avoid this unclear status by choosing an idealist instead of a realist theory of knowledge.

Disciplines are a central point of departure. Admittedly, they are often unclear and unstable, but they represent the real world, they are the best starting point, and they must fall within the objects of information science. It is the job of the disciplines themselves—together with philosophy (and hopefully classification research and LIS)—to make themselves more clear and more well defined and to illuminate their mutual relationships and their pragmatic consequences. Classification research should have a descriptive component (producing maps or atlases of science, e.g., by bibliometric methods) and a critical component: illuminating problems and negative tendencies in sciences and knowledge and distinguishing knowledge from pseudoknowledge, and true relationships and structures from mere fads and populistic trends. Information science should combine a study of communication patterns with studies of the nature of knowledge.

The classification of subjects by disciplines is an old tradition in library and information science. The Dewey Decimal Classification (DDC) is an example. It states, for example, that "a work on water may be classed with many disciplines, such as metaphysics, religion, economics, commerce, physics, chemistry, geology, oceanography, meteorology, and history. No other feature of the DDC is more basic than this: that it scatters subjects by discipline" (M. Dewey, 1979, p. xxxi).

This thesis is important and central to my theory of subject representation. Its principles are opposed to those described above as objective idealism and subjective idealism.[18] Scientific disciplines are kinds of social institutions, whose function is a special kind of work (knowledge production or research) originating from the objects of the disciplines. If the subject of a document is expressed in the form of a name of a discipline, the relevance or potentialities of the document for the working process of that discipline are explicated. The emphasis on collective organizations such as scientific disciplines or knowledge domains in subject analysis rather than on individually perceived aboutness or topics or rationalistic forms of knowledge represents an alternative to a dominating viewpoint represented in library and information science.

Another consequence of this view is that different theoretical backgrounds, paradigms, world views or metaviews—which can be either disciplinary, interdisciplinary, or cross-disciplinary views—are central to subject analysis. A document has given potentials. For example, John Dewey's book *Reconstruction in Philosophy* has given potentials in relation to information science and information retrieval theory. These potentials can be more or less recognized by the relevant user groups in society. For a period of time, analytic philosophy supplanted John Dewey's work. But still Dewey's work exists and has given potentials (positive or negative, depending on whether my judgment of Dewey's work is correct or false). The recognition of these potentials presupposes insight in the problematic aspects of classical empiricism and other epistemologies. Scientific and epistemological progress is not—or should not be—a mere question of fads, but should be rationally justified. Therefore, theoretical progress in epistemology and science studies is important for the ability to distinguish between fruitful trends and less fruitful trends in knowledge production. Epistemological positions should not be "chosen," but worked out in basic research in order to solve theoretical problems. For the information seeker, it becomes equally important to be able to identify the most fruitful contributions to a given problem area. In my opinion this implies that a fruitful subject analysis should allow the searcher to identify different theoretical approaches in a given area. From the point of view of activity theory, the analysis of the implicit or explicit epistemological assumptions in documents forms a central aspect of subject analysis.

Subject analysis can serve scientific or scholarly purposes, professional purposes, educational purposes, and everyday, ordinary purposes.[19] Subject analysis can be narrow and goal-oriented or it can be more general or abstract. The farmer's classification and the zoologist's classification of animals are not the same. The narrow, goal-oriented subject analysis is perhaps the most user-friendly, immediately relevant and understandable, but the more general and basic classification is of a deeper nature, less arbitrary, relevant to a much larger community, and more durable. Such basic classification and subject analysis has also important educational functions in teaching the users to navigate in the structure of reality as described by science. Different purposes require different design criteria for subject data systems. Scientific classification is misplaced in many situations, where mere ad hoc classifications are needed and vice versa.

Subjects in themselves—the objects of subject analysis—must thus be defined as the informative potentials of documents (or of other messages or information sources). This view of text meaning, in which a text has no stable, objective meaning is related to views formulated by such sociolinguistic thinkers as M. M. Bakhtin; D. Brandt; M.A.K. Halliday; R. Rommetwei; and Nystrand & Wiemelt, who discuss the meaning potential of a text.[20]

A potential is a rather intangible property—hence the problem with defining subjects. But the potential of a thing is not an idea (subjective or objective). A potential is an objective possibility. Uranium held its potential as an atomic fuel before science was aware of these possibilities, and many authors have been buried before the significant potential of their work has been recognized (e.g., Peirce). Ideologies can guide or misguide the understanding of the potentialities of documents (cf. Hjørland, 1996a). Which potentials are realized or could be realized is determined by the current stage of society's development. At one stage uranium is a not particularly valuable metal with no recognition of its special potential. At another stage it is an important energy source, and at a third stage it is perhaps something else again. This is to say that it is the level of development of human society, the human practice, that constitutes the actual subjects.

Each individual document has its own unique set of potentialities. When communicating these potentials, one makes reference to some broader field of human activity. The content of the specific document is new, but the field in relation to which its potentialities are evaluated is generally known. Hence the earlier mentioned linguistic notion that the concept of subject is connected with what is presumed known for the receiver.

A subject description of a document thus is in one way or another an expression of the informational potentials of the document, such as these appear to the person who describes the subject. The better the description predicts the potentials of the document, the more correct, more objective, is the description of its subjects. The understanding of this should become more clear if one reads the two concrete examples analyzed at the end of this chapter.

An interpretation of a given description of a subject must therefore involve the qualifications (and interests) of the person who has carried out the subject description. Patrick Wilson (1968, p. 92) wrote (with regard to what the user can expect to find within a particular location in a library's classification system): "For nothing definite *can* be expected of the things found at any given position"; this statement is only correct from this subjective prerequisite. We can affirm with the adherents of hermeneutics that perception of the potential of documents depends on the pre-understanding of the person who carries out the determination of the subject. In contrast to many adherents to hermeneutics, I, however, following John Dewey, wish to retain the concept of the objective classification (or potentials or subjects) of documents.

A subject description is thus a prognosis of future potentials. This prognosis can be based on positive as well as negative judgments. This leads us to a new question: Are there documents without subjects? In theory one has to answer no to this question; we cannot imagine documents without any possible informative potentials.[21] And it is a rare experience to consider in practice not assigning any subject designation. In specific cases the lack of clear possibilities for classification usually reflects that the document in question was inappropriate for acquisition or inclusion in the particular database. Thus the lack of a subject usually expresses an inconsistency between policies of accession and indexing.[22]

The subject description can be seen as both a kind of vision and as an evaluation in relation to current research. The most important prerequisite in subject description is not a special kind of method, but rather horizon and maturity in judgment. Overall, an important aspect is to allow the searcher to identify different theoretical approaches to a given problem. Analysis of the implicit or explicit epistemological assumptions in documents should be given priority. This implies that a relevant educational background for subject analysts should include courses or degrees in theories of knowledge and science.

The use of subject systems thus also assumes interpretation. The user must enter into the universe of the system and its devising. This is hardly exceptional. In some cases documents are ordered by the so-called principle of provenance, which requires that documents remain in the collection in the order in which they were originally organized. This requires an insight into the organization that existed when the collection was established. Ordering of documents and knowledge is always based on particular premises, worldviews, and assumptions. Knowledge of these premises is often necessary to obtain a satisfactory return from descriptions of subjects. The necessary degree of interpretation depends upon the extent to which the subject description has anticipated and met the needs of the user. In the principle of provenance only a low degree of anticipation is attempted, because the principle makes no attempt to consider the current user's context. In contrast, the above mentioned pharmacology Ringdok database exhibits a high degree of accommodation of user needs. Information systems which take into account the needs of the users are more expensive to establish and maintain, but are in return economical in use.

A description of a subject is rarely presented as a direct statement about the potential of a document. More often it appears in the form of a reference to an academic discipline ("the subject is psychology"), that is, a socially defined problem area within which the document particularly contributes to problem solving. As previously mentioned, subjects can also be expressed indirectly by merely emphasizing special qualities ("treats the architecture of Christian IV"), which can also be located in a discipline (history or art history) or which serve directly as the base from which the user himself evaluates the subject of the document (e.g., tourist attractions).

The issues of the expression of subjects, of information retrieval languages, and of representation in text go beyond the framework of this book. But since these issues presuppose a knowledge of what subjects are, the proposed theory of subject presented here is a prerequisite for more profound theories on these questions.

We can now return to Patrick Wilson's problem regarding the ill-defined phenomena of authors. Wilson is right that an imprecise use of concepts in a document should be reflected in the subject analysis of that document; the only question is how. Wilson (1968, p. 92) states: "A designation of a subject reflects the clarity or imprecision of a document."

The purpose of analyzing the subject is to determine whether a document has an informative potential in relation to future users of a given category or a given concept (e.g., hostility). If it does, it is classified under that concept; if not, then it is not put there.[23] Assignment of a subject to a document is indeed a clear judgment that the document has informative potentials within questions concerning hostility, even though this clear judgment is based on many deliberations of whether or not the document actually contributes to this subject, because it was imprecise in its use of concepts. In actual practice other possibilities often do exist that are preferable from an ideal point of view, for example, characterization of the methods or theoretical approach of the work, which well may give the work a higher profile in a database depending on its structure. In other words, decisions on the subject of a document are not typically an "all or nothing" judgment.

REALISM ABOUT DOCUMENTS

On the one hand, naturally, documents reflect the author's subjective view of the subjects treated. But we are interested in the objective properties of documents, not in the author's or any other person's subjective judgment. The objective properties are not the subjective judgments or evaluations contained in the documents, but it is objective properties which have cognitive or informative potential (provided that the reader can differentiate between false and true statements). My conception of the objective properties of documents is reminiscent of Karl Popper's concept "World III" (1972), in which he refers to books as "objective knowledge" and operates with thought experiments very similar to mine. Documents have given potentials in relation to specific goals and purposes. If all life on earth were extinguished, but libraries were left untouched, a civilization from another planet could reconstruct most of human civilization. However, my concept of the objectivity of documents is not borrowed from Popper, and there are great differences between our theories because Popper's theoretical base is dualism whereas activity theory is based on monism. There is not the space here to evaluate Popper's theory about the three worlds. It is controversial and has been seriously criticized both in philosophy and in information science (as to the latter, see Rudd, 1983), but it helps us to get a clear understanding of the objective potentials of documents.

In a narrow and ordinary understanding the properties of a thing are the sensory attributes of that thing. This narrow conception lies behind much theory about the description of documents, including subject analysis. In the broadest sense, however, a property of a document is every true statement that can be said about that document.

Objectivity means two different things in relation to judging the properties of a book: (1) "intersubjectivity" or independence of the person (subject) who apprehends, or (2) "in agreement with reality" in the above mentioned pragmatic and teleological meaning. In the first of these senses, the more readers who identify these same properties with the book, the higher the objectivity of the judgments. This kind of objectivity is related to the factual properties and is favored by positivism and adherents to indexing consistency. This kind of objectivity can only identify the more trivial properties of documents such as number of pages, language, form, type, and so on, which are important in descriptive cataloging, but rather trivial in relation to theories about subject matter.

In the sense of "in agreement with reality," the relationship is inversely proportional. Since special qualifications are necessary to be able to identify the significant properties in a scientific book, perhaps only a limited group can grasp the full potential of a work. In other words, the properties easily identified by the many will often be the less significant (or the more indiscriminate), and thus less objective in the second sense of this word.[24] Library and information science personnel with a deep degree of subject knowledge and with expertise in searching databases and evaluating searches done for professionals do often have important prerequisites for identifying such important properties.

This means that the most important properties (including the subjects) of a document cannot be determined by decision by a majority. The solution is an explicit and qualified argumentation. Such a determination is not a simple thing, susceptible to formal procedures or automation. When we maintain that the properties of a document are objective, even though the description of them requires special subjective prerequisites, this implies that reality, the testing of the document in practice, will in the final analysis decide its informative potential, no matter how many earlier misconceptions have been made. History becomes the final judge of the objectivity of statements about the properties of a document. Thus a subject evaluation should never be considered final. But neither should it be considered accidental or relativistic in the sense of "anything goes."

SUBJECTS AND THE PROPERTIES OF DOCUMENTS

Subject analysis builds on an evaluation of the document's properties with regard to optimizing the potential perception of the document among its actual and potential users. Which properties of documents are relevant, and which analytical functions are to be instituted with regard to these properties, are not given a priori, but are, among other things, dependent on contextual factors, including the existing volume of literature and the system of its access points.[25] To determine the subjects of a document, we must concern ourselves with *which* properties of documents enter into a subject description and *in what way* they play this part.

In practice it is very often the rather simple and hard properties of documents which form the basis of subject analysis (e.g., the title, headings, or introduction). Theoretically, however, this becomes extremely complicated, and as soon as an attempt is made to exclude a property, a hypothetical example pops up in which just that property would be part of determining a subject. The authorship of a document is hardly part of analyzing the subject? But what about the case of autobiographies (and as Boserup [1984] indicates, also hypothetically in other situations). In extreme situations, the language code can be used as a subject access point as one element in a subject search.[26] Also properties related to external reviews and evaluations of the document or its area must be included. I will not attempt to demonstrate here that all properties of documents enter into the subject function or to eliminate those which do not. My point of departure is this: There is not a well-defined or definable portion of the properties of documents which enter into the analysis of the subject.

Just exactly this situation led to Patrick Wilson's agnostic concept of subject matter cited earlier. In the same way, we would make the claim that the subject function cannot be a previously fixed procedure at analyzing properties, such as Ranganathan's PMEST formula attempts to set up. It is my opinion that the choice of specific properties of documents or specific functions of these properties inevitably leads down the idealistic path. Since librarians and information specialists (not to speak of computer scientists and researchers in artificial intelligence) would very much like to have clear and firm directives and procedures, an idealistic tendency continually lurks in the wings within the conception of the subject itself.[27]

Kröber and Segeth (1983) state that the concept of description is most commonly used about the perceptions of the senses, which are presented in a systematic and ordered way through deliberation and language. A successful description can achieve quite a precise picture of the item described, but it can only state how this object is constituted, not why it is constituted as it is. For the same reason, a description keeps to the superficial aspects of an object and does not pursue its essence, including the reasons for its existence. A description is thus a first step in cognition, which is later replaced by other modes of cognition that delve deeper into the essence of things. The requirement of a complete description of a phenomenon is both impossible and unnecessary. A complete description is impossible, because the infinite number of properties of a phenomenon would require an infinitely extensive description. A complete description is unnecessary, because both for scientific knowledge as well as for practical human purposes, an equally detailed description of all significant and insignificant, necessary and random, general and particular properties and relations is pointless. What is needed is knowledge of the significant, the general among the particular, the necessary, and the typical. Description can therefore only fulfill its function in the knowledge-gathering process insofar as it is not made absolute and discrete from other means of cognition, such as explanation, hypothesis, and prognosis. Description must, indeed, be viewed in the context of other such modes of cognition.

Comparison of the subject descriptions made by librarians and sociologists of sociological literature gives some insight into this situation (Krarup & Boserup, 1982). Because sociologists tend not merely to describe the documents, but to evaluate them in relation to their sociological value, the sociologists' judgments on subject were the most precise and useful.

It is naturally decisive for a theory of subject matter to recognize how to distinguish between the superficial and accidental properties on the one hand, and the significant properties on the other. Just as it is pointless to describe flora by superficial characteristics (such as color) instead of meaningful characteristics (e.g., categorization in plants with seeds or with spores), it is naturally just as necessary to describe documents according to meaningful rather than superficial characteristics. Thus, what is needed is an epistemological theory which facilitates the development of knowledge in the direction of the substance of things. Such a theory stands out in sharp contrast to conceptions which are based on research and analysis of subjects as an algorithm, a "trick," or an a priori method. It is rather the method which should be a reflection of the essence of the object.

SUBJECTS AND EPISTEMOLOGY

Jerome Bruner has recently criticized mainstream psychology:

I have written it [this book] at a time when psychology . . . has become fragmented as never before in its history. It has lost its center and risks losing the cohesion. . . . And the parts, each with its own organizational identity, its own theoretical apparatus, and often its own journals, have become specialities whose products become less and less exportable. Too often they seal themselves within their own rhetoric and within their own parish of authorities.

It is an effort to illustrate what a psychology looks like when it concerns itself centrally with meaning, how it inevitably becomes a *cultural* psychology and how it must venture beyond the conventional aims of positivist science with its ideals of *reductionism, causal explanation and prediction*. (Bruner, 1990, pp. ix, xii–xiii; emphasis in original)

Bruner's book could be seen as an epistemological analysis and critique of psychology in line with the discussion presented in this chapter.

Information science is concerned with the problems of epistemology at two levels:

- Level 1: Information science should develop a theory of subject for analyzing, for example, psychological literature. This literature, the object of subject analysis, is influenced by different paradigms or epistemologies as shown, for example, by Bruner's quotation above.

- Level 2: Information science is itself a science influenced by the same paradigms or epistemological positions as those influencing psychology and other human and social sciences.

If you claim that a subject literature should be analyzed from its own position, that a subject analysis of say empiricist psychology should be done by an information science theory of an empiricist nature, I disagree. As stated earlier, epistemologies are not chosen but are worked out in basic research. If you believe that Bruner is pointing to some relevant fact, this is of utmost interest for information specialists who are selecting, searching, and analyzing psychological information and documents. It would be a high-priority goal to make it possible for the users to differentiate between positivistic and cultural psychology, and to make a strong support for the minority who are trying to develop a more relevant psychology. Epistemological works such as Bruner's can serve as a theoretical guide for such information selection and organization.

Behaviorism, cognitivism, psychoanalysis, and activity theory are different theories or approaches to the same phenomenon: the human mind. But each of these theories implies its own subject matter for psychology. Behaviorism (empiricism) implies that the subject matter is behavior, learning, responses, discriminations, and so on. Cognitivism (rationalism) implies that the subject matter of psychology is information processing of the mind, short- and long-term memory, attention, top-down and bottom-up perceptual processes, and so on. Psychoanalysis (hermeneutics) implies that the subject matter of psychology is dreams, neurosis, unconscious processes, and so on. Activity theory (pragmatic realism) implies that the subject matter of psychology is human adaptation to various physical, biological, and cultural conditions, that is, how languages and cultures form human psychological capacities, processes, and personalities.

Therefore, subject analysis should reflect these different approaches and make the connections between approach and subject matter visible to the users (e.g., in thesauri). Epistemologies are never neutral, but have important consequences for the users of the produced knowledge. Subject analyses are not neutral either, but can make the different approaches in knowledge more or less visible.

It is my claim that it is difficult to identify the most relevant documents in modern science (see Hjørland, 1988, for an analysis of this problem with a case study). The effect of this identification being so difficult is that the theoretical basis of information systems assumes the status of an important scientific problem. The description of the subject of a document (i.e., the evaluation, assignment of priorities, and the consequent categorization of the potentials of the document) assumes an insight or understanding of which future problems can give rise to use of the document in question. The reason for this lies in two assertions: (1) Any document possesses an infinite number of properties (so that it is not possible to describe them all) and (2) the properties which are central to one context need not be so in another (thus a fixed set of priorities cannot be established once and for all, as the example from Ranganathan's system illustrated).

Information science should in my view regard itself as a tool for science (like statistics and other tools). The findings of the sciences should be taken as the starting point. Of course, the sciences are naturally neither uncontroversial, objective, or infallible, but at least as an ideal, the debate about the objectivity of scientific research is a part of science. In the same way, both a descriptive and a critical analysis of the subjects of the sciences should play an important role in information science. Thus an analysis of a subject is itself, at its most profound level, a part of the scientific process of knowledge gathering.

To sum up: As a science itself, information science faces the same problem as psychology: to choose a positivistic line of research or to choose a more cultural line. Information scientists thus need a solid grasp of epistemological questions, which can be utilized on two levels: (1) in building our own science and (2) in studying our object of analysis.

SUBJECT ANALYSIS: TWO CONCRETE EXAMPLES

Theories about subject analysis, subject matter, and information retrieval should in my opinion be able to give concrete examples on how their own analysis differs from those of other theories. If this is not the case, the theory cannot prove its importance to practice and hence—according to pragmatism—its theoretical value!

Example 1

Tinne Vammen. *Rent og urent: Hovedstadens piger og fruer 1880–1920.* København: Gyldendal, 1986.

The author is a Danish (female) historian. The title translates as: *Pure and unpure: The maids and mistresses of the capital [Copenhagen], 1880–1920.*

The author has written a book about the house in Copenhagen where she herself is living. It goes back to around the turn of the century. It focuses on the social-psychological relations between the women in the house: the mistresses and their servant girls.

The book covers a lot of different topics. It is about a very specific geographic place and a very specific historical period. It is about the relationship between two different social classes (bourgeois mistresses and working-class girls). It represents an attempt to develop "mental history" (history about mentality). We have a lot of information about the girls, where they came from, what the archives tell us about their relationship with the police, with their union, and much more.

"Pure and unpure" is used symbolically. It means that the girls had to clean the laundry. It also has a certain sexual symbolism: the girls typically came to Copenhagen from the countryside. Some of them ended up in prostitution.

Now that we have that information, we can ask what are the subjects of this work?

This book has distinctively different user groups. It is a rather obvious acquisition for a public library in Copenhagen as a contribution to local history. (It could also serve as an example of local history in the specific place in the countryside from which the girls typically emigrated). One subject is

1. Local history, social aspects. Copenhagen, 1880–1920

The book is a typical product of the Women's studies movement, the attempt to illuminate women's role in society. Therefore, the book is clearly an example of

2. Women's history. Copenhagen, 1880–1920

It is also an example of

3. Social history. Working-class women. Copenhagen, 1880–1920

It could serve sociologists and other social scientists interested in

4. Class relationships. Copenhagen, 1880–1920

It also represents an attempt to go beyond "material" history into the mentality of people. Therefore, other subjects of the book are

5. Psychohistory/The history of mentality

6. Family studies, sex, and prostitution, historical material. Copenhagen, 1880–1920

A library serving the relevant police or union could use this book to inform its readers about the relationship with the people. The subject is thus also

7. Police-population relationships. Prostitutes. Copenhagen, 1880–1920.

8. Union for housemaids, early history, aspects of

The final subject to be mentioned here applies to the symbolism of the title. The author or publisher might have tried to sell copies of the book because of its sexual symbolism. In this case, the implied subject could be related to

9. Pornography [though as such it would probably be a disappointment to most readers]

10. Books of general interest, easy readers

What then should be chosen as the subject of the book? The answer is that different epistemic communities have different needs: an information service should analyze the subject according to the potential questions of its primary user group. A public library in Copenhagen or an information service for the unions, should analyze according to their specific epistemic interests as indicated above. A general library like the Royal Library or Library of Congress should not mention all these specific subjects, but should estimate the book's most probable long-term utility. If the book represents an important methodological breakthrough in psychohistory or brings information about women's history which could serve as important sources for further study, this book should be classified as psychohistory or women's history, respectively. Otherwise, it should only be placed as local history, Copenhagen, 1880–1920 (this last proposal would be my suggestion).

If many libraries' different subject descriptions of this book are merged in one database (a union catalog), this book would be visible from many different epistemic interests. This would be an ideal situation.[28]

Example 2

Let us consider the book by Robert A. Wicklund with the title *Zero-Variable Theories and the Psychology of the Explainer* (1990).

According to the title of the book, it is about certain kinds of theories (zero-variable theories) and about the psychology of the explainer; the latter subject is related to the psychology of science.

If you read the book, you will see that zero-variable theories are not favorably evaluated. They are described as a kind of simplistic theory and the book tries to explain why this kind of theory is produced so frequently in modern psychology. Why do so many psychologists (or why do so many explainers in general) tend to use this kind of simplistic theory instead of more varied theories?

In the preface to the book in question, the following appears: "The reader should not suppose that this is a book about the philosophy of social science, or about moral pronouncement on what is good or bad in ancient and current psychological theorizing. Instead, the reader is invited to consider the psychological side of the *explainer.*"

The Library of Congress has made an analysis. It writes in its cataloging-in-publication data the following subject terms: (1) Psychology—Philosophy, (2) Psychologists—Psychology, and (3) Explanation. This means that the Library of Congress, in its first selection of subject terms, is disposed *not to follow Wicklund's statement in the preface.* While the two following subject statements can be said to be in accordance with the self-understanding of the book, this applies especially to the last subject expression.

My own subject analysis is the following. The book is important because it deals with a neglected issue in psychological research or psychology as a science: the apparent decay in the theoretical level in psychology.[29] This condition is illustrated by a number of concrete analyses of psychological theories, which in the succeeding psychological research have become substantially reduced. One such example is the almost classical theory of personality by H. A. Murray from 1938.

In my opinion, the most essential thing about Wicklund's book is in particular the concrete documentation of the apparent decline in psychological theory. There are many books about the philosophy and methodology of psychology, giving direction to the science of psychology, but there are relatively few books documenting the apparent decline in theory. It seems as if psychology does not exploit the best of its own theory and knowledge from philosophy and other sciences. How can this be explained?

Wicklund sees the documentation of the theoretical decline as something less important in his book. His main interest is to use this material to give an explanation not only about the condition of psychology, but about the psychology of explainers in general. The material which I consider to have the most potential value is for the author of the book only a minor thing.

This means there is a marked difference between the author's (Wicklund's) and my own judgment about what the potential value of the book is, what its epistemological potential is, and therefore what its subject is. This book has—as any book does—an unlimited number of properties. To analyze a book's subject is to choose the properties which have the greatest potentials for human knowledge. Therefore, my subject analysis is different from that of the author as indicated by the title and the quoted sentences from the preface.

The reason that Wicklund's and my own analysis of the central subject of the book differ so much lies in my professional evaluation of Wicklund's explanation, which I will characterize as being too individualistic: Wicklund seeks explanation of the decline in psychological theory in psychological mechanisms in the persons producing those theories.

Certainly Wicklund, in connection with his explanation, writes about interesting and relevant psychological phenomena (such as rumors and competition) which should be a part of the pattern of explanation, but in my opinion, a broader cultural and social description is needed as a background for the understanding of these mechanisms.

In my opinion the documented examples of decline in psychological theory can in part be traced to the market for psychological books (and the market for psychologists!). For a long period after World War II, the market for psychological books was a seller's market, and it was all too easy to sell even very poorly written psychology books (and to do poor research). This phenomenon is described in an article by Jürgen Kagelmann, psychological consultant for Psychologie Verlags Union of Munich in the magazine *Psychologie Heute* in October 1988. Kagelmann's main point is that the far too easy sales possibilities in the 1970s made for an overwhelming production of psychological books of a very doubtful quality. All that could be printed between two covers was thrown on the market, and the market was insatiable. This is an example of a nonindividualistic explanation, which in my opinion comes closer to the truth than Wicklund's explanation, even if this is not a full explanation.

Therefore, in my opinion, Wicklund has a tendency to individualize and psychologize a social problem, and his book contains in a way a contradiction. Wicklund acts in this book in the role of "explainer," and he too has a tendency toward a very simplistic, positivistic theory, which the book is actually meant to fight against.

The epistemological potential of Wicklund's book lies, in my opinion, especially in its documentation of certain conditions in psychological science which it is important to set right. Therefore, the subject of the book is the epistemology of psychology, methodology, theory of science, and philosophy. In my opinion, the Library of Congress was right in its first selection of subject terms (psychology—philosophy), which, as mentioned, was in contradiction to Wicklund's statement in the preface.

I would *not* consider zero-variable theories the subject of the book. It is hardly a concept with a future, not even as an explanation of the decline in theorizing. It is an open question whether what has been called "variable psychology" (Holzkamp, 1983, p. 522) is a valuable concept.

As regards the proposed subject "psychology of the explainer," it is for me a theoretical question whether it is meaningful to search for such a theory and—even supposing it is—whether Wicklund's approach is a contribution to such a theory. This should be evaluated in relation to research going on in decision theory, in philosophical theories about explanation, and in other fields, and that is not what Wicklund's book is about. I tend to doubt the value of the proposed subject "psychology of the explainer." This doubt also includes the Library of Congress's subject term "explanation." Wicklund's book is hardly a contribution to the concept of explanation in general.

The last proposed subject which I want to discuss is "psychology of psychologists" (Library of Congress: psychologists—psychology). Such a subject does exist, and books are written about it. They can describe, for example, the recruitment of psychologists, the motivation for choosing the profession, biographical matters, the professional socialization, and many other things. Wicklund's book is in my opinion not of this kind.

In my judgment—as already told—the subject of Wicklund's book is "philosophy and epistemology of psychology." My judgment is of course subjective and it could be wrong, in general or in part. The only way to decide this is to analyze the arguments. The arguments about the subject of a book are fundamentally the same as arguments about the advancement of knowledge.

CONCLUSION

The subject of a message is its informative potentials. That subject description which comes closest in the prediction of the role of a document in the advancement of knowledge represents its most correct or fruitful subject description. The evidence of the quality of the subject statement lies in the argumentation. If my above argumentation cannot be rejected it constitutes a better suggestion about what the subject of Wicklund's book is than either Wicklund or the Library of Congress has provided. If it can be rejected, my subject description of that particular book is not optimal, but this does not change my theory about what subjects are: the potentials of messages or documents for the advancement of knowledge and thereby practice.

NOTES

1. In Denmark, Tranekjær Rasmussen (1956) has formulated a theory about subjects (Danish *emner*), but it has never been translated.

2. The tables in this book representing classical empiricism, classical rationalism, and historicism are made by the author based on his philosophical reading. One book (Riis, 1993) has been of especially great importance in this connection.

3. Charles Sanders Peirce has another distinction: Realism is opposed to nominalism. Peirce is both a realist and an objective idealist.

4. The ideal of indexing consistency reflects the earlier mentioned empiricist ideal of intersubjectivity.

5. Malmkjær (1995d) describes the rationalist linguistics (Noam Chomsky), functionalist linguistics (1995b), behaviourist linguistics (1995a), and so on. In this way she analyzes linguistics from almost the same epistemological positions as I apply in this book.

Although Chomsky shares the computer model of the brain with researchers in artificial intelligence (AI), he is pessimistic about projects for natural language computer processing (cf. Putnam, 1992, p. 15).

6. These subjective categories may be more or less identical or intersubjective, but this is another issue; the principle is that they are individual, dependent on a subjective conception.

7. The way Ranganathan and others define the concept of subject implies a circular argumentation. Ranganathan's "facet" system applies combinations of elements into some organized structure. To demand that a subject be something organized is to provide a definition that favor his own theory and system. Such a conception cannot be used as a

fundamental concept for information science because one goal of IS is to investigate such assumptions.

A similar circular argumentation is given in a dissertation by Claus Poulsen (1994). He argues that the definition of subject provided by the present author (Hjørland, 1993) is limited to library and information science, while his own definition is what the researchers understand by that concept. Poulsen's "paradox" system uses terminology from the literature itself as subject representations. By defining "subject" as that which is expressed in the literature, Poulsen applies a definition which favors his own system and which makes it impossible even to pose the problem: Does a given text always represent the optimal subject representation of itself?

8. Peirce, who founded pragmatism, did not accept James's version of it and therefore changed its name to pragmaticism, a word he found so ugly that he could keep it for himself! Rescher (1995) describes two kinds of pragmatism in the development of American philosophy to the present day: objective (founded by Peirce) and subjective (founded by James). "Peirce saw subjective pragmatism as a corruption and degradation of the pragmatic enterprise, since its approach is not a venture in validating objective standards, but in *deconstructing* them to dissolve standards as such into the variegated vagaries of ideosyncratic positions and individual inclinations. And this is how objective pragmatists view the matter down to the present day—this writer included" (Rescher, 1995; emphazis in original). What I call short-term pragmatism is thus related to subjective idealism, not to scientific realism.

9. The etymology of the concept *subject* (Scandinavian *emne*) is as follows. *Nudansk Ordbog* (13. udgave) maintains that the word *emne* was borrowed about 1760 from Norwegian *emne* or Swedish *ämne*, the same word as *evne* [ability]. It mentions three meanings, of which only the first two interest in this connection: (1) material for treatment in speech or writing; theme; motive, (2) material ("raw material"), which is partly worked up, for example, about keys before the final filing. *Nusvensk Ordbok* mentions four meanings, of which the first is "raw material, something to produce out of."

Emne can be translated into "subject" in English. The concept of subject has eighteen main meanings in the *Oxford English Dictionary*, second edition (OED). Among those meanings is the Danish *subjekt* (e.g., a grammatical subject). Of the eighteen meanings in the OED the following should be mentioned:

5. The substance of which a thing consists or from which it is made.

7. Logic. a. That which has attributes; the thing about which a judgement is made. b. The term or part of a proposition of which the predicate is affirmed or denied.

8. Gram. The member or part of a sentence denoting that concerning which something is predicated (i.e., of which a statement is made, a question asked, or a desire expressed); a word or group of words setting forth that which is spoken about and constituting the nominative to a finite verb.

9. Modern Philos. More fully conscious or thinking subject: The Mind, as the "subject" in which ideas inhere; that to which all mental representations or operations are attributed; the thinking or cognitive agent; the self or ego.

The above meanings all come from *subjectum* (Aristotle's Greek: τὸ ὑποκείμενον) with the meanings (1) the material of which the things consist, (2) subject for attributes (qualities), and (3) subject for predicates (names). Additional definitions in the OED include the following:

10. The subject-matter of an art or science.

12a. That which is or may be acted or operated upon; a person or thing towards which action or influence is directed, or that is the recipient of some treatment.

13a. In a specialized sense: That which forms or is chosen as the matter of thought, consideration, or inquiry; a topic, theme.

14a. The theme of a literary composition; what a book, poem, etc., is about.

18. attrib. and Comb . . . (sense 14, chiefly with reference to cataloguing books according to their subjects) subject card, catalogue, cataloguing, entry, heading, index, list, reference.

The meaning of special concern to us is, of course, especially 14 (and the combinations in 18), that is, subject in the sense of "what a book is about." This definition does not, however, solve the problem. What does it mean that "a book is about" the subject x? OED does not differentiate the concept of subject from that of content(s). The *content* of the sentence "The Danish flag is red and white" is that the Dannebrog is red and white; the subjects of the sentence are, for example, the Dannebrog, colors, and national symbols. Subjects are thus *categories* to which a given content can be assigned. What we are searching for are, therefore, the principle(s) for determining which categories are relevant to a given content.

According to the meanings 12a and 13a—and the above mentioned definitions from Danish and Swedish—we find evidence of a pragmatic conception of subject or *emne* as being a "raw material" for humans to act upon.

In the German terminology, you will see that subject indexes and the like in libraries, books, and so on, are often called *Sach-* or *Fachregister*. *Fach* is a reference to professions or scientific disciplines. That means that in German there is a direct connection between the terminology used for my "subject" and the social groups which may be using those documents. That is, the concept of subject has no precise equivalent in German, but the corresponding concepts underline the function to refer documents to categories of users.

The etymological meaning of "raw material" underlines the fact that it is not the innate properties in the things themselves, but their functions for the human user, which make up subjects.

In the chapter we have compared the concept of subject with the concept of value. This gives a better grasp on the meaning of subject: Gold has its value not from the chemical properties in themselves (although they are necessary: that gold is precious is partly due to the fact that it is not easily corroded by chemical influences), but because of special cultural conditions. The value is not a built-in property in the things but is still a function of the properties of the things and of the human culture.

Thus we have seen that my conception of subject in library and information science is not in contrast to important meanings in general language. If such a contrast had existed, my position would have been weakened because we would then have to argue for a special usage of the word. Of course we are not claiming that the general concept emne or subject cannot have other meanings too, as seen in the OED, but we emphasize one side of the concept which supports my theoretical points.

Miksa (1983b, pp. 62ff) provides a very important historical analysis of the term subject, which explains the internal connection between the above mentioned meanings

13a, 10, and 14a. Unfortunately this work came very late to my attention through the citations provided by Frohmann (1994).

10. In the announcement for the Fourth International Congress for Research on Activity Theory (ISCRAT), to be held in Aarhus, Denmark, in 1998, this approach presents itself: "Activity theory originated in Russia and was founded by Vygotsky and his pupils Elkonin, Leontiev and Luria. Elkonin's followers, Davydov and Lektorskij, have contributed to its spread together with Michael Cole from USA and Klaus Holzkamp from Berlin."

In linguistics, M. M. Bakhtin (1981, 1986) represents a related theory.

11. One of the principles in dialectical materialism which I consider directly wrong is the claim that universal dialectical laws for both nature and human history exist. Another principle is the understanding of the concept of law. Novack (1975, pp. 99–102) offers a Marxist critique of John Dewey's understanding of scientific laws. He writes: "Dewey thereby erases the specific difference between a hypothesis and a law. A hypothesis may or may not be applicable or valid, whereas a law is a verified regularity."

In my opinion, this critique is wrong: a law is something formulated by a human being and can never be regarded as 100 percent verified or final in its description of reality. This is also a dominant theme in the philosophy of Karl Popper.

The concept of materialism is also problematic, because it is often used as a synonym for *physicalism* (see Moser & Trout, 1995, p. ix), as a metaphysical theory of matter. According to that book, "Materialism is now the dominant systematic ontology among philosophers and scientists, and there are currently no established alternative ontological views competing with it." In my opinion, such materialism is, however, more related to positivism and cognitivism than to activity theory. One of the main differences is that positivism and cognitivism are reductionistic, whereas activity theory is non-reductionistic. A new discussion of the challenge of historical materialist epistemology is Reed (1996).

12. On page 210 Bakhurst includes a quotation from Vygotsky showing the influence of Dewey on his thinking.

13. References about activity theory as applied to interface design includes Bardram & Bertelsen (1995); Blumenthal (1995); Bødker (1989); Kaptelinin (1992, 1993); Kaptelinin, Kuutti, & Bannon (1995); Kuutti (1990, 1991, 1992); Kuutti & Arvonen (1992); Kuutti & Bannon (1993); Linard & Zeiliger (1995); Mogensen (1992); Nardi (1996); and Nissen, Klein, & Hirschheim (1991).

14. Examples are Engestrom (1995); Timpka & Nyce (1991); and Holmgren, Timpka, Goldkuhl, Nyce, & Sjoberg (1992).

15. Not all modern researchers are of the opinion that things exist objectively and have objective properties. For example, the influential book *Understanding Computers and Cognition: A New Foundation for Design* by Terry Winograd and Fernando Flores (1987, pp. 73 ff.) takes the opposite position.

16. This view of subject analysis as a political activity seems strange, because databases and big libraries try to develop systems that can provide answers to every potential question. There is no question that modern technology allows more subject access points and thereby enables more precise questions to be answered. This could perhaps indicate that forms of information technology have a neutral function: that they are just more efficient. Basically, however, every choice of system, of subject access points, and of algorithms have qualitative and thus political consequences. An important

research question for information science should therefore be to explicate what the qualitative consequences of the different technical solutions are in the end.

17. For a further elaboration on this see also the quotation from Shapere (1984, p. 323) in Chapter 7.

18. You can say that just as John Dewey's thought fell out of favor for a long period in psychology and philosophy, similarily this approach to subject analysis was repressed by empiricist and cognitivistic tendencies in information science.

19. Karamüftüoglu (1996) has provided an interesting analysis of retrieval systems. Such systems may be used as channels to transmit information to the masses constituted as "subjects of didactics," for reproduction and consumption. They may be used equally as a means of production of new knowledge, by "inventing" new and unforeseen connections between texts. "Consumption of knowledge" is seen as analytically different from "production of knowledge." Consumption requires more denotative labor in subject analysis, while the more prescriptive labor can be used for creating new knowledge. Subject analysis should then be seen in relation to its social functions.

20. The Danish information scientist Peter Bøgh Andersen has proposed to me that my concept of subject is related to Peirce's concept of "final interpretant." Ransdell (1994, pp. 682–683) discusses this concept, which is illustrated by an example of legal semiosis. If a judge must interpret a law without benefit of recourse to any ascertainable basis in the immediate interpretant, he or she "makes a guess, in effect, as to what the final interpretant includes when he or she recognizes something as being a dynamic interpretant of that law at that time relative to that case. But it is the course of *future* [emphasis in original] legal interpretation of that law (in courts of appeal, in future juridical practice, and so on) that will determine whether the judge was or was not right in his or her attempt to anticipate the relevant content of the final interpretant—or, as we would ordinarily say, in the attempt to set a precedent that will be honored."

21. To claim that a document is without a subject would be to claim that the work and judgment of the author and publisher are misplaced. This would not be an unthinkable claim, but it would be a paradox to claim this and at the same time accept the document in a collection.

In some instances, such as national bibliographies, all published works must, however, be accepted and indexed. In such cases, the indexer can fall back on the concepts most related to the document's potentials or to the potentials claimed or intended by the author.

22. Unfortunately there can occur a contradiction in subject descriptions. Documents which correspond well to a classification system (or IR language) receive one (or few) classifications, which correspond to the respective category in the system. Vague or cross-cutting documents often receive far more classifications and thus achieve an unintended visibility. This phenomenon ought to be contained. Information systems ought to provide optimal use of the knowledge in the collected mass of documents. In the above case a document achieves visibility at the expense of other documents: if all documents were placed in all categories all value of categorization would be null and void. Rare situations can thus also occur where a subject description of a document does more harm than benefit, and such descriptions should be avoided.

23. If it is put there in order to illuminate the unclear terminology in the field, this could also be regarded as a kind of informative potential, even of a more indirect kind.

24. This situation is especially the case in basic research, where theoretical reorientations take place. In more everyday contexts or in "the normal process of

research" (in the Kuhnian sense) this expressed contrast between the two objectivity requirements need not obtain.

25. In practice there will often be several subject descriptions of a given document. Except for the subject descriptions the document will have properties, for example, as concepts in databases (from title, full text, and such). The function of subject descriptions should of course be seen in relation to such a system of possibilities. The aspect that is of interest here is the consequences of the information explosion (that is, the growth in the number of documents which need to be selected) in regard to the quality of the subject description. The greater the number of documents, the more difficult it will become to identify the most relevant ones. The more the number of documents grows, the more selective the subject description has to be. To put it in another way: the greater the number of documents, the greater the necessity for a real subject description rather than just an enumeration of the properties of the document.

The hypothesis can be formulated more precisely: the greater the number of documents, the more necessary it is to describe the subject of the documents from the point of view of the user (rather than document properties). There are simply too many properties and too many relations among properties for the user to decide which ones are relevant, and the work becomes too extensive.

26. You can, for example, identify Marxist psychology by the language code Russian; if you cannot read Russian, you can combine "original language = Russian" with "language = English" and thus have a list of Russian books translated into English.

27. But of course in the concrete development of information systems, procedures must be described, for example, in the use of classification systems and thesauri, and I myself in another connection have been a spokesman for definite and explicit procedures (check lists) in the description of subjects (Hjørland, 1988).

28. It is an ideal that readers do have access to subject data tailored to their specific interests. The proposed merging in a union catalog represents an important step toward improving the visibility of a book for all its potential readers.

However, subject data can also represent noise. It can be necessary to be able to identify the origin of the merged data and to opt out of some data from specified sources.

29. This evaluation of the state of psychology is not unrelated to my view of the neglect of the works of John Dewey, described elsewhere in this chapter.

5

Methodological Consequences for Information Science

In the first four chapters of this book I examined one of the core problems in information science: subject analysis and subject representation. I presented a specific methodological conceptualization that implies that individual decisions regarding the subject of a document need to be made on the basis of a "horizon" established by disciplinary and epistemological understanding and evaluation. In this chapter I will analyze and generalize this methodological principle and apply it to other fundamental information science problems.

INFORMATION SCIENCE

The American Society for Information Science (ASIS) defines information science in the following way:

Information science is concerned with the generation, collection, organization, interpretation, storage, retrieval, dissemination, transformation and use of information, with particular emphasis on the applications of modern technologies in these areas.

As a discipline, it seeks to create and structure a body of scientific, technological, and systems knowledge related to the transfer of information. It has both pure science (theoretical) components, which inquire into the subject without regard to application, and applied science (practical) components, which develop services and products.

Although the definition originated in 1975, it is here cited from *Key Papers in Information Science* (Griffith, 1980, p. 5). This definition is closely related to a definition given by Borko (1968).

There are of course many theories in information science, many horizons, paradigms, or ways to conceptualize this field.[1] One of the leading textbooks on information retrieval (D. Ellis, 1990) deals with the following approaches:

- Statistical and probabilistic retrieval

- Cognitive user modeling

- Expert intermediary systems

- Associations, relations, and hypertext

Other paradigms were presented at the ASIS annual meeting in October 1993. In a session entitled "Debating Different Approaches to Studying the Organization of Information" the formulations were as follows (quoted from the conference program, p. 22):

- "*The Object Paradigm*: the path to understanding how information should be organized is to analyze the nature of common information objects themselves" (Ling Hwey Jeng, UCLA)

- "*The Cognitive Paradigm*: the best way to approach the organization of information is to study how people think and to mimic those regularities of thought" (Donald Case, UCLA)

- "*The Behavioral Paradigm*: the best method for studying how information should be organized is to observe how people interact with potential sources" (Nicholas Belkin, Rutgers University)

- "*The Communication Paradigm*: the best way to understand information is to study information-seeking and use communicatively, examining how people construct questions and create answers to these questions" (Brenda Dervin, Ohio State University)

At the same conference, in a session on domain analysis, I formulated an approach in line with the activity-theoretical perspective: The domain analytic paradigm is a theoretical approach to information science (IS) which states that the best way to understand information in IS is to study the knowledge domains as discourse communities, which are parts of the society's division of labor. Knowledge organization and structure, cooperation patterns, language and communication forms, information systems, and relevance criteria are reflections of the objects of the work of these communities and of their role in society. The individual person's psychology, knowledge, information needs, and subjective relevance criteria should be seen in this perspective. (This formulation is also cited in Hjørland & Albrechtsen, 1995b.)

It is my view that what in reality characterizes information scientists most is a good working knowledge of electronic databases and some interests in bibliometrics, computer technology, and domain knowledge. Explicit theoretical works are rare. As Boyce and Kraft (1985, p. 165) state: "Our discipline has been more concerned with the facilitation of communication processes than with their explanation." However, if we are taking information science seriously as a science or discipline, the theoretical questions become very important. The theoretical questions are also very important for making explicit what the tacit knowledge of many information scientists might be and to formalize and strengthen this practical knowledge.

In considering theoretical questions it is important to distinguish between different levels of inquiry. Liebenau and Backhouse (1990) is one of the few introductions to IS which provides a description of the different levels from the physical to the social (see Table 5.1).

Often a distinction is made among, for example, cognitive approaches, physical approaches, bibliometric approaches and domain analytic approaches. However, if information means that *somebody* is informed (as Machlup, 1983, maintained), then information science must somehow be concerned with how people are informed. This imply that all theories and approaches—if they belong to information science—must have some connections with cognitive processes and knowledge either explicitly or implicitly. What distinguishes different approaches in information science must thus be such different epistemological assumptions as we discussed in Chapter 4 of this book: basic theories about language, meaning, and cognitive processes, whether they are holistic or atomistic, individual or social, subjective or objective, formalistic or content determined,

Table 5.1
Levels of Inquiry in Information Systems

Level of Theory	Object	Examples
Social level	The social role of information systems	Commitment, obligation
Pragmatics	Study the purposes and intentions behind communication and information systems	Motivation
Semantics	Study content and meanings in information systems	Subject matter, propositions
Syntactics	Study forms, formalisms, and structures in information systems	Language, rules, and protocols
"Empirics" or mathematical communication theory	Study means of communication, media, signals, and codes	Noise, echo
Physical level	Physical processes, apparatus, and computers	Telephones, cables

Source: Based on Liebenau & Backhouse (1990), modified.

historical or situational, symbolic or connectionistic, dynamic or static, and so on. All approaches to information science implies basic postulates and properties about cognition, meaning, language, and knowledge.

The important feature of activity theory is that it considers cognition as an adaptation to ecological and social environments. The difference between traditional approaches in psychology and some modern approaches, including activity theory, should be clear from the following quotation:

Why has there been so little progress in understanding the reasoning processes elicited by both tasks, despite an avalanche of studies since the 1960's? We believe one major reason to be the answers given to these two questions. These answers presuppose a *simple* dichotomy between structure and content, which is subsequently used to separate good from bad reasoning. However, this presupposition holds neither for modern logics nor for modern probability theory. . . . Each of these theories divides the information presented in a reasoning problem into two parts: relevant and irrelevant information. Relevant information corresponds to what is seen as the problem's structure. Irrelevant information corresponds to unimportant content. Different theories, however, make different divisions. . . . The general point is that there is no simple and unique division line between structure and content, or between information relevant and irrelevant to rational reasoning. What counts as the relevant structure for reasoning about a domain therefore seems to need a domain-specific theory. . . .

If human reasoning is, to some important degree, an adaptation to specific environments (where environments include social environments), then ecological analysis of reasoning mechanisms as adaptations to structures of important present environments, and evolutionary analysis of reasoning mechanisms as adaptations to structures of important present environments, and evolutionary analysis of reasoning mechanisms as adaptations to structures of important past environments, are indispensable. (Gigerenzer & Hug, 1992, pp. 168–169; emphasis in original)

Winograd and Flores (1987) understand language and cognition as "consensual domains." They build upon the Latin American biologist Humberto Maturana, who speaks of a mutual structural coupling between cognitive structures and given environments. But the philosophical influence in Winograd and Flores is much more hermeneutical than pragmatic realist. A similar view is also represented in the concept of "situated cognition" as used by, among others, Harold Garfinkel (1967), Jean Lave (1988), and Lucy Suchman (1987), which emphasizes the view of embodiment, that human thinking is determined by content and cannot be formalized and that abstraction, perception, concept formation, learning, and human development cannot be explained by formal systems. Instead, formalizations are seen as tools used by humans to systematize elements already formed and belonging to a closed space, where all elements and operations are determined in advance and where the formalisms can only be applied after the problem has been posed.

In Table 5.2 some major differences between the cognitive paradigm and the domain analytic paradigm are shown.

Table 5.2
Some Differences between Cognitivism and the Domain Analytic Viewpoint

Cognitivism	The Domain Analytic View
Priority is given to the understanding of isolated user needs and intrapsychological analysis. Intermediating between producers and users emphasizes psychological understanding.	Priority is given to the understanding of user needs from a social perspective and the functions of information systems in trades or disciplines.
Focus on the single user. Looks at the disciplinary context as a part of the cognitive structure of an individual.	Focus on either one knowledge domain or the comparative study of different knowledge domains.
Mainly inspired by artificial intelligence and cognitive psychology.	Mainly inspired by the information structures in domains, by the sociology of knowledge and by science studies.
The psychological theory emphasizes the role of cognitive strategies in performance.	The psychological theory emphasizes the interaction among aptitudes, strategies, and knowledge.
Central concepts are individual knowledge structures, individual information processing, short- and long-term memory, categorical versus situational classification.	Central concepts are scientific communication, documents, databases, disciplines, subjects, information structures, paradigms.
Methodology characterized by an individualistic approach.	Methodology characterized by a collectivistic approach. This should not be confused as a different political perception of the role of information systems, but a different theoretical approach to the study and optimization of information systems.
Best examples of application: User interfaces (the outer side of information systems).	Best examples of application: subject-representation/classification (the inner side of information systems).
Theory of knowledge: mainly rationalistic/positivistic, with tendencies toward hermeneutics.	Theory of knowledge: Scientific realism/ forms of social constructivism with tendencies toward hermeneutics.
Ontological position (implicit): subjective idealism.	Ontological position (explicit): realism (scientific and pragmatic).

THE CONCEPT OF INFORMATION

The literature about the concept of information is very large and scattered.[2] Bogdan (1994, p. 53) writes:

My skepticism about a definitive analysis of information acknowledges the infamous versatility of information. The notion of information has been taken to characterize a measure of physical organization (or decrease in entropy), a pattern of communication between source and receiver, a form of control and feedback, the probability of a message being transmitted over a communication channel, the content of a cognitive state, the meaning of a linguistic form, or the reduction of an uncertainty. These concepts of information are defined in various theories such as physics, thermodynamics, communication theory, cybernetics, statistical information theory, psychology, inductive logic, and so on. There seems to be no unique idea of information upon which these various concepts converge and hence no proprietary theory of information.

A definition of *information* in IS must thus be based on a particular theoretical perspective. The above formulation of a new paradigm for information science represents an effort to formulate the generalized methodological principle implicated by the approach taken by this author. This of course also implies a new understanding of the concept of information, which will be outlined here.[3]

Buckland (1991) analyzes the concept of information. The word *information* can be used about things, about processes and about knowledge (see Table 5.3). According to Buckland, things can be informative. A stump of a tree contains information about its age as well as about the climate during the lifetime of the tree. In similar ways, anything might in some imaginable circumstances be informative: "We conclude that *we are unable to say confidently of anything that it could not be information*" (Buckland, 1991, p. 50; emphasis in original). Just as anything could or might be symbolic, Buckland maintains, anything could or might be informative or information.

Table 5.3
Four Aspects of Information

	Intangible	Tangible
Entity	Information-as-knowledge Knowledge	Information-as-thing Data, document, recorded knowledge
Process	Information-as-process Becoming informed	Information processing Data processing, document processing, knowledge engineering

Source: Buckland, 1991, p. 6.

But if anything might be information, then the concept of information does not in itself provide any criteria regarding what to consider as information. A project such as LIBRU (Mariscal, 1993), which tries to quantify all information in the world, is absurd, not only because of the practical problems involved in quantifying maps, gravestones, slides, advertisements, sound recordings, video recordings, dissertations, periodicals, papyri, ostraca, Christmas cards, and so on. It is first and foremost absurd because information is not an objective thing which can be quantified in this way. One single Christmas card contains unlimited amounts of information about the producer of the card, the sender, the receiver, its motive, its paper, its printer, its colors, its stamp, and so on. This example might look extreme, but the same attitude toward information is often implicit in much library and information thinking. If the concept of information should be meaningful for IS, we clearly need some criteria of what to regard as information. What kind of advice can that concept provide with regard to what to represent in information systems?

The cognitive paradigm has rightly stated that information is always information *for somebody*. The users must play a part in a theory of information science. A thing can only be informative for a user if it is new to the user, if it is comprehensible, and if it is relevant: that is, if it changes the knowledge structure of the user (cf. Ingwersen, 1992, pp. 31ff). Buckland (1991, p. 50) finds that "It follows from this that the capability of being informative, the essential characteristic of information-as-thing, must also be *situational.*"

The domain analytic view develops this view further: users should be seen as individuals in concrete situations in social organizations and domains of knowledge. A stone on a field could contain different information for different people (or from one situation to another). It is not possible for information systems to map *all* the stone's possible information for every individual. Nor is any *one* mapping the "true" mapping. But people have different educational backgrounds and play different roles in the division of labor in society. A stone in a field represents one kind of information for the geologist, another for the archaeologist. The information from the stone can be mapped into different collective knowledge structures produced by, for example, geology and archaeology. Information can be identified, described, and represented in information systems for different domains of knowledge. Of course, there is much uncertainty and many difficult problems in determining whether a thing is informative or not for a domain. Some domains have a high degree of consensus and rather explicit criteria of relevance. Other domains have different, conflicting paradigms, each containing its own more or less implicit view of the informativeness of different kinds of information sources.

To sum up: The analysis of the concept of information made above implies that informational objects should not be analyzed and described only according to an objectivistic epistemology. It is not sufficient to describe information according to universalistic principles, as permanent, inherent characteristics of knowledge. Instead, information must be analyzed, described, and represented in information systems according to situational, pragmatic, and domain-specific principles.

THE CONCEPT OF MATCH IN INFORMATION RETRIEVAL THEORY

Information retrieval (IR) is usual regarded a "hard" and strong part of IS. However, Sparck Jones (1992, p. 684) finds that the general problem is highly intractable, and van Rijsbergen (1986, p. 194) points out that this field is in a crisis. The fundamental basis of all the previous work—including his own—is wrong because it has been based on the assumption that a formal notion of *meaning* is not required to solve the IR problems.

Belkin (1980) has provided a sharp logical analysis of the basic problem. The fundamental concepts in IR are, according to his article, as follows:

1. An unordered set, S, of documents, s [S = {s1...si...sn}]

2. A Request, R, put to the system which can presumably be satisfied to some extent by at least one of the members of S

3. An algorithm, A, which orders the members of S according to the probability of their being capable of satisfying the request, R. A document which completely satisfies the need underlying R is said to be relevant to R

4. A Rule, T, by which the meanings of the members of S and R are represented in the same language

In the "best match" hypothesis, which Belkin believes underlies all traditional IR system theory, "the probability of relevance for each document is assessed by the degree to which the document representation matches the request representation, or contains the request representation within itself. Then an exact match, or complete inclusion, results in ranking that document first, assigning to it the highest probability of relevance, no matter what other characteristics the rule A may take into account" (Belkin, 1980, p. 188).

Belkin shows convincingly that from these premises IR must be built on the users' premises and that the study of their cognitive processes in the communication system must play the key role in IS: "These problems with the traditional IR assumptions can be seen quite clearly, and alternative assumptions can be found readily, when the question of IR is treated in the context of a communication system specific to information science" (Belkin, 1980, p. 190).

Up to this point, I agree fully with Belkin. However, in 1980 the psychological study of cognition was mainly based upon the view imported from artificial intelligence, viewing cognitive processes as computer processes in the brain (the cognitivistic theory in psychology). Since then, Winograd and Flores (1987), as well as many others, have provided us with an alternative understanding of language and cognition.

Building on activity theory as well as on similar new views in cognitive science, my proposal is to view the users in relation to epistemic communities, with major or minor semantic distance to the knowledge producers (and thereby to the documents). For example, in physics, users without the necessary knowledge should be referred to introductory textbooks, popular expositions, and the like. In the same way, a user is always situated in a concrete place which has specific conceptual relations to different epistemic communities.

A domain—for example, the domain of physics—should be regarded as conceptually diversified, due to historical development, different approaches, and geographical and cultural diversity. The problem of matching now changes to a theory about database semantics. What does a given word in a given field in a given record in a given database mean in relation to a user X working with a problem Y?

As pointed out in Chapter 3, there need not be any formal linguistic similarity between related documents—as citation indexing can demonstrate—and thus "match" is not necessarily an indication of subject relatedness. An exact match could imply that a document had already solved the problem Y (or could retrieve obsolete views on the problem and miss current views). If X is a researcher this means that X has to formulate a new problem because Y has already been solved. This would not make X happy because it would indicate X had asked the wrong question. But when is a question wrong and when is it not?[4]

This example shows that it is meaningless to look at S and R in isolation from each other. R has been developed in relation to S either (1) individually: X learns about S until he is able to formulate R. The ability to formulate questions is a matter of an adequate educational background; or (2) collectively: X contributes to S, and S and R are developing together in what Humberto Maturana and Winograd and Flores (1987) call "consensual domains." Here the ability to formulate questions is a matter of an adequate organization of the scientific cooperation: knowledge of each other's findings, concepts, communication channels, and so on.

This view of language and cognition shares with activity theory a functional, ecological perspective, in which there exists a mutual, phylogenetic, and ontogenetic structural coupling between individuals. It is opposed to the view that language and cognition are a collection of mechanisms in isolated users or a semantic coupling between linguistic and nonlinguistic stimuli which the organism encounters. This view is prevailing in the traditional formalist/structuralist/cognitivist view of language and cognition. If we transform the former view to information science, we can say that producers, users, information systems, and intermediaries are often developed in a mutual structural coupling in the same domain or epistemic community and that their developments are mutually determined.

All this implies that the concept of documentary language could play a much more positive role than Belkin ascribed to it. A documentary language should not be constructed from the isolated user's "anomalous state of knowledge" (ASK), but first and foremost from the study of consensus and epistemic authority in the language, concepts and understanding among knowledge producers, problems of communication, and standardizsation of terminology. However, the psychological problems in intermediators' "translating" of basic research, such as the language and composition of textbooks and magazines, should be investigated: IS should start with an overview of given communication forms and channels and their development and functionality.

METHODS AND METHODOLOGY

The *methods* of information science denote the more or less sharply delimited procedures that exist for collecting knowledge in information science. In user studies we might use, for instance, sociological methods or thinking-aloud methods; in information retrieval we might use experimentation. An example of the experimental method is Cooper's (1978) influential article "Indexing Documents by Gedanken Experimentation."

The positivist theory of science has shown a preference for method rather than object; that is, it has defined what is scientific from the point of view of formal criteria, rather than from the point of view of the research object. It distinguishes sharply between scientific and nonscientific knowledge. According to logical positivism the only meaningful statements are those that can be verified either logically or empirically. This stance causes irresolvable problems, since the theoretical concepts in science are the result of abstraction processes, which represent real contexts. These concepts cannot be verified by purely logico-deductive methods or through simple sensory input. Within the positivist framework the research object is reduced to the empirical dimensions (e.g., user behavior) that can be registered and manipulated by using "recognized" methods. The concepts that express the research object are not viewed as something that science has reached in a process using alternately empirical and rational methods. If the research object is perceived in the manner just described, it implies that the research methods to a great extent are determined theoretically. Theories imply the relevance of various methods. If, for instance, "user need" is perceived as a psychological state within the individual, using psychological methods for studying user needs would be relevant. But when "user need" is perceived as a collectively determined dimension, using sociological methods is relevant.

For the time being, the conclusion is that a requirement for being able to write a methodology—a system of methods or a methodology textbook—for a discipline is that the discipline at least has a well-developed conceptual and theoretical framework. From there the methodological and disciplinary knowledge evolve in an interactive process. Often disciplines import methodology textbooks from other disciplines, perhaps just adding new examples. But even if methodological considerations originating in one discipline presumably can be useful for other disciplines, there is a danger that such methodology textbooks become "alienated," foreign elements in the disciplinary knowledge. This is demonstrated by the fact that often the important research in a discipline does not use these methods. I claim for instance that empirical methodology textbooks in the discipline of psychology have played a much less important role than, for example, clinical experiences and other "unofficial" methods. The same danger is obvious in information science.

Since several theories exist side by side in an academic discipline, it follows that there are also various perceptions of methodology. The philosophical and metascientific discussion of the relevance of various methods and their relation to the research object of information science belongs under the heading *methodology* of information science. Methodological and conceptual expositions of a discipline are closely connected. It is obvious that it would be appropriate for a young and immature discipline to work within methodological pluralism. A living discipline is one where internal as well as external dialog exists. A pluralistic foundation should, on the other hand, not be allowed to lead to a lack of awareness of the consequences of various methodological principles, since this in turn might lead to methodological and scientific stagnation. In practice it might be necessary to assume an eclectic stance, where all the fragments that appear useful are accumulated. But the eclectic stance should never become a principle that stops one from working toward theoretical clarification and coherence.

An important method which has been central to this book as well is conceptual analysis. Conceptual analysis is closely connected to theoretical studies. The way in which scientific concepts are studied and defined is in itself a philosophical problem. Operationalism, on the one hand, requires that one should be able to operationalize or measure scientific concepts. Such a requirement often leads to unnatural or "flat" conceptual constructions, which cannot be generalized outside the experimental situation. Ordinary language philosophy, on the other hand, takes as its starting point the real function of the concepts and their meanings in human communication. The concepts achieve more "depth" and offer more possibilities for a hermeneutic perspective. However, it is more difficult to use them as elements in a scientific model or causal theory. Clearly, a third perspective on concepts and meaning is needed.

The concepts of IS should be examined from a theoretical standpoint as elements in a theory of information seeking. Information seeking again should be viewed as a link in the cooperative processes of knowledge production and knowledge utilization. Scientific concepts are not arbitrary, but necessary. If they are incorrectly defined, they bring about theoretical blockage and implications which can be falsified either empirically or logically. For example, the psychological concept of need often leads to circular arguments: it introduces a concept that was meant to be an explanation, but is only a label, for example, if people smoke cigarettes, it is not an explanation to say that they do this because thay have a need for it. The findings of theoretical studies are different from the findings of empirical ones. The enumeration of methodological principles is the most important finding of theoretical studies.

An important methodological debate in modern social science is the question of the relationship between quantitative and qualitative methods. Quantitative methodologies give priority to statistical methods, while qualitative methodologies give priority to historical analyses, in-depth interviews, participant perspectives, interpretation, source criticism, and so on. Quantitative methodologies are related to (but not identical to) positivist epistemology, while qualitative methodologies are related to hermeneutic theory. This is not a relationship of absolute opposites, but a weighing of the relevance of the various methods. The general social science debate regarding qualitative/quantitative methodology is very relevant for information science.

In information science there has been such a debate between proponents for the quantitative and the qualitative methodology, respectively. Kuhlthau (1993) can be used as a model for the state of methodology today. Her studies build upon the following principles:

- User orientation instead of focusing on the information system itself

- Process orientation, that is, the perception of information seeking as a process

- Orientation toward both cognitive and affective processes

- Qualitative studies (interviews and case studies) and quantitative studies

- Longitudinal studies (i.e., the users and their development are followed over a number of years)

- Studies of real users with real problems in real libraries (as opposed to made-up experiments)

- Studies that build upon a theoretical framework of users as constructive information seekers. Authors such as John Dewey and Lev Vygotsky (the pioneer in a pragmatic and activity theoretical pedagogy and psychology) belong to this group.

As a whole, this arsenal of methodological principles looks very strong indeed. Kuhlthau emphasizes, rightly, that many user studies in reality do not show an interest in users, but in how the information system is being utilized. This is a very important observation. If research and education in the medical disciplines would not focus on the patients and their illnesses, but only look upon them as users of a health care system, then both the health care sector and the patients would be in trouble today. The reality as far as most user studies are concerned is that they do not focus on the users' real information problems.

Kuhlthau's arsenal of methodological principles is indeed impressive, and her research has provided important new knowledge. Its methodology is, however, still based on methodological individualism. She might, for instance, claim that users experience anxiety during such and such stages of the information-seeking process. However, if the consequences of this insight should be more useful in the design of information systems or for literature-searching training, we need more knowledge of the causes for this anxiety, of whether the provision of relevant information is helpful in both short-term and long-term perspective. What are the criteria of good information provision, of good information, of good study habits, of good scholarship and professionalism? Happiness and pride are related to the quality of the performance, and the causes are partly related to social norms. Do students in unclear fields experience more anxiety than students in well-defined fields? Are the emotions related to the content of the work or only to such formal aspects as the stage in the process?

The field of library and information science often appears to suffer from a fear of confronting reality or real information problems as opposed to user behavior and experiences. This is a well-grounded fear, since it is often very difficult to assess, for example, whether a user is performing an optimal information search or not.[5] It is equally difficult to tell whether the user's difficulties are due to circumstances relating to the knowledge domain within which he is working. Information seeking predominantly serves research (in the widest sense of the word, including project-oriented study). Most information scientists feel that only the individual researcher can evaluate the relevance of given references or information. If information scientists are experts regarding information-seeking strategies, they must, however, establish some knowledge of how different strategies influence the outcome both quantitatively and qualitatively. Since information overload seems a greater threat than the opposite, the qualitative factor seems especially important. Normally, information scientists may not have the same amount of concrete subject knowledge as their clients, but they may have a more general knowledge of information sources, structures, paradigms, and so on. The users approach information as a bottom-up process, whereas the information specialists approach information as a top-down process.

Kuhlthau's book describes the problems from the point of view of the individual's experiences. The "advantage" of this methodology is that the scientists won't be caught in incorrect interpretations and insufficient knowledge about knowledge domains, information sources, or their relevance in relation to the given problem. It is much safer to study the user's subjective experiences, mental states, and behavior as autonomous phenomena than to study reality and how it affects the users. The disadvantage is that information science does not gain enough knowledge about its central problems. It should be pointed out that John Dewey's and Lev Vygotsky's pedagogy, psychology, and philosophy are important milestones in the attempt to reach beyond mentalism, psychologism, subjectivism, idealism, or whatever we prefer to call it. They both emphasize the social aspects of experience as well as the fact that thought processes originate in actions and reality. This important fact is not pronounced in Kuhlthau's theory and methodology, even if she builds upon the work of these authors.

METHODOLOGICAL INDIVIDUALISM VERSUS METHODOLOGICAL COLLECTIVISM

If one wants to escape this mentalistic pitfall it is, in my view, essential to pay attention to a methodological principle called methodological individualism

(MI).[6] Furthermore, we need to establish an alternative to MI in information science. Methodological individualism in information science is the point of view that conceives of knowledge as individual mental states rather than—or in opposition to—knowledge as a social or cultural process or as a cultural product. This is why scientific methods (knowledge-producing methods) in this view consist of the study of cognitive processes isolated from the world. The world is represented in the cognitive processes and isolated from their development history (see Sinha, 1988). This has far-reaching consequences for information science methodology. Methodological individualism implies psychological methods (interviews, thinking aloud, recording of behavioral patterns, etc.). It should, however, be pointed out that also within psychology there are attempts to reach beyond methodological individualism. Examples of these can be found especially in activity theory (or the cultural-historic school of thought) within Russian psychology (see Leontiev, 1983) and further developed in other countries. More recent contributions include Resnick, Levine and Teasley (1991);[7] Sinha (1988); and Tolman (1992).

The opposite of methodological individualism I would prefer to call methodo-logical collectivism (MC). While the concept of MI appears to be a standard concept, including having a descriptor in *Philosopher's Index*, there does not appear to be a standard concept that mirrors MC. The well-known sociologist Emile Durkheim, who was one of the main opponents of MI, used the concept of "methodological holism." However, I prefer to operate with the contrasting pairs methodological atomism/holism and methodological individualism/ collectivism.

Within the psychology of language a corresponding analysis is presented by Forrester, 1996 (see Figure 5.1). Forrester's concept of the cognition dominant view shares the basic points of methodological individualism, while his language dominant view shares the basic points of methodological collectivism. According to Forrester, the language-dominant view often asserts that the language structure shapes and limits cognitive capacities, and maintains, that where we are concerned with examining concepts, we cannot ignore the particular social discursive context of the investigation. If we do that, we will fail to see the extent to which the evidence produced is interdependent with the task, the context, the underlying theory, and the philosophical position taken.

From a methodological collectivistic point of view, IS does not take as its starting point the individual's knowledge structure, but instead looks at knowl-edge domains, disciplines, or other collective knowledge structures. This implies other methods, for instance, bibliometric or informetric methods; however, these methods cannot stand alone. Buckland (1991, pp. 22–23), for example, claims that the overrepresentation of bibliometrics in IS is an important example of the pathological conditions in the field. Bibliometrics should not be seen as the answer to the problems of the cognitive view. Both approaches share some common problems in their positivistic view of knowledge. Instead we should develop a broader domain analytic methodology. Bibliometrics should be viewed as one method among others, its principle weakness being that as an "objectivistic" method it can only illuminate trends, not interpret or explain these trends.

The fact that information science takes knowledge domains as its starting point does not mean that information science is tantamount to the study of knowledge domains in the way that the metasciences are. The interests of information science are to a great extent connected with individual decision-making processes including subject analysis, information-seeking processes and information needs.

Figure 5.1
Two Views in the Psychology of Language

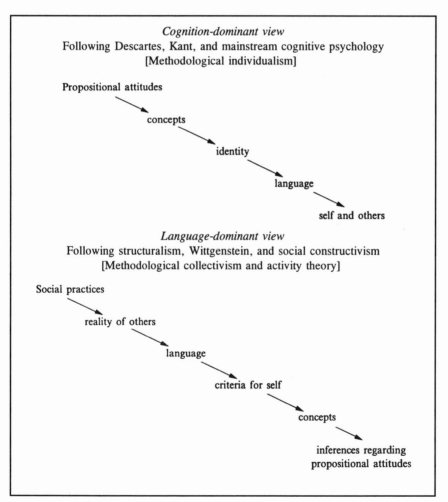

Source: Forrester, 1996, p. 28.

It means that the interests of information science to a great extent lie in the focal point of sociology, psychology, linguistics and philosophy.

However, it has been difficult to reach a synthesis that would put individual information needs, query formulations, search behavior, and so on, in a sociological perspective. The connecting link between the psychological and the sociological levels has been missing. The problem of information science is connected with the problems of psychology: information science has had to lean on psychology, the mainstream of which has not been able to rise above MI. In this chapter I intend to show that language is a central part of the key to the methodology of psychology, and thereby to the bridge building between psychology and sociology and between the subjective and the objective.

The debate over MI has more than academic interest. For library schools it is to a great extent a very real problem that concerns what type of professional background knowledge is needed for information seeking, recording of information, subject analyses, and so on. Should it be the study of individual decision-making processes, the psychology of reading, and cognitive structures, or should it be the philosophy, the sociology and the history of science? In terms of my pluralistic starting point all of these are relevant, but the latter have in my opinion not been well enough integrated into the efforts to build IS. It is of relevance to describe information processes on the individual level, on the machine level, on the level of "thought and discourse communities," and on the cultural-sociological level. However, it is of vital importance to know how these levels are connected.

The importance of the methodological exposition to the pair of opposites, MI and MC, is also related to the fact that the cognitive paradigm has won a large following in information science (as well as in cognitive science and artificial intelligence). This paradigm, which is not a real paradigm in the Kuhnian sense, represents methodological individualism.[8] Cognitivism in information science takes as its starting point the "mechanics" of the brain. We can study, for instance, Vickery and Vickery's diagrams in Chapter 6, "Semantics and Retrieval" (1987, p. 135, fig. 6.3). According to this model, concepts are born within the individual brain, which uses a referent in the environment. The concepts are a part of the subjective knowledge structures, where they are transformed into linguistic symbols. Collective knowledge, or public knowledge, is here seen as the sum of the individuals' knowledge. The authors describe a seemingly logical and self-evident chain: an individual's sense, conceptualization, and language, which are summed up in the whole of society's knowledge. This is a natural thought for a scientist who has not studied psychology, linguistics, or philosophy. However, from the point of view of activity theory and similar theories, this chain is incorrect. It builds upon a positivist perception.

Mos and Boodt (1992) write about the empiricist tradition in psychology, which they identify with a view of the self-sufficiency of perceptual knowledge and the view that language is merely the phonetic designation of an objectively perceived world. This view prevailed from Aristotle (who rejected Plato's world of ideas) to contemporary empiricism. A few researchers, however, objected to this view and considered speech a formative act of thought. For example, according to the philosopher Wilhelm von Humboldt, individuals do not merely think about the world, and express it, in language; the whole manner in which we live in the world including our perception of it, is grasped by means of language and therefore thought. Accordingly, the objectivity of our knowledge about the world is made possible only through language. There are no perceptual givens, and, hence, nothing for language or thought to "copy" or "reproduce. Mos and Boodt (1992, p. 199) further describes how the psychologist Karl Bühler, following Emile Durkheim, the late Dilthey, and Georg Herbert Mead, adheres to the irreducible social matrix of meaning; meaning always has an objective structure. This objective structure cannot find its origin in individuals but only in individual lives as lived in community (*Gemeinschaft*). Bühler's investigation into language came to regard language not only as a new field of application but also as essential to the methodology of psychology. Mos and Boodt point out an error both in the objectivist and the mentalist understanding of language:

The objectivist error, in its empiricist version, takes language as material forms that are to be tied to the world by primitive semantic relations such as of denotation. The mentalist error, in its rationalist version, takes these primitive semantic relations to be individual acts of expression prior concepts. In the first case, the conventional nature of the linguistic sign is relegated to privacy of perception, in the second, to the privacy of ideas. The first error leads to granting privileged status to observation sentences [i.e., logical positivism], the second, to the reification of meaning. Both objectivist traditions are skeptical concerning language. (Mos & Boodt, 1992, pp. 214–215)

A concrete example of how the meaning of a word is related to social cooperation not to individual perception is offered by Harvard philosopher Hilary Putnam:

Everyone to whom gold is important for any reason has to acquire the word "gold"; but he does not have to acquire the method of recognizing if something is or is not gold. He can rely upon a special subclass of speakers. The features that are generally thought to be present in connection with a general name—necessary and sufficient conditions for membership in the extension, ways of recognizing if something is the extension ("criteria"), etc.—are all present in the linguistic community considered as a collective body; but that collective body divides the labor of knowing and employing these various parts of the "meaning" of "gold." This division of linguistic labor rests upon the division of non-linguistic labor. (Putnam, 1975, p. 245)

Another book, by the Finnish sociologist Eskola and colleagues (1988), also deals with the dead ends that one runs into when applying this individualistic viewpoint to knowledge. Eskola et al. defend Durkheim's view that "the origin of social facts is not in the individual; their substratum can be no other than society." The whole book by Eskola et al. deals with this problem, which is why it would be too much to review the whole argumentation in detail. What we can conclude, however, is that human concepts do not evolve separately in each individual as a result of sensory input into the brain.

I therefore wish to emphasize that human concepts and human knowledge are a result of human cooperation and communication. The individual knowledge structures can only be understood based upon a group-oriented analysis of language users.

What a certain person knows or does not know, what benefits he or she might gain from using an information system, what barriers and problems his use of knowledge entails, are not primarily demonstrated by psychological studies of the capacity and mechanics of the brain, or the difference between long-term and short-term memory, or between semantic and episodic memory, but by a familiarity with his social role and work tasks, his educational background, and disciplinary connections.

Sinha relates cognitivism and methodological individualism:

The computational approach appears therefore to be committed to a radical nativism, predicated upon a dualistic distinction between mental objects ("lexemes" and expression in LOT [language of thought, a concept borrowed from Fodor]) and the actual objects of the real world. This neo-rationalist argument is used by Fodor to defend a general philosophical approach to psychology which he calls "methodological solipsism," consisting essentially in the proposition that the study of cognitive processes is to be seen as completely autonomous from the study either of the cognized environment or of developmental history.

The "methodological solipsist" stance also highlights another basic feature of the neo-rationalist position: that is, its tendency to cast the problem of knowledge in terms of the mental states of individual subjects, rather than, or in opposition to, knowledge being conceived as a social process and product. To this extent, Fodor's methodological solipsism is simply an extreme variant of a wider tenet of modern cognitivism, which may be referred to as "methodological individualism." (Sinha, 1988, p. 126)

When information science, inspired by artificial intelligence and cognitive science, in this way (e.g., Vickery & Vickery, 1987) takes as its starting point the individual cognitive processes, it appears to be a category error with great consequences. I will try to illustrate this with the following example. A Danish book about legal information, Blume (1989), describes quite well what is meant by sources (legal sources) within the discipline of law, how these are searched and used, and what their relation to the legal professional literature is. I will point to some of these.

The information sources on which the law is based are called legal sources. The legal sources are the elements that generally speaking can be assumed to play a role in the legal decision-making process. They are a collective name for the factors that influence the decision maker's, typically the judge's, decision or evaluation of the legal case. The legal sources aim to describe which legal sources should or could be used as a basis for the decision. The study of these thereby becomes the science of legal information seeking and information use.

The sources might be written or unwritten. Examples of written sources are laws, announcements, circulars, or guides. These types of documents form the consciously formulated state of the law. For various reasons, however, this part of the legal sources cannot stand alone. There are, for example, important interpretative problems that are connected with the laws and announcements that are written down. The next most important legal source is earlier legal decisions, which can be assumed to have importance for the solution of future legal disputes, the so-called precedents. These precedents are judgments reached by the courts, and in this connection it is first and foremost judgments reached by the highest court of justice that may have precedent-setting importance. Next to laws and precedents, judicial customs and usage play a role as legal sources. These sources are very difficult to trace in terms of information seeking.

The above example tells us that the legal discipline, including legal science, has a very conscious and explicit position as to which information sources belong to the discipline and which do not, which sources are primary and which are secondary. It is true for all disciplines, but it is especially clear when law is concerned. It is not primarily the individual jurist's decision, but it is a collective evaluation that is shared by the members of the profession.

In the example above the legal information-seeking process and the legal information structures are described on the disciplinary, the collective, and the sociological level. Blume does not describe the individual jurists' and citizens' individual knowledge structures—the psychological level is not his starting point.

Psychology is probably of some importance to all professions which communicate with people, including the legal profession. Jurists also use psychological knowledge. This is most directly seen in the area of witness psychology, where psychological techniques can be used, for instance, when small children are being cross-examined. Within criminology there is of course an interest in psychological causes for criminal behavior. And within the penal area there is an interest in psychological theories which have something to say about the conditions for resocialization. In law there has also been some interest in the rather vague connections to psychology in the concept of "the sense of justice." But jurists have not, as far as I know, made the category error of perceiving legal science as one of the cognitive sciences. The fact that a lawyer should understand the cognitive structures of his client and his opponent does not make legal science into a cognitive science. The jurist works with information much in the same way as the librarian does.

Wormell (1985, p. 27) and Ingwersen and Wormell (1990, p. 13) define the primary function of information transfer as bringing about harmony among various cognitive structures, for instance, the user's, the author's, and the system designer's cognitive structures. The model that the cognitivists within information science introduce would correspond to perceiving law as a cognitive science, the aim of which is to bring harmony between the lawmakers' and the users' cognitive structures. However, Frohmann (1990) points out that it is dangerous to make everything into psychology. The objective to bring about harmony among the cognitive structures of the knowledge producers and the knowledge users does not take into account that there might be conflicts of interest between the producer and the user, and that today many documents are being produced which are of somewhat questionable value to the discipline and its users. It is in the interest of the user to be able to single out that which is of high quality: the documents which actually can contribute to the solution of his problems and tasks, as well as to be able to see through and expose low-quality documents, including those which seek to manipulate. The cognitivist analysis does not allow for such insights.

We can therefore conclude, that approaches in IS based on MI does not offer tools for solving the user's real problem: to be able to search for the relevant literature and avoid the nonrelevant literature.

AN ALTERNATIVE TO MI: DOMAIN ANALYSIS

In the rest of this methodological chapter I will briefly look at the principles behind the positive alternative to MI. In the following chapters, I will apply these principles to some central information science problems, which up until now have been examined mainly from the point of view of MI.

Information scientists and information specialists should be able to perform analysis of the information systems in a domain and—based on their professional competence—to suggest improvements in these systems. Such suggestions (1) should not limit themselves to obvious or trivial problems caused by, for instance, too little resources and (2) should not primarily reflect competence in computer science or in other fields, although knowledge of the most efficient technology is important. Instead, improvements suggested by information specialists should reflect a genuine knowledge and methodology developed collectively in IS. This methodology I prefer to call domain analysis, but more research is needed before it has been worked out in detail.

Methodological collectivism in information science means that the object is collective information and knowledge structures. Collective knowledge structures are, for instance, the disciplines, the interdisciplinary structures, or, to use a broader term: knowledge domains. Information science is not alone in studying knowledge domains. Other disciplines also study domains from their own specific point of view. For example, philosophy of science studies scientific domains, linguistics studies languages for special purposes or sublanguages, the pedagogical discipline of didactics studies domains (there exists, for example, journals in the didactics of mathematics), artificial intelligence studies domains, and so on. Information science studies knowledge domains with the objective of being able to optimize the transfer, use, and mediation of knowledge, including the use of information technology, but from a less formalized and more social perspective than computer science and artificial intelligence.

Typical domain analyses might examine the information structure of a discipline, including the size of its literature, the distribution of the literature on various publication forms, its national/international structure, its citation patterns, cumulativity, diffusion, different paradigms, knowledge organization, interdisciplinary exchange etc. Familiarity with the information structure of a discipline has immediate consequences for the information seeking within the discipline.

Scientific and professional communication and information dissemination should be seen as part of a cooperative process of solving existing, common goals in more or less well defined groups. The model of scientific communication perceives the producers of knowledge, the intermediaries and the users as organized in thought and discourse communities, which form parts of the division of labor in society. These discourse communities have a high degree of synchronized thinking, language, and knowledge (the actual degree of synchronized thinking being an empirical question).

In the discourse communities, there is a constant flow of informal and formal information. The single document should be seen as an abstraction whose concrete design and meaning can only be understood from an analysis of its communicative role and of its disciplinary, technical, economical, and functional presumptions. To understand the attributes and functions of kinds of documents, it is important to look at them from a functionalistic and a developmental point of view.

The activity-theoretical approach to communication is somewhat opposed to what has—with ironical overtones—been described as "the postal package theory" by Rossi-Landi (cf. Petrilli, 1993, p. 241). With this expression, Rossi-Landi underlines the inadequacy of approaches which describe communication in terms of messages which, similarly to a package, are sent off from one post office and received by another. In other words, he criticizes the analysis of communication in terms of pieces of neatly formulated and univocally identifiable communicative intentionality. The signifier and the signified do not relate to each other on a one-to-one basis; the sign is not at the service of a meaning that has been preestablished outside the signifying process. Instead, he turns to authors in the pragmatic and materialist traditions, which place the sign in the context of dialogism, responsive understanding, and otherness. Peirce developed his semiotics in close relation to the study of the social behavior of human beings and the totality of their interests. It follows that the problems of knowledge necessarily involve considerations of an evaluative order. Interpreting messages can be done in different contexts. Peirce's *immediate interpretant* concerns meaning as it is used ordinarily and habitually by the interpreter and, therefore, it concerns the interpreter's immediate response to signs. Peirce's *dynamic interpretant* concerns the sign's signification in a specific context. Lastly, Peirce's *final interpretant* concerns the sign at the extreme limits of its interpretative possibilities. It concerns all possible responses provoked by a sign in a potentially unlimited sequence of interpretants: it alludes to the creative potential of signs.

According to the pragmatic epistemology, knowledge can remain silent and nondocumented or nonpublished, or it can reveal itself in human actions and products, including texts. The design of texts is governed by certain purposes and interests. The purposes and interests influence their functionality in ways which can make them less suitable to other purposes or interests.

Traditional approaches to information science have favored the similarities and the standards in documents and their representations. This is somewhat related to the empiricist and rationalist epistemology discussed in Chapter 4. Standards and structures in documents are becoming an important subject.[9]

However, from the point of view of domain analysis, it is important to study how different domains have different needs. From this perspective, the focus is not the uniformity or standards, but the differences: how different structures represent optimal adaptations to special needs and conditions in a domain. Tippo (1993) provides one important empirical example. She shows how historical abstracts should be designed to answer special needs of the domain of history, and that the international standard for designing abstracts is not well suited for this domain.

The overall communication system of IS is shown in Figure 5.2. As the figure shows, information can be communicated either directly (e.g., by Internet) or indirectly through primary, secondary, or tertiary services and documents. It is important for IS to study the information channels from a systems point of view because the channels compete with each other. Both systems analyses of communication in single disciplines and comparative analyses of the patterns in different disciplines are needed. An obvious problem to investigate includes suboptimal utilization of information due to lack of visibility, for example, unsatisfactory coverage of the primary information in the secondary systems.

Another very central question in IS is what kind of knowledge the information producer is selecting, including how knowledge is transferred between disciplines. Figure 5.3 shows the input and output from knowledge producers. The producers' selection of information sources are determined by domain-specific criteria. However, to some degree the selection is guided by epistemo-logical assumptions, which can be generalized. Rationalists prefer knowledge from within their own heads, empiricists prefer knowledge from natural sources, and historicists prefer knowledge from human cultures. Epistemological debates in social constructivism, for example, point to the importance of broad cultural information, even in sciences understanding themselves as natural sciences. Bibliometrics can study the actual use of different kinds of sources, but we need epistemological theories in order to interprete these patterns.

An interesting example is an empirical study that shows that American sociologists use the PsycINFO database more than they use Sociological Abstracts.[10] There are many possible explanations for this: for instance, the coverage of PsycINFO may be more in-depth, broader, or more up-to-date. An epistemological explanation might be that American sociologists are more oriented toward methodological individualism, and therefore they look for explanations for social conditions on the individual level. This epistemological explanation is an important working hypothesis because it suggests that American sociologists' preferences for databases might be based upon assumptions that are open for discussion.

Information science has an important partner in composition studies, a new, interdisciplinary research area, attracting researchers from literature and linguistics, psychology and cognitive science, sociology and the philosophy of knowledge. The aim is to understand the nature and process of creating documents, especially in relation to specific contexts and domains. Composition studies is grounded in epistemological assumptions that could be very fruitful for information science: Information and its users are not regarded from individualistic, mentalistic, or mechanical viewpoints, but in relation to historical and social developments in scholarship.

In the coming cyberspace all documents and their representations, citations, links, and so on, will be available in electronic form susceptible to investigation. The core problem of IS is the problem of document storage and retrieval, subject access points, and database semantics. By increasing our understanding of the creation and nature of documents, their different kinds and functions, their elements and relations between documents, and the relation between documents and different user groups, information science can come closer to its goal.

A basic point of view in domain analysis is that different scientific, scholarly, or professional domains each have unique structures of communication and publication and unique types of documents. Each unique structure is an expression of an adaptation to the special needs in the domain. Some examples of unique kinds of documents are the following:

In music:	Sheets of music
In geography:	Maps and atlases
In law:	Codes; bodies of law
In astronomy:	Almanacs
In genealogy:	Pedigrees and genealogical trees
In psychology:	Tests

Scientific documents have special characteristics which in particular are connected to the need to document or make probable claims about new research results and knowledge. Of course, standards exist, and many scientific articles, bibliographical databases, and encyclopedias have very important similarities across disciplinary borders. The existence of widespread or universal attributes in the information structures must, however, be looked upon as an adaptation to very fundamental and widespread conditions and needs.

Figure 5.2
Knowledge Dissemination from Producers to Users

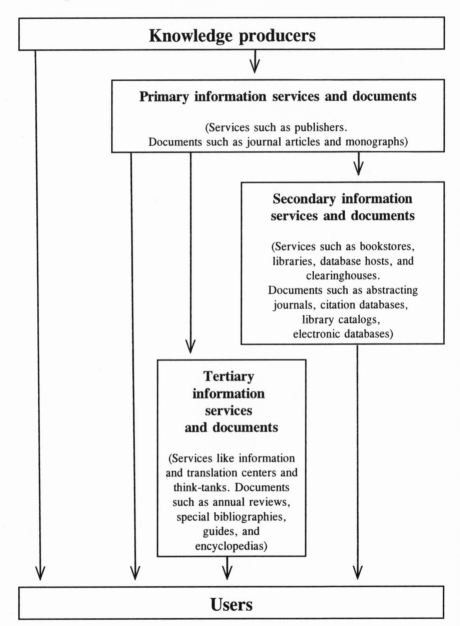

Knowledge producers

Primary information services and documents

(Services such as publishers.
Documents such as journal articles and monographs)

Secondary information
services and documents

(Services such as bookstores,
libraries, database hosts, and
clearinghouses.
Documents such as abstracting
journals, citation databases,
library catalogs,
electronic databases)

Tertiary
information
services
and documents

(Services like information
and translation centers and
think-tanks. Documents
such as annual reviews,
special bibliographies,
guides, and
encyclopedias)

Users

Figure 5.3
The Input and Output from Knowledge Producers

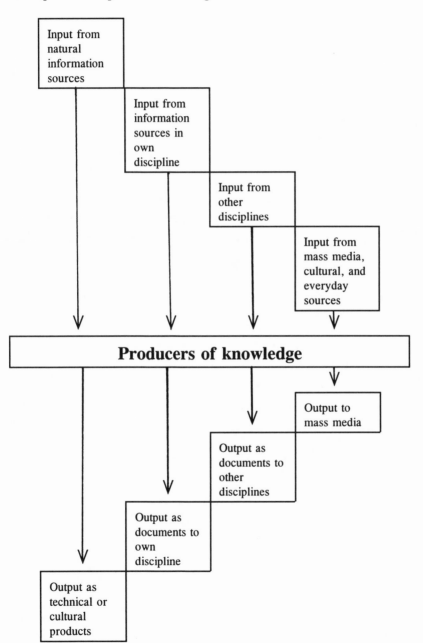

Methodological and epistemological norms have an influence on the architecture, rhetoric, language, and so on, of documents. Different scientific paradigms imply certain special needs in relation to information and documentation structures. There is the real danger of an ideological regimentation of subject literatures, which can lead to stagnation. In psychology and the social sciences a positivist influence on document typology from natural science can be traced (cf. Roberts, 1985). This need not be the optimal typology or structure in these fields.

In the scientific information system the primary literature is the point of departure. Other kinds of literature, for example, source literature, bibliographic literature, methodological literature, and review literature could be seen as developments of independent and explicit forms of materials inherent in the primary literature in embryonic form. This development to independence of certain kinds of literature is dependent on the kind of knowledge: whether it is possible to make a division of labor in the scientific field and to rely on others' selections, reviews, and evaluations. The more developed a science is, the more diversified, explicated, and formalized are the subroutines in the field, including the document typology.

Traditional disciplinary bibliographical work is often regarded as an end in itself and as a recording activity that does not have the character of scientific work. It might, however, also be viewed as a very time-consuming element in the empirical research process to ascertain the information structure of the knowledge domain.

Another name for the domain analytic approach in information science could thus be the sociological-epistemological paradigm. Taking our starting point in Mammen (1983), we can say that the survival of library and information science depends on whether it can present a domain analysis which contains a general, concrete, and specific perspective. A general perspective implies that it should be possible to generalize from an isolated instance. A concrete perspective implies that it builds upon concrete characteristics and phenomena, which are reflected in its concepts, models, and theories, and that these are not given a priori. And finally, a specific perspective implies that the same perspective is not a part of another already existing science.

Information science should primarily be understood as a social science, in that its research object is socially produced and transferred information and knowledge. In the social sciences there are various methodological paradigms, of which we have already discussed several.[11]

Can we—based on analyses of the debate on the methodologies of the social sciences—gain a better view of the corresponding problems of information science? Little (1991) discusses several types of explanations in the social sciences, including causal analysis, rational decision-making theory, and interpretation theory (hermeneutics). In regard to the latter he sums it up in the following way:

The interpretive approach to social phenomena amounts to the following thesis: All human action is mediated by a subjective social worldview; no social science is possible that does not penetrate the individual's social world. Thus all social action is framed by a meaningful social world. To understand, explain, or predict patterns of human behavior, we must first penetrate the social world of the individual—the meanings he attributes to the environment (social and natural), the values and goals he possesses, the choices he perceives, and the way he interprets other individuals' social action. Only then will we be able to analyze, interpret, and explain his behavior. But now the action is thickly described in terms of the meanings, values, and interpretive principles the agent employs in his own understanding of his world. (Little, 1991, p. 85)

Should this viewpoint be seen as a normative principle that pertains to all social science research? Is it reasonable to assume that all social sciences can use the hermeneutic approach? If this is the case, says Little, causal analysis and rational decision-making theory have to be rejected as explanatory models. His conclusion is that the interpreting model is a legitimate explanatory model for some social science problems, but that the assumption that all social science studies should be undertaken using this approach is not convincing. In Little's view there are substantial areas within the social sciences where the problems associated with meaning and interpretation are of no importance and in which objective factors—material interests, social structures, compulsory institutions—play a central explanatory role. There are many research areas within the social sciences in which hermeneutic analysis is neither necessary nor noteworthy.

The question as to information science can thus be seen as a question of the extent to which information science problems are suited to hermeneutic methods, and the extent to which they are suited to more objective explanations and methods such as causal analysis or rational decision-making theory.

There is in my opinion no doubt that there exists an ideal within information science to strive toward causal analyses and rational decision-making theory. Research in subject data systems of databases and libraries builds upon such strong assumptions. In this book I have made references to hermeneutic research which show that a text cannot be said to have a meaning that exists in and of itself; it only exists in the interpretation. This hermeneutic perspective has demonstrated that there are erroneous assumptions in the existing theories of subject data systems, and the hermeneutic perspective has demonstrated its importance.

On the other side, however, my work is based on clear ideals to build a theory that can be designated as rational decision-making theory: to make it possible to design information systems based upon principles that not only are built on interpretation and insights into function and content, but also can be represented as rational solutions, possibly of a system theory nature and based upon causal analysis. In my opinion, the pragmatic-realistic starting point—as developed in activity theory—therefore appears to be best suited to the interests of IS.

In the remaining part of this book I will attempt to reinterpret some central problems of information science within a framework that builds upon this methodology.

NOTES

1. Sometimes the theory of information science is referred to as information theory (e.g., Wersig, 1996). Normally, however, this last term has a much more limited meaning as a statistical theory about transmitting signals developed by Claude Shannon in 1948. Wersig (1996) provides a useful, modern overview of developments in the theory of information science including its connection to information theory in Shannon's meaning and action theory as a modern approach. (Action theory being very much related to activity theory.)

2. Mingers (1996) is an important evaluation of some of the most central theories about the concept of information.

3. This conception is also discussed in Hjørland & Albrechtsen (1995a).

4. The most important function of an IR system is not necessarily to satisfy a given request, but to help the user to formulate meaningful requests by providing structure, relations, and feedback on his initial ideas.

5. An attempt to do this can be found in Hjørland (1988, 1989).

6. Methodological individualism is fairly thoroughly treated by Little (1991, pp. 183–210), who defines MI as the viewpoint that social explanations and descriptions should be based upon facts about the individuals. This doctrine comprises several related, but distinct statements: a thesis about social units, a thesis about the importance of social concepts, and a thesis about explanation. The various versions of the thesis are, according to Little, not equivalent. The ontological thesis about MI is true, but fairly trivial; the importance thesis is completely unconvincing; and the explanation thesis is a correct but often misunderstood insight that macro-level explanations should be able to offer satisfactory explanations about micro-level processes. Little also shows how MI is connected with the reductionistic program: that sociological explanations should be reduced to psychological ones, and these again to biological ones, until one reaches subatomic physics. This reductionist program was one of positivism's main assumptions, but Little (p. 192) notes: "Most philosophers of science now agree that reductionism is not a plausible requirement of scientific concept formation and explanation when we look at specific areas of science." I will not discuss Little's views any further, but only note that even if Little differentiates the debate, he does not offer any arguments which change the thesis of this book, which seeks to base information science upon the opposite of MI: methodological collectivism.

7. Resnick et al. (1991) is marketed somewhat bombastically and is mentioned as "an emerging revolution in cognitive theory." The book is presented in advertizements in the following way: "Do humans do their thinking alone? Is thought confined within the boundaries of each individual mind? Today, psychologists are pioneering a new alternative to this classic view, claiming that our thinking is shaped by others, in a process known as socially shared cognition."

8. The cognitive perspective within information science is more thoroughly treated in Hjørland (1991).

9. For example, in a call for papers in 1995, the *Journal of the American Society for Information Science* announced a forthcoming special issue titled "Structured Information/Standards for Document Architectures."

10. The study of American sociologists' preference for PsycINFO was published in the *Note Us* newsletter, which is distributed by Sociological Abstracts. Final verification has not been done.

11. The positivist paradigm is officially a bygone era, but as this book shows, this invisible theory of science still has a dominating position, among other reasons because it is a spontaneous or naive theory. Within information science there has yet been no real debate about positivism. The concept of positivism, its definition, its forms in the information science literature, the counterarguments, and the alternatives seem to be unknown. It is unfortunate, since positivism represents a form of anti-intellectualism. In its attempts to avoid the metaphysical, positivism unfortunately oppress intellectual analysis and interpretation. Since libraries should be strongholds of intellectualism, an anti-intellectual theory appears grotesque. Nevertheless, theories about, for example, material selection in libraries are often built upon statistical analyses of user preferences without interest in the contents of the literature or the trends in knowledge production.

6

Science, Discipline, and Subject Field as a Framework for Information Seeking

Science, subject area, cognitive field, discipline, and so on, are complex concepts because they contain several definitions. From Plato and Aristotle up to Locke and Hume the word *science* was reserved for knowledge of what is necessarily the case. Such knowledge was thought to be acquired only by rational intuition. Knowledge derived from empirical inquiry was not called science. What today is called natural science was usually called natural philosophy until the end of the eighteenth century. Thus the concept of science is closely related to the concept of knowledge and to epistemological theories of how to obtain knowledge.

The notion of science can be viewed on the one hand as an institution in society, and on the other hand as an epistemological concept. Science as a social institution is studied mainly in the sociology of science. Science as an epistemological phenomenon represents an ideal (to be scientific or to qualify as science) and is studied mainly in the philosophy of science. The latter definition presumes, among other things, that there exists a concrete object or a concrete problem area with corresponding methodological clarifications and constructions. These two definitions are not independent, but represent mutually interwoven external and internal evolutionary conditions. The realistic theories of science tend to emphasize the internal demands of the field, whereas the constructivist philosophies tend to emphasize the influence of external factors on the development of science.[1]

The pragmatic understanding views science as a form of human activity or work. Whether something deserves to be called science or not is thus dependent upon value norms that determine what kind of work one finds relevant. Hardly anybody would claim that fruitless effort is relevant. Therefore, normative, philosophical criteria will be part of the definition. These criteria are historically determined, and they can be strongly connected with developments in the scientific method.[2] Society has problems, for instance, health problems, educational problems, or economic problems. The role of science—both applied and pure—is, among other things, to be a part of the theoretical and empirical framework that contributes to the solution of these problems. The methods, organizational forms, and so on, that prove—in the short or long term, directly or indirectly—that they contribute to the solution of relevant problems in society are recognized as science. There are no eternal or unchangeable criteria for science; the conception of science itself is historically determined, and it is a controversial issue. This book presents a pragmatic theory of science that may dissolve many purely metaphysical issues.

The concept of science obviously has several connections to information science. In addition to the question of whether information science meets the criteria of being a science, it should be pointed out that information science historically has its roots in scientific communication and documentation. The most important issue is, that the concept of science can serve as a methodological approach in IS. Information problems should not primarily be analyzed from the point of view of the subjective universe of an individual, but from the point of view of knowledge domains. One can, for instance, claim that individuals have fuzzy, unclear information needs (see, e.g., Ingwersen, 1992, p. 117). On the other hand, one can also analyze the problem by postulating that the user asks questions within a science or a domain where historically or currently there has been "strategic task uncertainty" (see Andersen, 1985). In Chapter 5, I discussed how the analysis of the information problems of a science, a subject, or a knowledge domain may offer an alternative to the tendency to methodological individualism and psychologizing within the field of information science. In this chapter I will propose a theoretical outline for information seeking understood as cooperation within the framework of the scientific disciplines.

What can we say about information seeking outside the scientific communities? If primary, secondary, and tertiary documents, libraries and information systems, and so on, are to be designed, there must exist a collective need for them and the possibility to pay people for the development and management of such systems. If a given group of people, say florists, begin in a systematic way to collect information about botany, chemistry, gardening, color perception, and so on, then we could say that they are in fact beginning to establish an applied science, where specialists are trained to collect, organize, and disseminate information of relevance to the group. The question thus changes from an extra-scientific situation to a situation where we could ask what kind of "science" it is, and what kind of information need the community has. On the other hand, if there is no collective group with such well-defined information needs, the information system cannot be optimized along *the same sort* of need-oriented principles, and we are moving from an information science perspective to the perspective of, for example, mass communication.

INFORMATION SEEKING UNDER CONDITIONS OF NORMAL SCIENCE AND REVOLUTIONARY SCIENCE

From the domain analytic perspective, information-seeking behavior is perceived as stages in a cooperation process between producers and users of knowledge within the framework of disciplines or discourse communities. It is a type of cooperation that is often organized as a scientific discipline, where the goals and definitions are derived from the object of the research or the research problems.

The goal of information seeking is to identify potential knowledge, data, information, or raw material—whatever one prefers to call it—that will contribute to the theoretical or empirical development of the field or to the solution of a practical problem. The latter can of course be the education or informing of others outside the discipline as well, since a discipline also serves intermediary functions in relation to external agents. For such purposes special kinds of documents are developed (e.g., textbooks and science magazines).

Some of the information that is needed represents a type of routinized information gathering, whereas other kinds of information are dependent upon theoretical transformations on the research front. A scientific or professional discipline usually takes its information needs very seriously. Economists, for instance, are interested in certain kinds of statistical information, which they need in order to be able to issue political-economic prognoses and for their own theoretical development. This means that the economics field will actively advocate the improvement of the country's descriptive statistics. Correspondingly, medical researchers will actively promote better descriptive health statistics, historians will actively work toward securing both print and nonprint sources for posterity, and so on. The disciplines set up special channels in order to secure the continuous supply of information to meet such recognized and important information needs. Such channels are, for instance, journals, handbooks, or whole institutions or libraries. Within the law discipline almost every serious practitioner in Denmark subscribes to *Ugeskrift for Retsvæsen* [*The Judicial System Weekly*], which publishes the supreme court's decisions. This is an example of what I call routinized information gathering, linked with the normal phases of science (see Kuhn, 1970). An important part of the education in any given field is instruction in the identification and preparation of information that is relevant to the common goals. This is of course especially true about information-rich fields such as law and history, which actually almost solely work with information gathering, interpretation, and preparation. But it is remarkable that even professionals working in fields which are not generally thought of in connection with information activities can be characterized as efficient information gatherers. A characteristic of good craftsmen, for example, is that they are efficient gatherers of information about materials, tools, prices, regulations, and so on.

During times of theoretical transformation, that is, when science—or an isolated branch of it—enters a revolutionary phase (Kuhn, 1970), this information need might change. At the very least, new types of information will be needed. Most likely, consensus will not prevail, and some scientists will try to introduce one kind of information into the discipline, while others will introduce other kinds. An example of this type of theoretical transformation is the augmentation of the biological "engine failure"-model in medicine with a multicausal socio-psychological view. Diseases, for instance infectious diseases, are no longer viewed exclusively as the function of a single source of influence (e.g., bacteria or viruses), but are also viewed in relation to the resistance of the organism, which might be damaged by, for instance, psychological stress (see, e.g., Wulff, 1985).

Ill-defined disciplines may often look all over for information and may retrieve a great deal, while the real problem remains to formulate a coherent knowledge base. The theoretical base of a science implies what information is particularly important for the science in question, as well as what type of information is less relevant or perhaps completely irrelevant. To take an extreme example, one's theoretical view on astrology determines whether one looks for information about the destiny of people in the skies or on earth. Since some of the proposed theoretical paths are more fruitful than others—it is difficult to see it any other way—both the individual scientist and the whole discipline have to work toward making the most fruitful information as visible as possible. A scientist does this first of all by utilizing it in his work, including citing the sources that he most directly uses in his research. A special problem in relation to this is the discipline's possibilities of influencing and controlling its own information dissemination. This would include, for example, its control over journals, publishers, libraries, and institutions. In cases where commercial or special institutional interests counteract professional and scientific interests, one may talk about anomaly in the described (ideal) model.

When a user turns to an information specialist with a question (and a problem that lies behind it), the information specialist analyzes the question and the problem both from the point of view of his or her subjective understanding of the nature of the problem and from the point of view of existing information resources and information-seeking alternatives. It is an unlikely scenario (but not at all impossible) that the information specialist would be the first one within a discipline to connect a problem with a new type of information, or with a new conceptual framework that has not yet been seen in connection with the problem. It is more likely that a scientist within the discipline already has noticed the association and argued for it in an article and that the user or the intermediary has noticed the article and has thus been able to track sources outside the discipline. As more scientists notice the relevance of these sources, the new association is institutionalized in the conceptual apparatus of the discipline, in communication channels, perhaps in thesauri, and so on, and we are approaching the situation during the normal phase.

For example, if we examine the sociopsychological paradigm within medicine that was mentioned above, we can say that the establishment of courses in psychology, social medicine, and the theory of science for medical students; the founding of special journals and institutions for social medicine; and the addition of a permanent psychology descriptor in the database MEDLINE in connection with all types of diseases are examples of the normalization of this paradigm. In this way, the medical profession is setting up information channels in order to secure the supply of relevant sociological and psychological knowledge into the field.

In the example above, we cannot identify clearly defined phases, but each science may, at any given moment, have tendencies both to normal science and to revolutionary science. (I am using Kuhn's terminology without taking it literally.) The revolutionary tendencies may range from the almost invisible to the almost completely dominating. In the career of the individual scientist it can be assumed that there typically will be a development in which the scientist gradually gains a better view of the existing knowledge in the field. In other words, the scientist's cognitive structure is starting to resemble the collective knowledge structure. From being a more or less comprehensive and passive reflection of the collective knowledge, the scientist will—depending on his or her individual development—form an opinion of the extent of the collective knowledge, its problems, and its "holes." A scientist will concentrate on producing more independent knowledge, focusing on deficiencies within the existing knowledge base. Starting from a given point of normal science (the majority view) he or she will gradually develop a personal understanding of a given set of problems and thus approach a more independent view. This view represents a minority view that might resemble a revolutionary state. The scientist's whole information-seeking behavior may therefore consist of more and more individual (and idiosyncratic) methods; the scientist will be using more and more untraditional information sources. There are, of course, big differences among research areas. Within medicine the patterns are much more similar than among the humanities, which are characterized by extreme individualism. It is, of course, relevant to study the background to these differences field by field.

It is important to note that fields set up more or less broad or strict limits for the information (seeking) behavior of the individual scientist. Individual information-seeking behavior takes place within a social framework, for example, a discipline. The more consensus in a discipline, the more restricted is the individual search behavior. A discipline "disciplines" its members.[3]

In this connection it should be repeated that the epithet of scientific discipline implies that the scientist disciplines himself or herself by agreeing to abide by the specific game rules that are manifest in the field. This disciplining concerns among other things standardization of the professional discourse and communicative behavior (e.g., selection of publication channels). The higher the degree of standardization, and the better the discipline functions as a collective enterprise, the more limited is the freedom of the individual scientist. When this freedom is limited by demands from the research object, it is a sign of developed science. When the freedom of the scientist is limited by social norms within the research group that are not caused by the research object, it is a sign of a lack of openness and of an immature and unhealthy discipline. With this I have reached the question of the fundamental uncertainty of information seeking.

THE FUNDAMENTAL UNCERTAINTY OF INFORMATION SEEKING

Information seeking is both practically and theoretically characterized by uncertainty. For instance, in looking for literature to support a scientific hypothesis, it will always be possible to use more databases, more alternative sources, more index terms, and to test new combinations. Not even the most sophisticated search profile can guarantee that all the important data in a database will be found. The only certain search method would be to go through all the documents one after another. This method would be unrealistic for most fields, where the monthly growth alone is so enormous that to use this method would in fact only distance the information seeker from the goal.

It is of course easy to come up with examples of unproblematic questions: Napoleon's birth date, the boiling point of mercury, Swedish tax laws, and so on. Such information can be tracked down with certainty. This is first and foremost due to the fact that this information is highly visible. This can be seen as a question about the relationship between signal and noise in information theoretical terms and of effectiveness in the organization of the information. However, it can also be seen as consequence of the fact that no interpretation is needed: one knows when the correct answer is found and when the search can be terminated. If, for example, the boiling point of mercury was problematic, and one wanted to look for a complete list of determinations of the number in order to estimate the most likely boiling point, then this example would represent uncertainty in information seeking. Information seeking is problematic in connection with a qualified determination of when all possible search alternatives have been exhausted, the search activities can be suspended, and the found results be viewed as being in reasonable agreement with human knowledge in the area (and not only an expression of an accidental and possibly completely inaccurate source).

The understanding that information seeking is a practical and fundamentally uncertain process is based upon the assessment that unproblematic questions of the type described above are exceptions, whereas the majority of, and the most important, information-seeking questions belong to the problematic category where interpretation and uncertainty are the rule.[4] Information seeking is uncertain, but this does not mean that we don't find enormous differences as to database construction as well as in the way that searches are performed in databases and libraries. It is a serious mistake to draw an agnostic conclusion on the basis of fundamental uncertainty, that is, to fail to work on improving the information-seeking options simply because one cannot reach a 100 percent perfect result. On the contrary, even in poor databases there is a great deal one can do in order to improve the searches, and there are many possibilities for improving the search conditions for future users at the database construction stage.

It stands to reason that databases which are based largely on document title searching are less efficient than databases which in addition to titles offer search options through, for instance, descriptors or abstracts, references or full text. It also stands to reason that the quality of the system of descriptors, the indexing, and the referencing may vary a great deal. As a searcher one is dependent upon the existing search options (subject access points), but even in a title database providing only titles as subject access points the quality of the search may vary immensely, depending on how many synonyms the searcher is capable of producing and which limiting variables he is capable of selecting in order to optimally reduce the loss of relevant references. As a rule, there is a great deal of variation in the databases in real life. Also, there are big differences between qualified and unqualified search profiles or search dialogs (see, e.g., Hjørland 1988, 1989).

This means that the practical uncertainty in connection with information seeking is a question of the resources (and qualifications) that are put into information and documentation work, as far as both database production and information seeking are concerned. In the final analysis, it is a question of economy: how much is worth investing in database production in order to facilitate the search process, and how much should be spent on information seeking instead of on giving more resources to the scientists so that they can reinvent the wheel? When do we reach the limits for what information seeking is worth? The situation in the 1990s varies from discipline to discipline, but is characterized by serious financial trouble among many database producers. Furthermore, the costs for monitoring and registering the literature in sufficient breadth are such that the quality of the indexing often comes second. Many database producers feel—rightly or wrongly—that free text searching in existing data, for example, titles and abstracts, offers good enough retrieval rates and that it is more important to include more literature in the automated systems than to invest in more thorough indexing. This state of things is probably due to the fact that we are living in a transitional phase between print media and electronic databases as primary channels of communication in science. One would guess that as soon as the electronic media have reached a stage where they include the majority of the scientific literature, competition as well as research and development will contribute to a shift from quantitative toward qualitative parameters. Hopefully we will move from the practical uncertainty in information seeking that is caused by the less than perfect utilization of existing principles and standards in the existing information systems, to the theoretical uncertainty that is caused on grounds of principle within the framework of known theoretical solutions. I will now consider this more fundamental form of uncertainty in information seeking.

First I would like to point out that the information science literature has put forward a controversial "law" that postulates a fundamental limit for information retrieval. It is the so-called law about the inverse relationship between recall and precision in information retrieval. As defined in Chapter 2, Note 12, *recall* stands for the proportion of relevant documents in a database that can be retrieved by using a given search profile. This is measured by the number of documents found in relation to the total number of relevant documents. *Precision* stands for how much noise is included in the results. This is measured by the number of all relevant retrieved documents in relation to all retrieved documents. The law was proposed at the beginning of automated retrieval systems. It was inspired by the experience that if you attempt to improve the retrieval rate in a given free-text database by, for example, including more concepts, precision will suffer. Such conditions may exist (see Cleverdon, 1972), but in terms of being a law, this statement is in my opinion fairly misleading. Buckland and Gey (1994) demonstrate that a tradeoff between recall and precision seems unavoid-able whenever retrieval performance is consistently better than retrieval at random. However, the interpretation of this fact is controversial. Fugmann (1994) demonstrates by thought experiment that it is possible to improve the precision of a retrieval system dramatically, without any drop in recall (e.g., by introducing first names in a directory). In my opinion the basic purpose in developing retrieval systems is to make systems that improve recall and precision at the same time, as has also been suggested in the literature (e.g., Soergel, 1985, pp. 121–122; Fugmann, 1994).

When I am talking about fundamental or theoretical limits to literature searching, I do not mean that there are fixed or inflexible limits. On the contrary, I mean that even if the ideal information system is an unreachable goal, practical and theoretical improvements of the information systems produce more and more efficient systems that are constantly extending the boundaries of what the systems can do. A thought experiment will illuminate the situation. If you assume a given ideal search function, you can easily construct a hypothetical example of a document and its subject description that will not be captured by this search function. The ideal character of this function is thereby refuted. Conversely, we could construct another search function that would start out from the constructed example—and be an improvement—and so on.[5]

If one examines information seeking in currently existing databases within psychology, one can point to obvious weaknesses in the existing systems: until a few years ago PsycINFO did not have adequate coverage of the monograph literature, an it still only sporadically covers a number of language areas (see Hjørland, 1989); subject description lacks permanent, explicit descriptive dimensions (see Hjørland 1988, 1989) and is often quite insufficient. Only when such conditions have improved will it be possible to examine the next level of development. PsycINFO indexes many of the psychological, psychiatric, biological, and other similar journals with a view to the needs of the discipline of psychology. But some psychologists are working with mathematical models, and ideally one should browse the mathematical literature in reference to the needs of the discipline of psychology. Some psychologists also admit that fiction and the scholarly study of literature often contains important psychological insights. Ideally this type of literature should also be examined with a view to selection and description for the discipline of psychology, and so on. Some information systems already go quite far in this respect. (As an example, Chemical Abstracts registers literature from many psychology journals as well as from, e.g., *Norsk Pelsdyrsblad* [*Norwegian Fur Journal*].) But there is always the possibility of going even farther, and selection as well as indexing and referencing policies can always be discussed.

Ultimately, what sets the limits for the effectiveness of a system is the understanding (Capurro, 1986, and many other hermeneutically oriented scholars call it pre-understanding) that lies behind the selection and description of the needs of a science and the scientists at any given point in time. It is a question of making explicit the boundaries of a given discipline, its methodology, and its epistemological problems, including its movement from the surface to the essence of things or from the particular to the general. Such a recognition is an infinite process, in that still-deeper layers of reality can always be explored. Electronic databases as information systems are by nature both expansive and unselective, making possible the tracking of alternative theories and very specific data. For this reason alone, they should not depend on a narrow or one-sided view of a discipline. This should not, however, be mistaken for a basic lack of theory, since the success of any information system ultimately depends on its ability to predict the needs it is expected to meet. An uncritical accumulation of documents and subject relations in the database will at some point in time reduce efficiency instead of improving it.

I will conclude by saying that currently existing databases typically exhibit many practical flaws, which can be corrected on the basis of existing knowledge about information retrieval and databases. At the same time, there is continual development of the theoretical and technical foundations for information systems. The search options and the possibilities for potential innovations in the existing systems are improving at a tremendous rate. However, information seeking will always be fundamentally uncertain, and ultimately this uncertainty is determined by the self-comprehension of the scientific disciplines, their methodology, and their ability to predict and describe their own needs in such a way that it is possible to define what kind of literature should be made visible for various user groups. In information science, various bibliometric studies of the most-cited journals are common, but such studies are rarely combined with analysis and discussion of the discipline within the framework of a theory of science. This appears to be somewhat problematic.

METHODOLOGICAL ASPECTS OF INFORMATION SEEKING

Swanson (1986b, p. 115) offers as an example of information seeking the mathematical analysis of how a child pumps a swing. He ascertains that this literature cannot be found under "pumping" or "swings," but in the literature on "parametric amplifiers." Swanson uses this example to demonstrate that information seeking is fundamentally uncertain. I find that the same example in a much higher degree illuminates two other principles:

1. Information systems are not primarily pedagogical systems that are meant to mediate between everyday terminology and professional terminology. Rather, they are scientific systems that assume that the user is capable of analyzing a problem from a professional point of view.

2. As pointed out above, scientific knowledge is characterized by a shift from surface qualities to more generalizable and abstract expressions for the nature of things (from children and swings to parametric amplifiers). On the other hand, I see no reason why information systems cannot maintain a high professional standard. Therefore, I do not find that the example in and of itself shows fundamental uncertainty with respect to information seeking. It would be absurd to imagine an information system that for each law (or each mathematical function) would attempt to enumerate all actual or potential concrete uses of this law.

INCIDENTAL VERSUS SYSTEMATIC MOMENTS

Swanson (1977, 1986a) describes information seeking as fundamentally a trial-and-error process. His opinions are fairly widely cited and followed. He is strongly influenced by Karl Popper, who views scientific theories as guesswork that can be falsified by other scientists. In the same way, Swanson views a search function as a guess that can be falsified (but never completely verified). I don't want to reject the notion that a not insignificant part of almost all realistic information seeking is based on trial and error, but I would like to defend the opposite viewpoint: that information seeking fundamentally—but perhaps not in praxis—is a systematic and methodical process and *not* incidental guesswork.

In order to show the conscious and methodical character of information seeking we can observe a scientist who has produced new knowledge in a given area. He will usually make great efforts to formulate this new knowledge by using concepts that make it possible for him to communicate his knowledge to relevant colleagues. He will also carefully consider the title of the article, which journal the article should be published in, how to inform colleagues at conferences, and so on. He is often a member of scientific associations which invest a great deal of money in the publishing of new knowledge and perhaps in the recording of new knowledge in databases such as PsycINFO or Chemical Abstracts as well. Subsequently, the database providers invest in search tools that index the literature in such a way that it is most visible for potential users. They invest in the development of thesauri and terminology, so that the concepts used by the scientists are put in relation to the collected literature in the field. The concepts might be borrowed directly from the literature, they may be put under a similar concept, or a completely new concept might be constructed. Corporations, libraries, and others hire personnel with a disciplinary background to assist in retrieving information from these databases. All things considered, it is a carefully planned, conscious attempt to make sure that the knowledge producer and the knowledge user reach each other. Trial and error makes it sound as if this were only a game of chance. As far as the search itself is concerned, the success of the communication process is largely determined by the parameters of the bibliographic control and the terminological level of the discipline. Fields that are reasonably well defined both systematically and as far as terminology is concerned are almost by definition proof that information seeking is no casual test such as Swanson describes it.

Information seeking on the individual level to a lesser or greater extent looks like a casual guessing process, but the frame for this process can be found on the level of the collective. The degree of casualness is based on the organization of the cooperation. Science is work and information seeking is a process within the cooperative process framed by the discipline. In cases where cooperation is poorly organized (or when it is a parody to even speak of cooperation, for example, when formal qualifications have become an end unto themselves regardless of the advances in knowledge), information seeking will start resembling a casual process. After a while the situation will become unworkable, as trivial contributions start to overshadow the valuable ones. This means that information seeking's conformity to "laws" is not connected to the search process, nor to the search technology (like the technology-fixated part of the information science world would like us to believe), but rather to the knowledge base, the structure of which is determined by the scientific organization. The key to a general theory of information seeking therefore lies in an analysis of scientific organization from an epistemological and sociology of science perspective!

Swanson's fairly powerful emphasis on the trial-and-error nature of information seeking is, in my opinion, first and foremost a question of anomalies in connection with the above outlined idealized communication process. First, the person who performs the search might not have a good enough background in the specialized terminology in the area. In such a case his search behavior will to a large degree look like a trial-and-error process. Second, the bibliographic control and the terminological level of the field may still be underdeveloped. The degree of bibliographic and terminological control should be seen as a result of various sociological conditions of the knowledge production process, for instance, the knowledge producers' potential for mutual cooperation and coordination. The information producer may also consciously or unconsciously fail to use such things as simple quality checks (e.g., spelling) or common terminology or may publish in unpredictable contexts (it might, e.g., be more prestigious for psychologists to publish in medical journals). Such circumstances reduce the methodical character of the information-seeking process and strengthen the random element. Another important matter is the degree of professional organization in the scientific disciplines, and whether scientific disciplines are organized according to internal demands that are part of the problems of the discipline, or according to external political or organizational conditions (sociologists of science talk about internalistic versus externalistic criteria for the development of science). Today there is a strong tendency away from basic research toward applied science, which takes us away from universality and generalizable theoretical integration of knowledge. This in turn reinforces the element of chance.

As far as I can see, the boundary between on the one hand strictly systematic access and on the other hand trial-and-error access is quite fluid, which is due to the scientific and terminological level, the organization of the knowledge base, and the professional qualifications of the user. The ideal professional qualifications of an information specialist are not identical to those of a researcher within the field, in that the information specialist needs to have a broader information perspective, which includes, among other things, knowledge of the research organization and the information structures.

In addition to the above mentioned anomalies in the communication process, there are also other circumstances that contribute to making information seeking into a trial-and-error process. Reality and language are extremely rich and multifarious, and the knowledge-producing process consists of more than just identifying pieces in a jigsaw puzzle. Within many fields knowledge is created and expressed in a specialized language, and although it is relevant to scientists in other fields, they tend to express the same knowledge (or the same need) but within another frame of reference, through the use of other concepts.

The fact that the research problems in various scientific fields to a growing extent are overlapping, in that knowledge more and more often is imported from other disciplines, is another circumstance that works against systematic information seeking. Naturally it is more difficult to master the tools and concepts of several scientific disciplines. Our time is, apart from purely technological innovations like the Atlas of Science mentioned earlier, characterized by a sense of exhaustion or resignation when it comes to grasping the overall connections and describing the multitude of scientific fields, interdisciplinary fields, and so on. A vigorous effort in this area could strengthen the transfer of knowledge across fields and lead to cooperation among various fields. Information science, with its tradition of scientific classification systems (e.g., the UDC), should have an obvious role to play in this connection. Unfortunately, the prevailing ideology today works against such classification work.

This is why there are basic limits to how methodical information seeking can be (see above section on the fundamental uncertainty of information seeking). On the most profound theoretical level the information-seeking problems originate in the same scientific problems as all scientific methodology. As computers solve many of the practical problems as to storage and transfer of data, the search problems will be even more tightly connected to the scientific methodology, of which they should be regarded as a part.

Further development of the methodological aspects of information seeking can be broken down into two aspects: (1) problems concerning the conceptual structuring of the objects of information seeking and (2) problems concerning the structure and properties of the search tools that are available to the user (e.g., primary, secondary, and tertiary documents). Generally speaking, both sets of problems have not to date been examined quite thoroughly. An examination of these problems on a general level seems to have been too abstract for most writers (whereas there exists an extensive literature on special search tools and special problems).

Concerning the first aspect is it no easy task to say something general about how concepts are structured during the information-seeking process, when one attempts to identify something as yet unknown by using these concepts. The most well-developed theory of this kind in information science is facet theory, which is connected with Ranganathan's name. I have attempted to use this theory in a search model within psychology (Hjørland, 1988, 1989). Facet theory gives the option of either constructing a universal structure of the search concepts or analyzing a field and constructing a facet structure for that field, which subsequently is used for searching. It is in line with the epistemological starting point of this book to view the last possibility as the most satisfactory. Here I will not discuss this model more closely, except by saying that it seems to be on the one hand absolutely necessary, and on the other hand—as I hinted earlier when I talked about Ranganathan in the section on the concept of subject—epistemologically problematic (which implies an internal conflict in the theory, which hopefully will be fruitful to research further).

Instead, I will briefly outline a theoretical approach that is characterized more by internal, organic connections than by the rigid structure implied by rationalism and objective idealism. In Hjørland (1993b) a case concerning a literature search regarding premenstrual syndrome is reported.[6] In this case I attempted to deduce some general principles about the structuring of concepts in information seeking.

During literature searching, concepts, search symbols, or search tools representing four categories are being used:

1. The research object itself, its properties, structure, processes, and so on

2. Scientific theories and methods concerning the research object

3. Scientific disciplines, traditions, and paradigms that deal with the research object

4. Formal aspects of the communication process, for example, publications, where knowledge about the research object is documented

The example using the menstrual cycle is an expression of the fact that there is an internal connection among these four conceptual categories. In the actual search situation one of the things that contribute to making literature searching into a qualitative method, rather than just an expression of external and superficial technical knowledge, is the awareness of this internal connection.

The research object is the mental effect on women of the menstrual cycle. Most researchers within psychology and medicine use a highly positivistic and biological-theoretical approach to this subject. This approach in turn determines to a large extent the methods used for exploring this subject (e.g., by using psychological tests) and the publication channels that are chosen (so-called prestigious international journals, which are indexed in Psychological Abstracts or MEDLINE).

If one wants to find "alternative" knowledge, this might build upon a theoretical approach based on a social scientific framework. The phenomena that the biology-based theories take for granted can be put into perspective by studying, for instance, the views on menstruation among various cultures. The knowledge of a concept like "the discipline of psychology" implies knowledge of the fact that there are great differences among the various disciplinary traditions in American, European, or the former Soviet psychology. This might be a part of the search design and of considerations regarding formal limitations of the search (publication forms), for instance, selection of databases. One might, for example, decide to give priority to the German database PSYNDEX.

The fact that I have chosen an example where "alternative" stands against "traditional" should not be interpreted to imply that I have proposed a theory of seeking nontraditional information. What I have attempted to express above is a general internal connection among an object, the theories and methods dealing with the object, scientific structures and traditions, and publication patterns. This theory is obviously especially meaningful in areas where these internal connections aren't obvious, such as psychology and the social sciences.

Now I have proposed the very first outline of a general theory of literature searching, one that starts in the classical philosophical problem of empirical and rational knowledge, incorporates findings from the history of science and sociology of science regarding scientific disciplines and paradigms, and, in including the teachings of bibliography and document types from library science, finally brings all this together in one thesis that has the pragmatic goal of prescribing a method for literature seeking.

In regard to the search tool structure, the second methodological aspect of information seeking, I have touched upon such problems in my earlier work.[7] In my opinion, there does not yet exist a single publication that even somewhat satisfactorily reviews the document typology within the theoretical frame of reference that I have outlined here, that is, that views the field-specific document types as developed in relation to specific communication tasks. In this book, I will limit myself to discussing the relation between bibliographic searching and chain searching (that is, properties of bibliographies and reference lists[8] used as search tools).

BIBLIOGRAPHICAL SEARCHING VERSUS CHAIN SEARCHING

Many librarians appear to hold the view that bibliographic searching is a more methodical process than unraveling the literature using informal contacts and through references in already located literature (i.e., chain searching). I would like to show that neither of these methods—as far as they can be viewed by themselves at all—can be said to be more methodical than the other.

The value of chain searching is often quite high. An example of how this can be highlighted is Welwert, 1984 (reported in Hjørland 1988, 1989). A search for the subjects reading comprehension versus listening comprehension resulted in 79 relevant references using database searching, 47 references using manual sources, and 82 relevant references using chain searching in the references that were located. The last 82 references could, of course, not have been found without the previous bibliographic search, but nevertheless, the example gives an indication of the relatively great significance of chain searching. Or perhaps it is an indication of the high degree of uncertainty of bibliographic searching that so many references were not found by a thorough search of databases and printed bibliographies. In my above reported treatment of Welwert, I indicate that there may exist relevant literature of a completely different theoretical orientation, which Welwert failed to locate. If this assumption is correct, it offers yet more evidence in support of the belief that the superiority of bibliographic searching is overrated (at least as it has been developed to date within this field).

The efficiency of bibliographic searching is, of course, determined by how much of the relevant literature has been recorded, analyzed by subject and described in a way that allows us to locate it via bibliographies, databases, and reference literature. The bibliographic approach is characterized by its formality. There are often formal rules that determine what is included in a bibliography or database and how it is described (e.g., by using descriptors). The description is an expression of the competence that is tied to the administration of a set of rules. The efficiency of the result depends in particular on whether the formal rules are able to ensure the design of a product that meets the needs of the users. The strength of the formal approach is that little of the material is excluded because of value-based criteria. The weakness of these systems is that they—by virtue of being formal—do not give priority to materials according to relevance. A lack of resources to carry out the planned, formal program might lie behind the random inclusion of both the highly relevant and the hardly relevant references. In real life, there is almost always a lack of resources, which means that the most relevant references often are absent (e.g., because they are excluded on formal grounds or because the bibliographic apparatus is inadequate, consisting of a number of "torsos" or uncompleted works).

The efficiency of chain searching—assuming that one gets a start—is determined by how well the document identifies and cites relevant information in the reference list. The method presupposes that the scientific literature in the field is neither unrelated to other research in the field nor simply redundant. In other words, it assumes that researchers are extremely conscientious in their literature searching and their referencing to relevant sources and that the references are selected with a view to informing the reader of important literature. It also presupposes that the scientist does not cite, for instance, on purely formal or presentational grounds.[9]

In fact, today we do know something about scientists' citation behavior. Smith (1981, p. 84) mentions fifteen reasons for authors to quote other documents:

1. Paying homage to pioneers

2. Giving credit for related work (homage to peers)

3. Identifying methodology, equipment, and so on

4. Providing background reading

5. Correcting one's own work

6. Correcting the work of others

7. Criticizing previous work

8. Substantiating claims

9. Alerting to forthcoming work

10. Providing leads to poorly disseminated, poorly indexed, or uncited work

11. Authenticating data and classes of facts—physical constants, and so on

12. Identifying original publications in which an idea or concept was discussed

13. Identifying original publications or other work describing an eponymic concept or term

14. Disclaiming work or ideas of others (negative claims)

15. Disputing priority claims of others (negative homage)

Seglen (1996, p. 29) lists a range of problems concerning selection of references:

1. References are selected because of their usefulness for the author, which is something different from their quality

2. Only a small fraction of all used material is cited

3. General knowledge is not cited

4. Knowledge is often cited from secondary sources

5. Documents supporting an author's arguments are cited more often than other documents

6. Flattering (citing editors, potential referees, and other authorities)

7. Showing off (citing hot new "in" articles)

8. Reference copying (references provided by other authors)

9. Conventions. In biochemistry, for example, methods are cited but not reagents

10. Self citations

11. Citing colleagues (often reflecting informal transfer of information)

Further references about this exciting area of citing behavior includes Brooks (1986, and 1987); Cronin (1984); Harter, Nisonger, and Weng (1993); MacRoberts and MacRoberts (1989); and Mustelin (1988). This research says something about the usefulness of references versus descriptors in information seeking. To the degree that the conventions can be described they are of immediate relevance. With the knowledge given above, we are able to state that citation indexing should perform well on a search for biochemical methods, but rather badly on a search for a reagent.

The evaluation of the possibilities of chain searching is therefore connected with studies of cooperation among scientists and subsequent citation behavior. Again, studies in the sociology of science and in epistemology are relevant. It is not difficult to se the importance of, for example, Kuhn's (1970) theory. To the extent that the demands on optimal citation behavior are met, the reference list of every document represents a perfect, "selective" bibliography in the field—or, together with other articles, is part of a network that represents a perfect bibliography. Inclusion in the bibliography that is formed by the reference list is characterized in particular by the fact that it expresses more limited disciplinary priorities. The strength of chain searching is that within a scholarly discipline there is relatively little risk of overlooking the most important documents. The weakness of this method is especially related to the fact that any given assumptions within a field can be revaluated, and the documents that become relevant after a revaluation (e.g., a paradigm shift) typically will not be found by chain searching, since the selection of references is performed based on paradigmatic norms. In addition, the motives of the scientists are not always pure, in that it might lie in their interest not to inform the reader of important sources since they wish to reap the fruit of these at some later date.

Bibliographic searching and chain searching are both dependent on certain conditions that determine their efficiency. None of these methods can a priori be said to be the most systematic, and to some degree they are prerequisites for each other. In areas where quality bibliographies exist, bibliographic searching will be strong. In areas where the scientific standard is very high, chain searching will be strong. In the end, scientific work might develop into an efficient bibliography, and efficient bibliographies into products of scientific quality. Under these conditions the subject bibliography will represent the best map of the research area, an empirical mapping of the structure of a field, while the article or book and its reference list will be the most accurate answer to a well-defined question, a sort of microsounding in its structure. In other words, bibliographies are more metascientifically oriented. The two products will be able to make use of each other in this process. Welwert's work is—in addition to the studies reported below—one of the very few examples which give an idea of how far we are from a reasonably efficient situation.[10]

Chain searching versus bibliographic searching can be further illustrated by field studies (see Pao, 1993) and controlled studies (see Pao & Worthen, 1989), in terms of literature references versus terms as search criteria. These studies, which were performed in medicine and which built upon a pool of common references in MEDLINE (which is considered to be a database that maintains a high level of indexing quality) and SCISEARCH (a science citation index), cannot be regarded as definitive, but they do indicate

- that the level of overlap is low (4–5%) when terms and references are used for searching
- that term searching seems to be a more efficient form of searching than reference searching (term searching in MEDLINE gave a mean recall of 77% and a precision level of 56%; reference searching in SCISEARCH gave a recall of 33% and a precision level of 60%)
- that compared to term searching alone, reference searching was capable of increasing recall by a mean of 24%. Moreover, it turned out that the overlap between the two search strategies had high precision

What is lacking in studies like the ones mentioned above is a closer analysis of the nature of the terms and references that result in noise or no results. These kinds of studies are typically quantitative rather than qualitative. If recall can be increased by 24% by including reference searching, it would be highly relevant to analyze what kind of concepts typically should have been included in the bibliographic records, but weren't! Might these kinds of experiences lead perhaps to a formulation of new instructions for the indexers, so that indexing practices can be improved?

My conclusion is, therefore, that questions regarding the efficiency of chain searching versus bibliographic searching have to be analyzed from the point of view of the norms regarding specialist language, citation practice, and document analysis in a given field. Thus my hypothesis is that the quantitative results that can be seen in, for instance, medicine reflect special conditions in terminology and citation practices within the field, which most likely are different in other fields. For this reason, a given subject access point (which is what we might call the descriptors, references, and so on) can't be expected to have a fixed information value regardless of knowledge domain. This means that the research focus must shift from isolated consideration of search methods and access points to domain-specific conditions.

THE ROLE OF THE INFORMATION SPECIALIST

The core role of information specialists is to identify information from different sources and to contribute to the organization of knowledge in order to increase its retrievability. Many people in society identify and organize knowledge, but they do this from some narrow perspective in a buttom-up mode. Information specialists are concerned with the macroperspective of information retrieval and knowledge organization. Overview or employing the top-down mode is important. Subject specialists are specialists in knowledge resources within a discipline, or sociologists of knowledge in a particular discipline. From this perspective general information specialists are specialists in problems related to the philosophy of knowledge, sociology of knowledge, database semantics, and so on. (In practice, however, general information specialists often tend to focus on the technological tools and formal rules used in information retrieval and knowledge organization.)

Under conditions of normal science, the information specialist typically has a command of the search tools and the special terminology that allows him or her to function as a research assistant of sorts. But naturally (s)he has a significant area of competence that is fairly independent (nonacademic librarians can of course also be of assistance, if they receive sufficient training in the terminology of the field and its bibliographic tools). This research assistant, who may be in charge of specialized administration of the databases and "maps," can hardly be used for other research-related functions. The potential conceptual relations would typically be built into the thesauri. Information retrieval capabilities are mostly exhausted with the ability to use the field's reference literature, thesauri, systems, and so on. This role may be typical for information specialists working in, for example, chemistry.

In a typical revolutionary or unclarified situation the role of the information specialist becomes more independent and a more integrated part of the research work within the discipline. Everybody's role is less clear during such a phase. The information specialist does not work for a user who has a clear picture of his information needs, and he or she is not only the keeper of a system which others know better than he or she does, but his or her knowledge and experiences of the totality of the system make possible a particular horizon, with a potential for supplying the scientists in the field with insights that are highly relevant in the formulation of search queries. In addition to drawing on semantic relations in thesauri and the repertoire of bibliographic tools, an information specialist in such a field has to draw on his experiences with the history of the discipline (and its experiences with both successful and dead-end tracks), limitations, theoretical conceptions, relations to other disciplines, and so on. In this kind of situation the information specialist will not typically be a research assistant, but rather something of a metaresearcher, or a generalist. Nevertheless, the information specialist will have a very goal-oriented information function, which prevents a general migration of the field and ensures real cumulative activity. This kind of role may be typical in, for example, the social sciences.

The conditions described above may partly explain one phenomenon that is described in the literature: humanities scholars are far less inclined than their colleagues in the natural sciences to delegate information searches to information specialists or "documentalists" (see Stone, 1982, pp. 294–295). In the natural sciences the scientists are more bound and disciplined by "reality" and thus more bound to common views and paradigms.

As pointed out above, all fields incorporate various degrees of normal science and revolutionary science, but these are different in different fields. Here I will not discuss in more depth which fields represent one or the other. I will only ascertain that all fields have a need for an infrastructure and an expertise that focus on a strengthening of the information structures of the field. That is, all fields need initiatives that use an information science perspective.

NOTES

1. In a sociological (or more descriptive) sense, science is a part of the division of labor in society, and its official function is the production of new knowledge. Scientists or researchers are people who are paid for producing knowledge. This conceptualization of science is more explicit in the term "the institution of science."

Science is organized in scientific disciplines. Research is carried out within these disciplines or as interdisciplinary collaboration. The sciences are social organizations which are made up of scientists, assisting staff, facilities, journals and publications, computer systems, libraries, and so on. A formal criterion for science may be that there is ongoing documentation of the knowledge production; that is, the existence of journals and handbooks within the field is an important indicator that a science really exists.

There have been discussions of whether disciplines such as library and information science, audiologopedics, parapsychology, education, and so on, are really scientific disciplines. Regardless of the fact that there are people who are paid for doing research within these fields, and the fact that there are disciplinary journals and handbooks, the right of these fields to call themselves "sciences" is being called into question. That is, the concept of science is being defined normatively. These norms are often connected with the methods of the discipline. Psychology was acknowledged earlier than education as an independent science because psychology used the experimental method. Both philosophy of science and epistemology study these kinds of norms.

Mammen (1983, pp. 26ff) deals with the requirements that need to be met in order for psychology to be called a science: generality, concreteness, and specificity. That a science should be general means that its experiences can be generalized from the individual instance. The object of a science is concrete means that its categories are not made a priori, preceding the empirically studied phenomena, but reflect general characteristics that have been discovered in the phenomena. The categories of a science can therefore not be defined independently from these phenomena. That the object of a science should be specific for the science in question, since otherwise it might disintegrate into other already existing sciences, even if the concrete object area may overlap with other concrete object areas.

The question of whether all sciences deal with general objects is discussed in philosophy, where some theorists (Windelband, among others) make a distinction between nomothetical sciences (the natural sciences), which work toward finding general laws, and ideographic sciences (the human sciences), which describe individual instances and their special properties, for example, historical events, descriptions of individuals in psychology, and so on.

The question of the concreteness of scientific objects is closely connected with ontological questions about the materialistic or idealistic nature of the world.

The question of whether each discipline should have its specific object is discussed by Giesecke (1981), who argues that some disciplines, for example, education, do not have specific objects, but are aporethical.

When a discipline is "accepted" it often becomes institutionalized, for instance by professorial positions at universities and institutions of higher learning. The institutionalization may become a driving force in itself; that is, regardless of epistemological confusion and disagreement—including an abandonment of the original theoretical basis—the discipline may continue its existence, depending on the forces that want to save versus destroy it.

2. Psychology was institutionalized as a discipline a long time before educational research was. The reason for this was that psychology employed the experimental method. Later the humanistic movement in psychology questioned the relevance of the experimental method. The lesson is that the methodological criteria play a very important role in the constitution of a discipline, but that these criteria themselves are a subject for discussion and historical development.

3. An important analysis of the concept of discipline is made by Foucault (1979). His book is about discipline in the prison and about how this kind of discipline creates disciplines in the scientific sense (especially the rise of the behavioral sciences). Foucault is skeptical about such discipline(s). This is, however, not the issue to discuss here.

4. Regarding general and practical uncertainty in information seeking, it can be pointed out that many libraries and administrators strongly wish/plan for a screening of the information-seeking tasks (see, e.g., Thorhauge. 1993, p. 93), such that more simple tasks are attended to on the first level, while more difficult ones are sent on. I am convinced, based upon practical experiences, but also upon the theoretical considerations presented above, that such screening should not be performed. Only the most qualified professionals can routinely decide whether a question is "simple."

The text offers examples of information-seeking tasks that I think are unproblematic. An example of a task that seems simple, is the following: Find statistical data on the grain harvest in China. The question fools us, since answering this question presupposes knowledge of the fact that one has to make a political evaluation. There are many sources which all give different numbers concerning the volume of the grain harvest in China.

An example from real life: a user calls the Royal Library and is connected to the reading room, where an assistant answers the phone and gives it to someone else only if he thinks it is necessary. The user asks: "Are there as many words in the Danish language as in the English language?" After giving it some thought the assistant answers: "Well, that has to be the case. There has to be a name for everything in Danish and in English." The academic librarian on duty (myself) interrupted and asked to take over.

5. Swanson (1986b) describes what he calls the "essential uncertainty of information retrieval." Since he is very much inspired by Popper, he views the uncertainty of information seeking as a parallel to Popper's ideas on scientific theories: they can be falsified but never really verified. This idea of verification and falsification of a search function is discussed by the hermeneutician Capurro (1986, pp. 173ff), who does not find Swanson's terminology particularly useful, since one does not talk about truth and error in information seeking, but about a hermeneutic process that lacks absolute criteria. Capurro therefore suggests the term "seek-and-find" method instead of trial and error. One of Capurro's points is that an error in the information-seeking process is informative for the user.

6. A psychologist went to the Royal Library and asked for literature on the psychological aspects of the menstrual cycle. It is not difficult to find literature on this subject. It is even easier to find a lot. The main bibliography of the field, Psychological Abstracts, lists it as a subject heading. Most students, researchers, or practicing psychologists will find more than enough. If the psychologist in our example were to sit down with, for example, PsycLit on CD-ROM, she would probably become so overwhelmed by the number of references that she would not ask the psychology information specialist for

help in finding more. If the psychologist in question is something of a perfectionist, she may go to the Science and Medical Library (DNLB) and perform additional searches. There are a large number of other sources, but if only free and electronic sources (understandably) are used, there may be a risk of missing out on the most important ones.

During the interview I mentioned these possibilities first, and then I asked her about her theoretical interests in the field, in order to orient myself as to the relevance of continuing. In many cases the user indicates directly or indirectly that the above mentioned search possibilities are enough. The user can disclose this, for instance, by revealing research interests in the problem that are close to those that dominate the psychological literature and Psychological Abstracts.

In this concrete example the psychologist revealed an interest—after having been asked—in critical examinations of this problem area, for example, feminist viewpoints. Such information—which would not have been brought up if the librarian had not operated with this possibility in mind and hence interviewed the user—throws new light on the search strategy. Other sources should be used, as well as other concepts on the whole, a whole new strategy. A question like the one of whether the menstrual cycle affects the woman's psychological state of mind is psychologized and biologized in much of the psychological and medical literature. Serious research, however, cannot disregard the literature within the field, and in my opinion a search in Psychological Abstracts should be performed, as well defined as possible. A formal limitation to including only review articles (which many librarians use in order to avoid overload) does not generally ensure that the critical material that was asked for is located, but they may be useful as "maps" of the more traditional treatments of the subject.

The above mentioned considerations are, of course, the subjective notions of the librarian, and one should always be open for the possibility that they are incorrect. But decisions have to be made, and one only has one's own subjective experiences. The question is therefore how one's professional values are supported, not how one disregards one's own professional ideas. The consequence of the form of "objectivity" that disregards the disciplinary views is that quantitative considerations (which bibliography contains the most references) will dominate, and thereby priority is given to the dominating paradigms in the research literature. In other words, the exact opposite of critical and independent thinking occurs.

As a result of the above I suggested to the user that in addition to a search in Psychological Abstracts she should try to trace more cultural-historical expositions, as well as supplement with searches in more social science oriented databases. Since German psychology has a more society-oriented tradition, I suggested a search in the German database PSYNDEX. I asked the user to tell me whether the resulting references improved the quality of the search, and this was confirmed. This confirmation was partly a verification of my theory (even if there is always a risk of a Rosenthal effect, that the user will give a friendly thank you by agreeing).

7. In particular, Hjørland, 1989, is an attempt to describe the situation regarding search tools in an actual discipline. Hjørland, 1990b, is an attempt at investigating various document types from a communication theory perspective. In Hjørland, 1995 (under "Document Typology"), a framework is outlined (and therein is referred other, as yet unpublished works). The above mentioned work sketches the view of the various document types as developed in relation to specific communication tasks.

8. The use of reference lists in articles and books for information seeking means the use of primary documents as a source.

9. The habit of scientists to include pro forma citations can be illustrated by the following quote from Lancaster, Zeter, and Metzler: "Nevertheless, it is also necessary to point out that many of the references are very superficial ones, acknowledging some intellectual debt to Ranganathan without actually explicating Ranganathan's work or even explaining in detail the nature of the debt. A few authors seem to make such non-substantive references to Ranganathan in more or less every article they write." (Lancaster et al., 1992, p. 276).

10. In this book, I have only discussed subject bibliographies. As a consequence of my theoretical position I change the concepts *general bibliography* and *special bibliography* somewhat. The traditional understanding is that the national bibliography is the key concept, the general bibliography, while the disciplinary bibliography is special and presupposes the existence of the general bibliography (see Munch-Petersen, 1980, especially p. 42).

In my opinion, subject bibliographies, for example, Chemical Abstracts and MEDLINE, are the central bibliographic tools in their fields and useful for everybody who needs chemical or medical literature. These bibliographies are not based upon the national bibliographies (and therefore do have holes in their incorporation of the monographic literature). The national bibliographies almost always play a secondary and supplemental role in the professional context (special libraries rarely acquire them). If the discipline has a good subject bibliography, the national bibliography perhaps plays a more important role in terms of interdisciplinary tasks and as supplements. The most central tool in my theory is the subject bibliography. I choose to view the national bibliographies as interdisciplinary tools rather than as general tools. As such the national bibliographies of course play an extremely important role, for instance by defining the public aspect of the publications. I also argue that the increasing accessibility of national bibliographies online and on CD-ROM will give support to national bibliographies as professional tools.

7

Information Needs and
Cognitive and Scientific Development

In the previous chapters I have assumed that the goal of information seeking and subject analysis is to meet information needs. Now I will examine the concept of *information need* more closely, including an evaluation of a dominating, psychologically based theory of information needs. In addition, I will try to add to it a social dimension that corresponds to the methodological collectivism developed in Chapter 5. It stands to reason that an incorrect understanding of the concept of information need may be an important impediment both to a general theory of information seeking as well as to practical information retrieval.

The goal of a library or information system is, of course, to meet the needs of users and potential users of documents or information. A user's information needs may be related to education, research, culture, or recreation or may be professionally oriented. It is essential not to confuse the concept of need with the concept of demand. The demand for documents or information may be low, for instance, because libraries seem impractical or inaccessible to the user, but the user's information needs exist nevertheless. The user's information needs may be more or less conscious or acknowledged. In the LIS literature a distinction is made between need as an expression of objective information need and demand as an expression of a subjective need, which is expressed in the user's queries to the librarian or information system. However, more extensive analyses of this problem are rare. As a rule most writers only draw attention to the distinction, and need is treated as demand all the same.

The concepts of subjectivity and objectivity are difficult ones. The Norwegian philosophers Foellesdal, Walløe, and Elster (1992) suggest the following definition: "A document (e.g., a thesis, a television program, a journal article) is *objective*, if and only if the opinions and attitudes it evokes in the receiver would not change if he or she had had full knowledge of the case with all information and all alternative hypotheses" (p. 283; emphasis in original; translated by the author). In the same way we can say that the determination or diagnosis of information needs—whether done by the user himself or by others—is objective if it would not change if he or she had had full knowledge of the case with all information and all alternative hypotheses.

"Hard" or objective methods (e.g., behavioristic and positivistic methods) can only measure the demands or attitudes of the users. "Soft" or subjective methods (e.g., hermeneutics) can interpret the attitudes and demands. Many user studies have shown that users tend to be satisfied with libraries and information services because they have a low level of expectation. Only research methods that allow an interpretation of user behavior on the basis of broad understanding of the available information sources can approach the real, objective information needs as defined above. Thus, so called objective methods tend to produce subjective results and vice versa!

The Danish psychologist Jens Gudiksen (1979) has published a brief overview of the psychological concepts of need and their consequences in relation to information transfer and library work. Among other things, he emphasizes that need should not be viewed statically, but as something that is produced.[1] The goal of an information system is not only to meet certain needs, but also to make it possible for users to develop their needs. Users cannot acknowledge their need for certain documents (or subjects) until they are aware of the existence of these documents (or subjects). Well-functioning libraries and well-functioning information services not only satisfy needs that have already been articulated, but are also a part of the process of making it possible to acknowledge and articulate these needs in the first place. An information system should ideally—this point will be elaborated below—be proactive in relation to the user's information needs, that is, acknowledge them before they are articulated in a query.

Information need is different from other types of needs, for instance the need for food, sex, and achievement, by being a means to meet the more primary needs. The information need of a lawyer in an actual situation is a secondary need in relation to a more primary need, for example, to win a case. Thus the structure of information need is subordinate to the structure of more immediate needs, and they can be viewed as informational prerequisites to the solution of a given problem. The solution of a problem represents a person's need. The prerequisites for solving these problems—among these, the information oriented prerequisites—are derived and secondary needs. Itoga (1992) emphasizes that

Within the alternative framework, information needs should not be treated as psychological or physiological states but as a hypothetical agent for information seeking behavior. . . . the discussions above suggest that the human act of having information needs is a dynamic process rather than a state or a step, and that we should assume other basic human needs than information needs in order to explain the cause-effect relationship. This finding is in line with the view by Wilson [1981] who notes: "it may be advisable to remove the term information needs from our professional vocabulary and to speak instead of information seeking towards the satisfaction of needs." (Itoga, 1992, p. 341)

However, I have not postulated that there is no such thing as, for instance, an intellectual, creative, or musical need. I have only pointed out that information needs in information science typically should be viewed in relation to other problems, which are rooted in completely different, underlying problems and needs.

Moreover, the concept of need is peculiar in that there is not necessarily a mental aspect to it, as Green (1990) and Jørgensen (1963, p. 393), among others, have observed. Jørgensen directs our attention to the fact that a bicycle tube may need air, even though it is really the user of the bicycle who has the need for the air in the tube. The bicycle does not feel a need. Similarly, we might ascribe information needs to other people: needs that they do not experience or agree upon. For instance, an employer or a university teacher might have a different idea of one's information needs than oneself. The concept of need thus has an important normative aspect.

A comparison of informational and educational needs takes into account the social character of the information need, and it thereby removes something of the mystical and idealistic from the concept of information need.[2] Furthermore, it is made plain that in the same way that participants in the educational debate may have different views on the need for education, information needs are also connected to ideas on a higher level, for instance, views on humanity, science, or society. The comparison may also put into perspective the relation between more general and more specific information needs. The information retrieval literature largely ignores this problem of more general needs, or the relationship between the more specific and the general needs, but at the same time implicitly presumes that more specific problems are being discussed. IR theory thus builds upon implicit and ill-defined assumptions regarding information-seeking situations and knowledge (cf. Chapter 5).

In order to differentiate between the individual and the collective in regard to the concept of information need, it may be relevant to include the concept of *epistemological interest*, since this concept should not be understood in an individual or psychological sense. Epistemological interest is a theoretical concept that can be traced to Jürgen Habermas's (1968) theory, which characterizes the difference between the epistemological interests of the natural sciences, the social sciences, and the humanities.[3] The concept is essential to information science, since it can be used for making important nonindividualistic statements about the information needs of various disciplines. I introduced this concept earlier in relation to subject analysis and discussed how the same document can be analyzed from the point of view of various epistemological interests, for instance, feminist, local historical, and psycho-historical epistemological interests. I deviated a little from Habermas's original meaning.[4]

Michajlov, Cernyj, and Giljarevskij (1980), information scientists from the former Soviet Union, find that the communication of information needs is made difficult because of two things: (1) the completely individual character of the scientists' and specialists' information needs and (2) the inability of all human beings to communicate their own information needs in an adequate way.[5] The goal of research on information needs is the communication of the real information needs of the scientists and experts and not their subjective opinion regarding this need. Michajlov et al. write:

Studies using sociological methods to investigate the information needs and information use of scientists and experts take us deeper into the psychology of scientific creativity. This problem, which goes well beyond the boundaries of information science, has up until now not been satisfactorily worked out, even if in various countries hundreds of research papers are produced annually regarding this question. . . .

By and large this type of research has not yet shown desired results. The investigations are carried out in isolation, they are based on biased methodologies, and their results can only to some degree be compared. But the lack of results should not be blamed on the above mentioned conditions alone. In the majority of the cases the methods used to discover the information needs are based on the opinions of the information users themselves, which is a serious limitation, since they express themselves in a very subjective way. In addition, the user's continuous association with the information system teaches him not to demand more than it can offer. The habit that develops is transformed into a stable psychological factor that distorts the data in questionnaires, interviews, analyses of reader surveys and even collected bibliographic data. (Michajlov et al., 1980, pp. 222ff; our translation)

Michajlov et al.'s opinions are incisive for much user research, but they do not contain a real clarification of the concept of information need. In my opinion most of the empirical studies in the field are premature, since some of the most basic epistemological problems have not been solved. This concerns especially the relation between the individual and the collective information need, the subjective and the objective in the information needs, and the general development patterns of these needs. Even if Michajlov et al. are aware of the subjective-idealistic in the information need studies, they nevertheless seem to have a fixation on this concept as a distinctly individual phenomenon.

R. S. TAYLOR'S THEORY

Within the LIS literature Robert S. Taylor's theory (1962, 1967, 1968) on information needs has played an important role. Almost all textbooks for librarians in reference work or public service refer to this theory. It is frequently cited and it has, for instance, been appointed a citation classic in *Current Contents* (Taylor, 1985a, p. 234). The librarians talk about the needs that lie behind the user's inquiries. It is a common experience that a query is not necessarily a good representation of the information need that the user really has, and that lies behind the query, and that might come up in a dialog. Taylor's theory offers an approach for tackling this important problem. When it was first published it was a great inspiration, since it made it possible to combine information science problems with psychology, and it thereby functioned as a methodological approach for the young information science. Even if it is fairly old, it has never really been challenged or revised. One notices that Taylor (1985a) himself is a little surprised at the continued referring to this old work.

Taylor's theory is characterized by a mentalistic approach, according to which the information need progresses in a relatively independent fashion inside the head of the user.[6] It develops continuously and goes through the phases Q1, Q2, Q3, and Q4, from a "visceral information need," via a "conscious need," and a "formalized need" to a "compromised need."

At the first level, Q1, there is the conscious or even unconscious need for information not existing in the remembered experience of the inquirer. According to Taylor, it may be only a vague sort of dissatisfaction and it is probably inexpressible in linguistic terms. This need will change in form, quality, and concreteness as information is added. At this stage there is no social exchange, and no question is yet formed.

At the second level, Q2, Taylor describes a conscious mental awareness of an ill-defined area of indecision. It will probably be an ambiguous and rambling statement. At this stage the inquirer may talk to someone else to sharpen his focus. He presumably hopes that two things will happen in this process: (1) his colleague will understand the ambiguities; and (2) these ambiguities will gradually disappear in the course of the dialog.

At the third level, Q3, an inquirer can form a qualified and rational statement[7] of his question. Here he is describing his area of doubt in concrete terms and he may or may not be thinking within the context or constraints of the system from which he wants information.

At the final level, Q4, the question is recast in anticipation of what the files can deliver. The searcher must think in terms of the organization of particular files and of the discrete packages available—such as books, reports, papers, drawings, or tables. Unless the inquirer knows the information specialist well, he is—according to Taylor—inclined to pose his first question in positive and well-defined terms, even to the point of specifying a particular package (Q4). If, however, the specialist is accepted as a colleague, the negotiation process can start earlier and be much more fruitful. An important necessity for such acceptance appears to be subject knowledge. "A person with a technical background will handle a technical subject in less than half the time and with more competent and thorough results" (Taylor, 1968, p. 183).

According to Taylor, these four levels of question formation shade into one another along the question spectrum. They are stated only as convenient points along a continuum. I will here attempt to show that it is hardly possible that the information need, as Taylor implies, can progress in a continuous manner, since a given piece of information may disturb the whole problem that triggered the need. At the same time it will be shown that what develops inside the head is not primarily the need, but the knowledge of the problem area that gives rise to the information need. *Cognitive development* is thus a better label than information need development.

Taylor sees the compromised question (Q4) as the information specialist's business, because it deals with the representation of the inquirer's need within the constraints of the system and its files. The skill of the reference librarian is to work with the inquirer back to formalized need (Q3), possibly even to the conscious need (Q2), and then to translate these needs into a useful strategy. "This is a directed and structured process, although there are of course many different styles and many levels of competence and knowledge on the part of both librarian and inquirer. There are certain obvious traits which will help the librarian: empathy, sense of analogy, subject knowledge, and knowledge of files, collection, and clientele" (Taylor, 1968, p. 183).

Markey (1981, p. 217) asserts that: "It is clear that Taylor's theory remains untested and unchallenged, but subsequent reports appear to support and reinforce his work. His model does little more than delineate the levels of visceral, conscious, formalized and compromised needs in the interview." Markey's conclusion is still valid: there has been no major explicit challenge of this theory up to now. Markey revises Taylor's model somewhat, but her revision is not fundamental enough that I need to discuss it here, since it will also fall under the same criticism that I will present below.

Taylor quotes D.M. Mackay, and writes in this connection: "The inquirer has what D. M. Mackay calls 'a certain incompleteness in his picture of the world—an inadequacy in what we might call his "state of readiness" to interact purposefully with the world around him' (10) in terms of a particular area of interest. He comes to the library or information center as one of several possible alternatives, for information to fill out 'his picture of the world.' These alternatives themselves pose an important problem"(Taylor, 1968, p. 180–181). However, an inquirer does not necessarily have a certain "incompleteness in his picture of the world." This might be the case, especially if the queries pertain to something factual, but it might be that the query involves verification or confirmation of an already formed picture of an area or object. People who know the least about something often do not realize it themselves. The quotation brings to mind a picture of a container inside the head which needs to be filled up. This way of thinking is related to "the postal package theory" of communication, which has been criticized from newer interpretative approaches (see Chapter 5).

It is often the case that the more one knows, the more one knows what one does not know (including knowledge of potential information sources). Taylor's conception is thus connected with a theory of knowledge that views knowledge as a continuous addition of new knowledge, a compiling process (in contrast to a process where knowledge is viewed as more or less proven theories or hypotheses which one seeks to verify or falsify).[8]

When Taylor describes the need development from Q1 to Q4, he makes the assumption that the information need follows an independent trajectory in relation to cognitive development. However, during the user's problem-solving process, he gradually develops an understanding of the problem and of the kind of information that might contribute to the solution of the problem. At the same time, theoretical development takes place, which has ramifications for the subsequent information-seeking process. What we are talking about is therefore not primarily development of need, but development of knowledge or cognition. There occurs a derived change in needs, but not an independent development of meanings that moves from a vague to a more conscious level following some kind of internal line. Taylor's four phases thus represent a confusion of two different things: the development of the knowledge of the primary problem and the change in the information need as a consequence of this primary development.[9]

KNOWLEDGE DEVELOPMENT

An Example of Need Development: Research in Psychopathology

Within psychopathology there is disagreement over how important a role biological or psychosocial factors play in the development of mental illnesses. This is just an extremely simplified conception of what in reality is represented by an abundance of different theories. The individual researcher will—hopefully—undergo a cognitive development, during which he situates his own conception and finds a resource upon which to build or modify his own ideas. If, during this process, he starts testing some hypotheses, for example, concerning the diagnostic practices at various hospitals, his information needs will change as well. The problem is, of course, in the most profound sense to solve the mystery or the mysteries of psychopathology.

The information need that is connected with such a wide-ranging problem is so extensive and amorphous that in practice it is not operational. The various hypotheses that might arise during the research process give rise to derivative information needs, which may go in various directions. One hypothesis might indicate that information about cell biology constitutes the information need, while another hypothesis might indicate that knowledge about the patients' psychological and social conditions constitutes the information need.

Within comprehensive problems such as psychopathology, researchers often divide themselves according to theory or paradigm, for example, in psychodynamic theories, biochemical theories, learning theories, and so on. Each paradigm can establish its own journals, conferences, concepts and terminology, databases and handbooks. This represents a new division of labor in science, and this means, that some of the burden of the individual information processing is transformed into a collective responsibility. The information need has become public, and the collecting of the specific information that can satisfy this need has become a collective responsibility.

The essential difference between Taylor's and his followers' psychological conceptions and the perspective of activity theory is that the latter maintain that the information need is not seen as located in the user's head. It changes according to the information that is retrieved, and that is largely a result or an implication of the hypotheses or theories that exist at any given time. This implication is not primarily individual or psychological but subject related and logical and may be explicated in public. If the data that support, for example, Gregory Bateson's theory of the origin of schizophrenia as a result of the mother's double bind interaction with the child are shown not to corroborate this theory, the researcher has to revise his hypothesis, and the information need becomes a different one, shifting from studies of mother-child interactions to perhaps biochemical studies. The fact that reality is not as uncomplicated as the example, and that both theories may in fact coexist, does not alter the fundamental validity of the argument.

Sometimes the learning process develops in a continuous manner (a gradual mastering of more and more materials); at other times the process is discontinuous, for instance, when new data completely destroy the foundation of a theory. The underlying need development follows a discontinuous path and is determined by breakthroughs in the knowledge process. This is opposite to Taylor's theory, where the phases Q1–Q4 are described as points on a continuum.

Individual and Collective Knowledge Development

Taylor's model of need development can thus be replaced by a model for knowledge development, as shown in Figure 7.1. In the research process we talk about an integration of two lines of development: individual cognitive development (psychological) and collective knowledge development (sociological).

Individual knowledge development is in the research process normally characterized by a process where the researcher gradually approaches the collective knowledge level concerning a given problem. The individual researcher gets more familiar with what colleagues know about a certain subject and what the

Figure 7.1
Model of Knowledge Development and the Derived Need Development

Knowledge level Q1 ----> Need state Q1

:

:

Knowledge level Q2 ----> Need state Q2

:

:

Knowledge level Q3 ----> Need state Q3

:

:

(and so on)

literature has to offer, and is able to better evaluate his own possibilities for making a contribution. Unless this is the case, it is difficult for the individual researcher to contribute to the solution or the development of the research problem. Individual knowledge development is first of all expressed in information needs that are, or can be compared to, educational needs. Later there is increased individualization, and this educational process inevitably has to proceed as a highly self-directed process, where the "compass" is the given research object. The given information need is determined primarily by the research object and secondarily by the relevant parts of the researcher's own previous work. The individual researcher will become more and more aware of the deficiencies and holes in the research up to that point and will move closer to the minority at the research front. It is extremely important that researchers are free to follow their internal compass and not be forced to follow externally or ideologically given norms.[10]

According to disciplinary history within the more descriptive sciences (e.g., anatomy), *collective knowledge development* is characterized by more and more detailed description of the object. In more theoretical fields, the development is characterized by gradual progress from a superficial characterization of the research subject to a deeper knowledge of the more abstract and general essence of the research object.[11] This kind of knowledge development is evidenced by the great scientific theories, discoveries, and handbooks. Unless this is the case, the research area will stagnate, and large amounts of papers, isolated empirical data, and half- or completely falsified scientific theories will accumulate, such as is the case within some knowledge domains. Such a critical or pathological situation within a knowledge domain will cause the individual users to experience information input overload. If knowledge development occurs along these lines, we end up with advanced domains in which information needs cannot be determined by similarity between ordinary concepts and document representations.

There are, of course, huge differences among the disciplines, research environments, and periods in collective knowledge development. In terms of understanding the connection between the individual and collective knowledge development, it is especially relevant to consider the sociological patterns in science, which are studied, for instance, by means of bibliometrics. Derek J. de Solla Price characterizes the research fronts in science in the following way: "New papers use the other half of their references to connect back to the relatively small number of highly interconnected recent papers. In a particular field each recent paper is connected to all its neighbors by many lines of citation. A convenient image of the pattern is to be found in knitting. Each stitch is strongly attached to the previous row and to its neighbors" (Price, 1972, p. 167).

Such knitting is, according to Price, typical of the sciences, but not of the humanities or technology. The knitting model tells us that the individual researcher works with information that is produced almost simultaneously by his colleagues. There are, of course, also great internal differences within the sciences, but as background for understanding the mechanisms between the individual and the collective the model provides a good starting point. Inherent in the researchfront model is that some areas develop quickly, by the year.[12]

This means that individual knowledge development happens quite fast: the researcher gets a quick overview of the status of the research area, rapidly identifies a research problem he can work with, and produces new results that become part of the collective structure, and so on. Research development in this model is quite public, and individual development adapts to this collective process of knowledge creation. The given collective information need is determined primarily by the research object and secondarily by the given collective knowledge level regarding the research object, including the theoretical and methodological level of the discipline and the research organization. The individual knowledge is to a high degree subordinate to the collective knowledge.

The model is of course described here in a highly idealized version, and it is naturally a completely different matter to translate it into concrete history and sociology of science. The purpose of this exposition has been to supplement Taylor's extremely individualistic information need development model with a collectivist model of development, in order to move from philosophical idealism to philosophical realism, from the primacy of thought over reality to the primacy of reality over thought. Behind the concrete information seeking-process lies an information need that is an integration of the individual and the collective information need.[13]

If a research area or a researcher is at a fairly immature stage, the subjective information need, expressed in, for example, queries to databases or libraries, can often be characterized by superficial similarities with the research object. This might occur as concepts that are close to everyday characterizations of the research object in question or as an immature transfer of methods or concepts from disciplines that are essentially different from the object under investigation (e.g., the positivist tendency to force scientific methods and nonintentional conceptions on the humanities disciplines).

For a university teacher, an important part of working with the students is to challenge and correct their notions of a given problem, so that the students' conceptions will start corresponding to the objective needs. It cannot, of course, be guaranteed that guiding the student will lead to increased objectivity, but in practice it is often necessary to assume that this is the case—if the opposite were true one could not operate with formalized educational systems. Correspondingly, the task of the librarian or information specialist can sometimes be compared to that of the university teacher, that is, to try to problematize the subjectively presented information need in order to reach a formulation of the information need that corresponds more closely to the objective parameters of the problems.

If the discipline is at too immature a level, there is a special need for collective efforts to bring the field up to a higher level, for instance, by placing priority on basic research or by methodological analysis and discussion.

I have earlier—in the context of the discussion of the concept of subject— pointed out that scientific information systems cannot (as Belkin, Oddy, & Brooks's ASK model seems to imply) be viewed as being oriented toward individual needs or the scientists' educational needs. In my opinion information systems should be viewed as being oriented toward solving the collective problems of the discipline, such as they appear at a given point in time. It is the responsibility of the individual scientist to attain the knowledge needed for a scientific treatment of the problem. A theory of information need, therefore, cannot be just a psychological theory about individual development, but rather, it has to build upon a conception of the theory of science and has to be investigated from a historical and sociological point of view.[14] If there is no epistemological starting point, there is no way to grasp the relationship between collective and individual need development; individual development is isolated. Something that in fact is not an independent process of development is singled out and treated as such. In short, one ends up in psychologism or subjective idealism.

John Dewey's Theory

In the year 1902 John Dewey formulated a theory of knowledge that seems astonishingly modern in the light of this discussion. Dewey's theory emphasizes that thinking and doing are not individual, but functions of social life, and that consciousness as a whole is social in nature. For Dewey, thinking and doing were two sides of the same thing. When a person doing something is confronted with a problem that stops him from doing it, "thoughtful action" is developed, which includes the following five stages, quoted from Dewey (1902):

1. Puzzlement, confusion, doubt, which can be attributed to the fact that one has ended up in a situation that is not yet clarified.

2. An anticipatory idea based on guesswork—that is, an attempt to analyze the consequences that the elements of the situation are assumed to lead up to.

3. A careful inspection (investigation, inspection, research, analysis) of all accessible information that might define and illuminate the problem in question.

4. A final formulation of the anticipatory idea with the goal of making it more precise and consistent, since it is now adapted to a large number of facts.

5. Adhering to the idea as a plan of action that is being used in the current situation with the goal of bringing about the anticipated result and hence being able to test the idea.

Dewey especially emphasized stages 3 and 4. It is by virtue of the work that is put into these that thoughtful action rises above ordinary trial and error, even if he concedes that every genuine action always includes a residue of trial and error.

The use of the word idea attracts special interest. In the classical theory of knowledge idea and reality are separated, but in the pragmatic theory the idea is an integrated part of the action. This integration is reached by making the idea into a plan of action. This integration is also present in Jürgen Habermas's concept of knowledge interests or epistemological interests. This conception is also related to the cultural-historical tradition in psychology in the view held by the Russian psychologist Vygotsky on language, thinking, and consciousness, which is developed further in activity theory (see Leontiev, 1983).

The American pragmatic psychologist William James was somewhat skeptical of the development that dominated American psychology at the beginning of our century (see, e.g., Misiak & Sexton, 1966, p. 136). American psychology (and philosophy) lost interest in pragmatism and thus one of its most fruitful theories, and it evolved, in my opinion, in a rather sterile and unproductive theoretical direction. This meant, among other things, that consciousness and the concept of need came to be viewed as something very individual. Information science also came to be dominated by the same positivistic and rationalistic tendency. This is the reason why information science—the discipline for which literature seeking is the core problem—still has not been able to see the pearls that can be found in the pragmatic tradition and to integrate them into its own methodology.

REALIZATION AND FORMULATION OF INFORMATION NEEDS

Hakkarainen, who works with the psychological concept of need, writes: "In selecting material from the extensive literature on motivation for a critical analysis, the criterion has been whether motivation has been used as an explanatory principle. An attempt has been made to examine the concept of motivation as a whole. The category of 'activity' has been taken as a conceptual frame of reference" (Hakkarainen, 1990, p. 273). This quote may be viewed as an example of a researcher's conscious formulation of his own information need: literature on motivation that uses the concept as the explanatory principle and that covers the whole concept. This represents a formulation that theoretically could be posed in a library or to a database. However, the formulation would be extremely difficult to work with in practice, with IR languages constructed as they are today. Many librarians would think the information need quite vaguely formulated. Hakkarainen further formulates a conceptual frame of reference, the concept of activity; it is somewhat easier to deal with this concept, even if formal search strategies for it are difficult, since only a very small fraction of the literature uses the concept of activity in the sense that Hakkarainen employs.[15]

Our problem here is how Hakkarainen has been able to develop his knowledge of his own information need in order to verbalize this need. It is obvious that one needs to know something about the literature in advance in order to be able to formulate the need. If one did not know beforehand that one would drown in a sea of trivial documents, one would just have formulated the same information need as "literature on the psychological concept of motivation" or perhaps just "literature on motivation."

Many researchers and students are not able to formulate their information need as adequately as Hakkarainen (even if it may look vague). In many cases researchers' notions of their own information needs are built upon incorrect and unrealistic premises. For instance, they tell the information specialist: "I need literature on the psychological concept of motivation. Only the most central ones. The 25 most recent references." What they do not know is that a search for the 25 (or even 100) most recent references is almost guaranteed to result in extremely narrow references, which will not say anything essential or general about the concept of motivation as such (but there may be, for example, a user study of motives for buying a certain detergent). Queries such as this one also document the incorrect notion that the most recent is necessarily also the best.

Artificial, formal limitations may also be used: motivation among children, among users, among scientists, and so on. Behind such an inquiry lies an implicit rationalistic assumption: that the general concept of motivation is developed and searchable in a formally limited segment of the literature. Automated retrieval systems contribute to creating such formal limitations, because they are well suited for combining them. But one ends up in the same unsatisfactory situation: with references that formally deal with one's interests, for example, motivation among school children. But one easily ends up being overwhelmed by trivial studies of a concrete nature, and one's knowledge of the subject is not increased, since there is no presentation of the essential motivation theories.

Based on such experiences a researcher works backwards, all the way to the basic concepts and problems of the discipline (which again are rooted in the basic philosophical problems). From here it often seems to be easier to get back to the concrete and specific problems. Hakkarainen's problem formulation can be found in his dissertation. This formulation of the information need is thus preceded by years of studies of psychology and by many possibilities for determining the fruitfulness of various psychological theories, until the author finally decided upon activity theory as the theoretical frame of reference.

How the researcher reaches the theoretical frame of reference and the formulation of his information need is another problem. The fact that there exist researchers who incorrectly assume that they themselves are important need not be documented here, and neither does the existence of scientific disciplines and theories that follow blind leads. In both cases we are talking about a false interpretation of their contributions and hence their information need. In the first case we are talking about a form of individual subjectivity, and in the second about a form of collective subjectivity. Qualified debate and argumentation can of course determine whether a researcher or a whole discipline is characterized by false evaluation or problematic tendencies. This should be worked out by using scientific methodology, theory of science, and so on. But scientific problems cannot be solved by majority rule (as bibliometric analyses often implicitly assume), as the Danish philosopher Søren Kierkegaard so strongly emphasizes:

The truth is always in the minority; and the minority is always stronger than the majority, because the minority is ordinarily composed of those who do actually have an opinion, whereas the strength of the majority is illusory, composed of the crowd which has no opinion-and which therefore the next minute (when it becomes apparent that the minority was the stronger) embraces the opinion of the minority, which now becomes the majority, that is, the opinion becomes rubbish by having statistics and the whole crowd on its side, while truth is again a new minority.

As far as truth is concerned, the same thing happens to this awkward monster, the majority, the public etc. as we say happens to the person traveling for his health: he always arrives one station too late. (1850, X(3) A 652)

The researcher's formulation of his information needs is, in addition to conceptualizations of the objects under study, based upon realistic or unrealistic assumptions of the structure of the knowledge base that is being searched and upon assumptions of an epistemological nature. Hakkarainen's formulation of his information need is in reality a formulation of a document relevance criterion.

Information need is connected with *the relevance concept*: how subjective and objective relevance criteria develop during individual and collective cognitive development. The expression "N has an information need" is the same thing as "documents or information of relevance to N can be found."[16] A person N may need information already existing in society, or N may have a problem which eventually could be solved if relevant information could be produced. In the latter case, we could speak of a need for research rather than for actually existing information.

Awareness of one's information need at the same time implies an awareness of relevance—of more or less vague relevance criteria. The development of the information need is to some extent the development of relevance criteria. The relevance concept has been treated quite extensively in the literature, and we shall not go too deeply into this concept here. An important analysis is made by Prieto and Dascal (1994, p. 795). According to this analysis knowledge cannot exist without relevance. Relevance and truth constitute the two criteria of validity of a given knowledge. While the truth of a given knowledge depends upon its relationship to the known reality and is therefore independent of sociohistorical conditions,[17] the relevance of such a knowledge results from its relationship to practice. Indeed, the practices are chosen by the subject, but by the subject socially conditioned, since it is the social group he belongs to which decides whether a practice is obligatory, forbidden, or permitted. Thus, relevance appears—according to Prieto and Dascal—as the sociohistorical dimension of knowledge.

From this analysis it is not difficult to accept that the question of relevance criteria in IS to a large extent is a question of the norms of scientific methodology. A good theory about a subject matter helps to deliminate what is not relevant, and therefore what can be sorted out in IR. If the criticism of methodological individualism in information science is justified, it means that knowledge of domain structures, paradigms, and so on is relevant in information science approaches, and that knowledge of individual, subjective conditions recedes into the background.

For collective as well as individual knowledge development, philosophical, theoretical, methodological, and conceptual clarifications are the road to more insight into relevance criteria and hence into information need. The more immature the research area in which a researcher works, the more difficult it is for the researcher to reach an individual clarification of his information need. In addition, the social mechanisms in immature and ineffective research areas may impede the study of their information needs, while simple honesty is viewed as a threat to their survival and growth (see Ravetz, 1973, pp. 377–378). Researchers in such disciplines may be pressed into more or less unrecognized insistence on immature methodological notions in order to prop up their self-respect and "keep the show going."[18]

Even if the most central part of the concept of information need, as shown above, touches upon document relevance criteria, it also includes something more. Studies of information need often involve the relevance of information sources and channels, for instance, formal and informal communication, scientific meetings, journals, libraries, and databases. I maintain that the most central part of the concept is the relevance criteria regarding the information, but I also include relevance criteria regarding the various information channels that intermediate access to the information/documents. This expansion of the concept of information need is desirable, because it is the expanded part of it which is most central for the information specialist.

How users evaluate their own information needs in a given situation and how this evaluation develops can, according to the ideas set forth above, to some degree be understood as their evaluation of the value of various information sources. It is something in which researchers working within psychological decision theory have shown a great deal of interest (see e.g., Connolly & Wholey, 1988). Their studies appear to show that the users' estimations—of course in very simplified and explicit situations—are wildly inaccurate, and that these inaccuracies occur both in the evaluation of information sources, in the selection of sources, as well as when information from several sources are combined. It seems that on a higher level there is probably some serious miscalculation, and the user acquires either too little, too much, or the wrong information. It is not my task to discuss these conditions here. These studies do not typically deal with bibliographic information, which is what information science primarily deals with, and one might question whether this research can be generalized from the laboratory to the real life.[19]

The study of information needs in the expanded sense has to build upon a more holistic theory of how adequately the system of information sources works within a given knowledge domain, and how the individual information sources work from the point of view of a systems analysis. Such a theory has to incorporate knowledge about the nature of the knowledge domain in question as well. If we are talking about a very interdisciplinary domain, there are other requirements than if we are talking about systems within scientific domains that are quite self-sufficient or well demarcated. The individual researcher's needs can only be understood within the framework of a systems theoretic model of the communication structure of knowledge domains. If there are diverging ideas of the goals and methods of the knowledge domain, there will also be diverging ideas of the structure of the ideal information system. An analysis of the information needs in the expanded sense suggests that the domain analysis that I introduced in the methodological chapter should be utilized.

I have now presented the view of the concept of information need from the point of view of activity theory and tied the analysis and understanding of information needs to the general notion of methodological collectivism. Above I have redefined Taylor's model of information needs as a model of cognitive development. Each new hypothesis, and each new step in knowledge development, corresponds to new information needs. I now return to the model of knowledge development and derived need development, which is depicted in Figure 7.1.

Would it not be possible to rehabilitate Taylor's model by claiming that his outline of need development is simply a microprocess that happens at every step in the knowledge process? Does Taylor's model actually represent a microevent in cognitive development? The above analyses of information needs show that the answer to these questions has to be no. Even the horizontal line of development represents knowledge development that is determined by the external situation (e.g., methodological knowledge and knowledge of the information structure of the knowledge domain). There is no question of an internal, psychological development of need. There is an internal cognitive development, which *implies* information needs. This implication may or may not develop to consciousness about the information needs.

At the same time, however, we can see that it is possible to analytically separate out several lines of development. One line of development concerns the recognition of the research object itself. Another line of development concerns methodological and theoretical principles. A third line of development in the knowledge base concerns the system of information channels within the discipline. Ultimately, there is an internal connection between these lines of development, but to some extent they can be isolated theoretically, and they are connected with various forms of expertise. The recognition of the research object concerns the core of the research within the discipline (subject expertise). The recognition of methodological and theoretical principles is also based on the discipline, but it is connected especially with philosophy of science (methodological and philosophical expertise). The recognition of the system of information channels and their attributes can also be regarded as part of a given discipline, but it is especially connected with the fields of library science, scientific documentation, and information science (information expertise). Its relative independence from the knowledge about the object itself and about methodological knowledge represents one of the premises on which information science exists.

Taylor's fourth phase—Q4—only concerns the communication process (e.g., the communication between the researcher and the librarian). Taylor pictures this as an independent phase on top of a fully conscious and verbalized information need and claims that it is an extension of the continuous development in stages Q1 through Q3. Taylor implies that during Q4 something that can be called a "distortion of the signal" occurs, that the user—in order to make himself understood—expresses his needs in a way that corresponds to the librarian's view of reality: He compromises between his real need and that which he thinks the librarian can understand and help him with. (The idea in Taylor's model is that the librarian is supposed to learn an interview technique that makes it possible to receive the undistorted signal by working back toward phase Q3 and, possibly, toward Q2.)

In my view, however, Taylor's Q4 is not the extension of the knowledge development, but is a parallel line of formulation, which in principle can take place on all levels. The user might, for instance, go to the library with a vague idea of writing an assignment about labor unions (that is, Q1–Q2) and nevertheless express it as a compromise (Q4), that is, without going through the phases Q2 and Q3. He might, for instance. ask about the address of a specific labor union or something such as "Where can I find the directories?"[20]

Taylor has made a correct observation when he points out that in a conversation between the inquirer and the information specialist, one often finds that the information specialist can contribute something different and more than what the researcher is asking for, or even that he knows of a book that makes the whole problem inexpedient or redundant. However, this shows that the information specialist has relevant knowledge of the information system or of the literature in the field that might be of use to the inquirer. Taylor's perception of the problem is a psychological tendency by the user which can be obviated by psychological understanding. I, however, tend to view it as an expression of the inquirer's lack of knowledge of the possibilities that the information specialist has to offer. If the communication between the inquirer and the information specialist is to be optimal, they both need to have a precise and extensive picture of each other's knowledge.[21]

The prerequisite for a better dialog between librarian and user is better knowledge of each other's prerequisites. The information specialist can get closer to the user by paying more attention to methodological problems and by viewing the information-seeking process from this angle. It offers better prospects for having relevant communication with the user. The user also needs more knowledge of the information structure, databases, and so on, and he can get it more easily if the information specialist studies such questions and tries to transfer the results to the users, for instance by arranging courses. It would be strategically important if information specialists could win the bastion that consists of being responsible for well-functioning and respected courses for students, researchers, and other users, where information seeking is integrated into a scientific or scholarly methodological context.

My analysis of Taylor's Q4, that is, the communication between the user and the information specialist, shows that I do not attach as much importance to the psychological techniques in the communication process as to the contents of the communication. I also claim that philosophy of science and general methodology are a good and general enough background if one wants to establish a common general level of usability in the communication.

The notion of information need that I have outlined here differs from most of the recent literature in information science, which still views the concept of information need in Taylor's individualistic, psychological sense. Only a very few researchers have been interested in the variable "information" (Bates, 1987) or "subject area" (Mote, 1962; Amba & Iyer, 1992, p. 98) in relation to theories about information needs. However, new philosophical influences from semiotics, hermeneutics, and activity theory seem to prevail in IS.[22]

The conclusion of my analysis is that human knowledge is *object-oriented,* and that it is the object of inquiry (that is, the nature of the query) that determines the line of development. There is no "ghost in the machine."[23] The belief in the independent development of knowledge or needs inside the head of the user is an idealistic idea that can only lead to stagnation.[24]

NOTES

1. A comprehensive treatment of the psychological concept of motivation and need from a methodological collectivistic point of view can be found in Hakkarainen's dissertation (1990). Unfortunately, it is published in Finnish, but it has a twenty-page summary in English.

2. Information needs might perhaps most fruitfully be compared to educational needs. The concept of educational need is discussed in Jacobsen (1991), and even if this exposition is, in my opinion, too psychologizing (it considers the subjectively experienced educational needs at the expense of societal needs), it puts these problems of need in perspective.

It can be pointed out that Øhrgaard (1992), in a contribution to the pedagogical debate, expresses concern over today's students, who have worked with a great deal of specific subjects, but in his opinion lack a horizon, a perspective, an overall view. Such a pedagogical statement (which the students themselves may or may not be aware of or agree with) can directly be transformed into a distinction between more general information needs and more narrow, pragmatic information needs.

3. Habermas's theory assumes that the epistemological interest of the natural sciences is to control nature, the epistemological interest of the social sciences is "emancipation," and the epistemological interest of the humanities is pragmatic (understanding the human being and the culture).

4. The Danish psychologist Erik Schultz writes in his dissertation (1988, pp. 118–120) that if Habermas's concept of epistemological interest is confused with a psychological concept of motives, which refers to the scientist's mind, the whole point is lost. In this I agree with Schultz. Schultz's rejection of the concept of epistemological interest as a psychological concept of motives corresponds to my criticism of the subjec-

tive idealistic conception. It is possible also to be interested in how the personality of the scientist affects his or her choice of problems and thus the information need. Berthelsen (1992), for example, studied the difference between women's and men's self-selected written exam topics. He claims (p. 291) that women tend to be satisfied with nice reports and "toothless" topics and that they should be required to problematize and to be more critical. Such questions concern the psychology of research, but they require a clarification of the goals of research and an articulation of the problems, methodologies, and epistemological interests of the particular disciplines. Such an interest in the specific psychological aspects of information needs is, in my opinion, secondary to information science. Schmidt (1991, p. 21) expresses it in the following way: "scientific knowledge is de-subjectivized."

5. In order to illuminate these difficulties, Plato's dialog Meno is cited:

Meno: How will you look for something when you don't know at all what it is? What sort of thing, pray, among those that you don't know will you set before yourself as the object of your search? Or even if you were in fact to hit upon it, how would you know that it was the thing that you didn't know?

Socrates: I understand what you are saying, Meno! Do you realize what a belligerent statement you bring us? That a person can search neither for what he knows nor for what he does not know. That he cannot search for what he knows, because he already knows it and does not need to search any further, nor for what he does not know, because he does not know what he is searching for.

6. Whether information, needs, signs, and cultural products exist inside the head or elsewhere is an ontological question. Semiotic theories sometimes treat these problems at a deeper theoretical level. See, for example, Eco (1994).

7. Taylor may have adopted some views from Cleverdon, Mills & Keen (1966) who (p. 256) write: "The enquiry is expressed in the form of a 'stated requirement'... quite often the stated requirement is far removed from the real needs of the questioner." It was Cleverdon's view that objective testing could be obtained if only the stated requirements were used.

In this positivistic tradition the users need in solving a problem is considered as something private which can only be decided by the questioner himself. This is quite contrary to the view in activity theory, where problems are considered as having an objective character and objective solutions, whereas the users have subjective views of their needs, influenced by their educational background and other forms of socialization.

Also in the atomistic and mechanical research tradition there is a presumption about a need, simple expression, and a well defined set of documents sharing the same characteristics. However, as Doyle (1963, p. 199) pointed out: "The searcher needs an efficient exploratory system rather than a request implementing system" and that "exploratory capability, as it turns out, is provided by traditional libraries, but not by some of our modern machine literature searching schemes."

8. Behind it might also lie the fact, which I discussed above, that the phrase information need is a bit treacherous. While it is a fact that in order to solve a given problem, one might need certain information, the real need is to solve the problem; the information is only a means or a secondary need in relation to the primary need.

9. One reason for Taylor's ambiguity regarding this is that the writings on this matter do not address the time frame of this need development. Are we talking about years or minutes to complete the cycle? And what determines this duration?

10. Individual cognitive development is mainly studied by psychologists. There are obviously great differences among individuals in their cognitive development. This is due both to abilities in a more narrow sense and to differences in relevant stimulation, learning, and experiences.

One of the well known psychological theories about cognitive development is that of the Swiss psychologist Jean Piaget. According to his theory, children's cognitive abilities develop in global stages according to universal principles (regardless of culture). More recent researchers such as Keil (1989), are sceptical about such global and universal stages in development. They see cognitive development as much more domain specific, content oriented and culturally determined. Such new developments in cognitive psychology tend to connect the study of individual conceptual learning to the study of conceptual development in the arts and the sciences.

The individual cognitive development is more or less determined by the individual's role in society and by his or her motivation, intelligence, personality, morality, and independence. To make a contribution to a field depends on a long-term determination to understand the problem and to acquire the necessary knowledge. Some of the necessary prerequisites may be acquired incidentally in the culture, but most often a conscious effort to attain qualifications for the research area in question are needed. Often it is necessary to cross disciplinary borders and other formal criteria set up by others. Such learning might be inhibited by psychological motivation to appeal to other interests than those dictated by the research problem or by influences of an ideological character.

11. Shapere (1984) can illuminate this development:

> Although in more primitive stages of science (or, perhaps better, of what will become a science), obvious sensory similarities or general presuppositions usually determine whether certain items of experience will be considered as forming a body or domain; this is less and less true as science progresses (or, as one might say, as it becomes more unambiguously scientific). As part of the growing sophistication of science, such associations of items are subjected to criticism, and are often revised on the basis of considerations which are far from obvious and naive. Differences which seemed to distinguish items from one another are concluded to be superficial; similarities which were previously unrecognized, or, if recognized, considered superficial, become fundamental. Conversely, similarities which formerly served as bases for association of items come to be considered superficial, and the items formerly associated are no longer, and form independent groupings or come to be associated with other groups. The items themselves often, in the process, come to be redescribed, often for scientific purposes, in very unfamiliar ways. (Shapere, 1984, p. 323)

12. A particularly interesting example is given by Small (1977), who describes how a research area within just one year changed in a revolutionary way. This example is rather like an exemplary model of the development of a research area, illustrated by bio-chemistry.

13. It is very difficult in the literature to identify studies that provide models of the relation and matching between the cognitive development of an individual and the collective development of knowledge. The only study found is provided by Moneta (1993), who matches the cognitive structure of individual scientists with the development of a scientific field or domain in which the scientist is working. Moneta's point of departure is scientific creativity, but the model could be applied to information needs and other specific IS problems as well. It expands the cognitive approach with a social dimension.

In the case of a relatively inexperienced researcher there will lie a great deal of educational need behind a given information need; that is, he will have the need to get an overview of the structure of the field, its problems, and status. In the case of a very knowledgeable researcher such information may be redundant, and he can work directly with a very isolated problem. In a theoretically underdeveloped discipline the information need might include a great deal of philosophical material and material from bordering disciplines. If, on the other hand, we are talking about a scientifically rigorous discipline, the information need might be concentrated on very well defined data. When an intermediary wishes to interpret a concrete user query and the information need that lies behind it, the interpretation indicates a separation of the more collective/objective elements of the information need from the more individualistic/subjective elements.

From a sociology of science perspective certain subjective tendencies in science can be explained. For example Thomas Kuhn's (1970) well-known book about scientific revolutions contains an abundance of social-psychological explanations of the connection of paradigms to generation shifts in science.

14. This view of information needs as determined by the character of the different sciences and fields of study, is not new in library and information science. A book such as Webb (1986) Sources of information in the social sciences (especially pp. 3–22), does discuss the information needs of social scientists compared to natural scientists.

The problem seems to be that this approach to the study of scientific communication and information needs has been supplanted by a more individualistic view in information science. The collective, subject-based approach is powerfully embodied in the operating structures and traditions of academic/research librarianship, but it has never been integrated in the theoretical and methodological literature of information science. Most schools of library and information studies have increasingly oriented themselves to the theories in the cognitive sciences rather than the further exploration of communication patterns and information needs in domains of knowledge.

Reasons for this may be that most librarians find work in public libraries and that it has been difficult for schools in information science to develop a general methodology for the study of domain-specific needs.

15. As described in Hjørland (1987), in the PsycINFO database the word *activity* is used to denote, for example, nerve and gland activities, or the activity of older people (a gerontological activity theory) with no connection to the concept as it is used in this book. There is an obvious need for a descriptor related to activity theory—as in the INSPEC-database.

I will refrain here from discussing in more concrete detail how an IR language should be constructed to meet Hakkarainen's information need as it is formulated above. It is an extremely important problem, and it is part of the philosophical aim of this book to try to analyze such problems in order to make it possible for information systems of the future to better resolve tasks with which existing systems do not deal very well.

16. The needed information can exist either concretely (in documents) or only as a possibility. Whether it is possible to gather the concrete existing information is a question of information retrieval theory. Whether it is possible to get the hypothetical information is a question of epistemology and scientific methodology.

17. According to pragmatic philosophy, the truth of claims of knowledge is also determined by criteria of utility for practical purposes. The difference between truth and relevance must therefore be a matter of independence of given sociocultural practices versus the total human condition.

18. This reasoning explains why it is so difficult to measure information needs empirically in the way that library and information science repeatedly tries to do it. If one asks people empirically what they need, it is possible only to survey what I have called the subjectively perceived need. The real knowledge need is not measured by empirical studies, but they are a logical consequence of the objective level of the basic research that exists at any given point in time. Disciplines where there is little strategic task uncertainty (Whitley, 1984; Andersen, 1985, p. 19) will be very different from disciplines where there is a lot of this type of uncertainty. In cases where there is little task uncertainty, the information need of the discipline is of a relatively stable nature and can more easily be measured than in disciplines where there is high strategic task uncertainty. An effort to study the information needs empirically should therefore be supplemented with analyses of the problem areas, and disciplines and tendencies within these, from an epistemological perspective. This is the only way in which information systems can become proactive in relation to the needs.

On the individual level it is similarly more difficult to recognize one's information need the more superficial one's knowledge of the problem area is. Therefore, White (1992, pp. 146ff) introduces the concept of *magisterial relevance criteria* or information needs for cases where it is not primarily the individual himself, but rather his educational authorities, who determine the need. Superficial knowledge is not only a question of the size of the knowledge base, but to a great extent a question of structure and of understanding basic laws, principles, theories, and concepts.

19. This is the well-known problem of ecological validity in psychological research.

20. Taylor's development outline does not take into consideration some important insights from psychology. We have briefly become acquainted with Dewey's views on ideas as plans of action. On a more general level, within psychology, concepts like interiorization and internalization are used, which denote that processes concerning external objects are transformed into processes that happen on the mental level. The goal of these transformations is to be able to carry out actions that transcend the limits for the external reality. Hence it is possible to test possibilities on the conscious level in order to find more efficient solutions on the external action level.

Taylor's need development only denotes an internal line of development that in the end leads to external, conscious action. Concepts like "practical intelligence" and "thinking with one's hands" become a paradox in such a psychological view. This paradox is removed with the inclusion of the concept of interiorization.

The Russian psychologist Vygotsky (here quoted from Leontiev, 1983, pp. 98ff) is an important figure in the development of the interiorization theory. When a person acts, he uses a tool (e.g., in a physical sense, a hammer, or in a mental sense, a language). According to Vygotsky, the individual's mental processes are affected by the individual's handling of this tool, and they include experiences developed in the cultural history of humanity. This is why human beings' higher mental processes are created in the interaction among people, first externally, and thereafter as individual, intramental processes, which can be transformed, can solve problems, and can be brought to bear on the external level.

The circumstances are of course complicated. But it shows that Taylor's model is not valid on a general level. It is not always that the process passes from the internal to the external; it may also go in the opposite direction. The knowledge and verbalization of the needs can be assumed to happen in dialog with, for instance, an information specialist and in interplay with the information sources. The role of the information specialist, therefore, is not only to use a psychological technique that makes it possible to receive the undistorted signal that exists inside the user's head, but also to contribute to making the user recognize and formulate the information need through a dialog and by demonstrating various information sources.

21. In Denmark, the librarian Frede Mørch (1985) has contributed to the understanding of this problem by incorporating the Danish psychologist Steen Folke Larsen's work on the concept of egocentric speech. According to Mørch, the user's tendency to formulate his query in the Q4 phase can be seen as an attempt to avoid egocentric speech and formulate his query based on the premises of the information system or on his observations of the requirements, condition, and structure of the information system. Mørch writes about this:

Such a re-formulation of the subject that the user previously has made within his own semantic universe, based on his own general level of usability, and perhaps based on episodic requirements, often causes a vertical movement from a very intentional to an extentional level, with subsequent loss of precision.

Taylor's recommendation that the librarian should work backwards from Q4 to Q3 or Q2 is not unproblematic; the librarian first has to demonstrate to the user that such a movement toward the intention of the concept does not force the user into egocentric speech, in other words that the two parties have a common level of usability. (Mørch, 1985, p. 523; translated from the Danish original)

Mørch is not explicit about how the librarian can demonstrate the common level of usability. He avoids the problem of the fact that the user and the librarian do not have identical prerequisites. Above I have attempted to outline various kinds of knowledge. The user and the information specialist have dissimilar prerequisites.

22. Two Scandinavian examples which indicate this influence are Vakkari (1996) and Ingwersen (1992, 1994). Vakkari (1996, p. 225) explicitly states, that "its [the cognitive paradigm's] central challenge is to overcome its methodological individualism by enriching its theory with concepts of social nature." Ingwersen (1992) shows a influence of hermeneutical, interpretative philosophy, and his 1994 work on polyrepresentation analyzes collective cognitive structures.

23. The expression "ghost in the machine" originates from Gilbert Ryle's book *The Concept of Mind* (1949). This is one of the most important books in the modern philosophy of mind. According to Ryle's logical behaviorism, talk of mental states such as belief, desire, and emotion is to talk about dispositions of the organism to behave in certain ways. There is no such thing as "mind" as traditionally understood in the Cartesian tradition.

24. Kulkarni & Simon (1988), for instance, are dealing with how knowledge is developing during the scientific discovery process and how knowledge about the subject and the acquisition of knowledge from the literature as well as from colleagues play a part in the development of knowledge. In this field the term "domain-specific knowledge" is being discussed more and more, as well as the importance of knowledge for perception, memory, and so on (see, e.g., Fincher-Kiefer et al., 1988).

Within the field of user studies there have been many studies attempting to measure information needs and to study them empirically. That such an empirical approach to information needs may be problematic can be illustrated by the following example: when Dialog in 1972 introduced its retrieval service, there was a strong competitor called Orbit. Orbit performed an empirical study of the potential users' need for databases, but Dialog argued that one should follow a supermarket principle with as large a selection as possible. Dialog first entered and rapidly won the market, while Orbit never gained enough of a foothold and gave up after a few years. The difficulty in studying information needs empirically is, among other things, due to the fact that library and information services should not only be reactive, that is, not only adapt to the users' needs, earlier patterns of usage, and immediate information problems; they should also be proactive, that is, anticipate information needs of which the users have not yet become aware. An information system may be proactive if it has staff who take an interest in society, the environment, and the discipline that it serves and who pick up on trends and their consequences at the same time or before the users do.

Selected Bibliography

Ahlers Moeller, B. (1981). Subject analysis in the library: A comparative study. *International Classification*, *8*(1), 23–27. (Abbreviated English version of B. Ahlers Moeller, *Vidensklassifikation: En komparativ analyse af Statsbibliotekets systematiske katalog*. Århus: Statsbiblioteket, 1979. [Mimeograph].).

Aitchison, J. (1986). A classification as a source for thesaurus: The bibliographic classification of H. E. Bliss as a source of thesaurus terms and structure. *Journal of Documentation*, *42*(3), 160–181.

Albrechtsen, H. (1992). *Domain analysis for classification of software*. Master's thesis, Royal School of Librarianship, Copenhagen. (Available from the author, c/o Royal School of Librarianship, 8 Birketinget, DK-2300 Copenhagen S, Denmark).

Albrechtsen, H. (1993). Subject analysis and indexing—from automated indexing to domain analysis. *The Indexer*, *18*(4), 219–224.

Amba, S., & Iyer, H. (1992). Contextual information needs: Retrieval techniques and the research process. In *Cognitive Paradigms in Knowledge Organisation. Second International ISKO Conference* (pp. 95–107). Madras: Sarada Ranganathan Endowment for Library Science.

American Psychological Association. (1994). *Publication manual of the American Psychological Association*. (4th ed.). Washington, DC: American Psychological Association.

Anbro, K., Dahlkild, N. C., Nielsen, L., Staalfeldt, P., & Work, A. (1972). *Samfundsvidenskabernes filosofi og historie—set ud fra den kritiske teori*. København: Akademisk Forlag og Københavns Universitets Institut for Kultursociologi.

Andersen, H. (1985). Videnskabssociologiske perspektiver på udviklingen i fagene nationaløkonomi, erhvervsøkonomi, sociologi og datalogi. En projektpræsentation. In J.-J. Jensen (Ed.), *Har vi den rigtige forskningspolitik?* (pp. 12–23). Esbjerg: Sydjysk Universitetscenter.

Andersen, P. B. *See* Bøgh Andersen, P.

Anderson, J. D. (1996). Organization of knowledge. In J. Feather & P. Sturges (Eds.), *International encyclopedia of library and information science* (pp. 336–353). London & New York: Routledge.

Atherton, P. (1978). *Books are for use: Final report of the Subject Access Project.* Syracuse, NY: Syracuse University, School of Information Studies.

Bakhtin, M. M. (1981). *The dialogical imagination: Four essays.* Texas: University of Texas Press.

Bakhtin, M. M. (1986). *Speech genres and other late essays.* Texas: University of Texas Press.

Bakhurst, D. (1990). Social memory in Soviet thought. In D. Middleton & D. Edwards (Eds.), *Collective remembering* (pp. 203–226). London: SAGE Publications.

Bardram, J. E., & Bertelsen, O. W. (1995). Supporting the development of transparent interaction. In B. Blumenthal, J. Gornostaev, & C. Unger (Eds.), *Human-computer interaction. 5th International Conference, EWHCI '95. Selected Papers* (pp. 79–90). Berlin: Springer-Verlag.

Bartolo, L. M., & Smith, T. D. (1993). Interdisciplinary work and the information search process: A comparison of manual and online searching. *College & Research Libraries, 54*(4), 344–353.

Bates, M. J. (1987). Information: The last variable. In C.-C. Chen (Ed.), *Proceedings of the 50th annual meeting of the ASIS, Vol. 24* (pp. 6–10). Medford, NJ.: American Society for Information Science.

Bauersfeld, H. (1992). Activity theory and radical constructivism. *Cybernetics & Human Knowledge, 1*(2/3), 15–25.

Bazerman, C., & Paradis, J. (Eds.). (1991). *Textual dynamics of the professions: Historical and contemporary studies of writing in professional communities.* Madison: University of Wisconsin Press.

Bedney, G., & Meister, D. (1997). *The Russian theory of activity. Current applications to design and learning.* Hillsdale, NJ: Lawrence Earlbaum Associates.

Belkin, N. J. (1980). The problem of "matching" in information retrieval. In O. Harbo & L. Kajberg (Eds.), *Theory and application of information research. Proceedings of the Second International Research Forum on Information Science, 3–6 August, Royal School of Librarianship, Copenhagen* (pp. 187–197). London: Mansell.

Belkin, N. J., Oddy, R. N., & Brooks, H. M. (1982). ASK for information retrieval. Part I: Background and theory. Part II: Results of a design study. *Journal of Documentation, 38*(2+3), 61–71 and 145–164.

Bell, W. J. (1991). *Searching behaviour: The behavioural ecology of finding resources.* London: Chapman & Hall.

Benediktsson, D. (1989). Hermeneutics: Dimensions towards LIS thinking. *Library and Information Science Research, 11,* 201–234.

Berger, P. L., & Luckmann, T. (1987). *Den samfundsskabte virkelighed: En videnssociologisk afhandling* [Social construction of reality]. København: Lindhardt og Ringhof.

Berthelsen, J. (1992). Køn og eksamensopgaver: En eksplorativ undersøgelse. *Nordisk Psykologi, 44*(4), 271–292.

Blair, D. C. (1990). *Language and representation in information retrieval.* Amsterdam: Elsevier.

Blume, P. (1989). *Juridisk informationssøgning: En praktisk introduktion til retssystemets kilder* (3rd ed.). København: Akademisk forlag.

Blumenthal, B. (1995). Industrial design and activity theory: A new direction for designing computer-based artifacts. In B. Blumenthal, J. Gornostaev, & C. Unger (Eds.),

Human-computer interaction. 5th International Conference, EWHCI '95. Selected Papers (pp. 1–16). Berlin: Springer-Verlag.

Bogdan, R. J. (1994). *Grounds for cognition: How goal-guided behavior shapes the mind.* Hillsdale, NJ: Lawrence Erlbaum Associates.

Bookstein, A., & Swanson, D. R. (1975). A decision theoretic foundation for indexing. *Journal of the American Society for Information Science, 26*(1), 45–50.

Borko, H. (1968). Information science: What is it? *American Documentation, 19*(1), 3–5.

Boserup, I. (1984). Hvad er emnedata? In N.-H. Gylstorff, N. C. Nielsen, & M. Laursen Vig (Eds.), *Emnedata i online-alderen* (pp. 31–42). Danmarks Forskningsbiblioteks-forenings Internatmøde Nyborg Strand 7. - 8. februar 1984. København: Biblioteks-centralens Forlag.

Boyce, B. (1982). Beyond topicality: A two-stage view of relevance and the retrieval process. *Information Processing and Management, 18*, 105–109.

Boyce, B. R., & Kraft, D. H. (1985). Principles and theories in information science. *Annual Review of Information Science and Technology, 20*, 153–178.

Brand, J. L. (1996). Can we decide between logical positivism and social construction views of reality? *American Psychologist, 51*(6), 652–653.

Brooks, T. A. (1986). Private acts and public motivations: An investigation of citer motivations. *Journal of the American Society for Information Science, 36*, 223–229.

Brooks, T. A. (1987). Evidence of complex citer motivations. *Journal of the American Society for Information Science, 37*, 34–36.

Brooks, T. A. (1993). All the right descriptors: A test of the strategy of unlimited aliasing. *Journal of the American Society for Information Science, 44*(3), 137–147.

Bruner, J. (1990). *Acts of meaning.* Cambridge, MA: Harvard University Press.

Buckland, M. K. (1991). *Information and information systems.* New York: Greenwood.

Buckland, M. K., & Gey, F. (1994). The relationship between recall and precision. *Journal of the American Society for Information Science, 45*(1), 12–19.

Bødker, S. (1989). A human activity approach to user interfaces. *Human-computer inter-actions, 4*(3), 171–195.

Bødker, S. (1993). Historical analysis and conflicting perspectives-contextualizing HCI. In L. J. Bass, J. Gornostaev, & C. Ungar (Eds.), *Third international conference. EWHCI '93. Human-computer interaction, 3–7 Aug. 1993 in Moscow* (pp. 1–10). Berlin: Springer-Verlag.

Bøgh Andersen, P. (1990). *A theory of computer semiotics: Semiotic approaches to construction and assessment of computer systems.* Cambridge: Cambridge University Press.

Capurro, R. (1985). *Epistemology and information science* (Stockholm Papers in Library and Information Science, TRITA-LIB-6023). Stockholm: Royal Institute of Technology.

Capurro, R. (1986). *Hermeneutik der Fachinformation.* München: Verlag Karl Alber.

Chi, M. T. H., Hutchinson, J. E., & Robin, A. F. (1989). How inferences about novel domain-related concepts can be constrained by structured knowledge. *Merril-Palmer Quarterly Journal of Developmental Psychology, 35*(1), 27–62.

Cleverdon, C. W. (1972). On the inverse relationship of recall and precision. *Journal of Documentation, 28*, 195–201.

Cleverdon, C. W., Mills, J., & Keen, E. M. (1966). *Factors determining the performan-ce of indexing systems* (Vol. 2: Test results). Cranfield, England: College of Aeronautics.

Connolly, T., & Wholey, D. R. (1988). Information mispurchase in judgment tasks: A task-driven causal mechanism. *Organizational Behavior and Human Decision Processes, 42,* 75–87.

Cooper, W. S. (1972). A definition of relevance for information retrieval. *Information Storage and Retrieval, 7,* 19–37.

Cooper, W. S. (1978). Indexing documents by gedanken experimentation. *Journal of the American Society for Information Science, 29*(3), 107–119.

Cornelius, I. (1996a). Information and interpretation. In P. Ingwersen & N. O. Pors (Eds.), *Proceedings CoLIS 2: Second international conference on conceptions of library and information science: Integration in perspective. October 13–16, 1996* (pp. 11–21). Copenhagen: The Royal School of Librarianship.

Cornelius, I. (1996b). *Meaning and method in information studies.* Norwood, NJ: Ablex.

Cronin, B. (1984). *The citation process: The role and significance of citations in scientific communication.* London: Taylor Graham.

Cutter, C. A. (1904). *Rules for a dictionary catalog.* Washington, DC: Government Printing Office.

Dabney, D. P. (1986). The curse of Thamus: An analysis of full-text legal document retrieval. *Law Library Journal, 78*(1), 5–40.

Dahlberg, I. (1974). *Grundlagen universaler Wissensordnung. Probleme und Möglichkeiten eines universalen Klassifikationssystems des Wissens.* München: Verlag Dokumentation.

Dahlberg, I. (1992a). The basis of a new universal classification system seen from a philosophy of science point of view. In N. J. Williamson & M. Hudson (Eds.), *Classification research for knowledge representation and organization. Proceedings of the 5th international study conference on classification research* (pp. 187–197). Amsterdam: Elsevier.

Dahlberg, I. (1992b). Editorial. *International Classification, 19*(4), 187.

Danziger, K. (1990). *Constructing the subject: Historical origins of psychological research.* Cambridge: Cambridge University Press.

Dewey, J. (1902). Interpretation of savage mind. *The Psychological Review, 9,* 217–230.

Dewey, J. (1948). *Reconstruction in philosophy.* (Enlarged ed.). New York: Beacon. (Original work published 1920)

Dewey, M. (1979). *Dewey Decimal Classification and relative index* (19th ed., Vol. 1). Albany, NY: Forest Press.

Doyle, L. B. (1963). Is relevance an adequate criterion in retrieval system evaluation? *Proceedings of the American Documentation Institute 26th Annual Meeting.* Washington, DC: American Documentation Institute, 199–200.

Eco, U. (1994). Jacobson, Roman. In T. A. Sebeok (Ed.), *Encyclopedic dictionary of semiotics* (2nd ed., Vols. 1–3, pp. 402–408). Berlin & New York: Mouton de Gruyter, 1994.

Elias, A. W. (Ed.). (1971). *Key papers in information science.* Philadelphia: American Society for Information Science.

Ellenberger, H. F. (1970). *The Discovery of the unconscious: The history and evolution of dynamic psychiatry.* New York: Basic Books.

Ellis, B. (1990). *Truth and objectivity.* Oxford: Basil Blackwell.

Ellis, D. (1990). *New horizons in information retrieval.* London: Library Association.

Ellis, D. (1992a). Domain, approach and paradigm in information-retrieval research. *Journal of Documentation, 48*(3), 328–331.

Ellis, D. (1992b). Paradigms and proto-paradigms in information retrieval research. In P. Vakkari & B. Cronin (Eds.), *Conceptions of library and information science: Historical, empirical and theoretical perspectives* (pp. 165–186) (Proceedings of the international conference held for the celebration of the 20th anniversary of the Department of Information Studies, University of Tampere, Finland, 26–28 August 1991). London: Taylor Graham.

Ellis, D. (1996). *Progress and problems in information retrieval*. London: Library Association Publishing.

Engestrom, Y. (1995). Objects, contradictions and collaboration in medical cognition: An activity-theoretical perspective. *Artificial Intelligence in Medicine, 7*(5), 395–412.

Eskola, A., et al. (1988). *Blind alleys in social psychology. A search for ways out.* Amsterdam: North-Holland.

Fairthorne, R. A. (1969). Content analysis, specification and control. *Annual Review of Information Science and Technology, 4*, 73–109.

Farradane, J. E. (1961). Fundamental fallacies and new needs in classification. In D. J. Foskett & J. B. Palmer (Eds.), *The Sayers memorial volume* (pp. 120–135). London: Library Association.

Farradane, J. E. (1967). Concept organization for information retrieval. *Information Storage and Retrieval, 3*, 297–314.

Feather, J., & Sturges, P. (Eds.). (1996). *International encyclopedia of library and information science.* London & New York: Routledge. [The book wrongly indicates that it is published in 1997].

Fincher-Kiefer, R., et al. (1988). On the role of prior knowledge and task demands in the processing of text. *Journal of Memory and Language, 27*, 416-428.

Foellesdal, D., Walløe, L., & Elster, J. (1992). *Politikens introduktion til moderne filosofi og videnskabsteori.* Copenhagen: Politiken.

Folke Larsen, S. (1980). Egocentrisk tale, begrebsstruktur og semantisk udvikling. *Nordisk Psykologi, 32*(1), 55–73.

Forrester, M. A. (1996). *Psychology of language: A critical introduction.* London: SAGE Publications.

Forsman, B. (1984). Vi måste ha ett värderingsfritt klassifikationssystem! [Contribution to Hansson, 1984a]. *Biblioteksbladet,* (5), 112–113.

Foskett, A. C. (1982). *The subject approach to information.* (4th ed.). London: Clive Bingley.

Foucault, M. (1979). *Discipline and punish: The birth of the prison.* Harmondworth, England: Penguin. (Translated from French).

Frohmann, B. (1990). Rules of indexing: A critique of mentalism in information retrieval theory. *Journal of Documentation, 46*(2), 81–101.

Frohmann, B. (1994). The Social construction of knowledge organization: The case of Melvil Dewey. *Advances in Knowledge Organization, 4*, 109–117.

Fugmann, R. (1992). Illusory goals in information science research. In N. J. Williamson & M. Hudon (Eds.), *Classification research for knowledge representation and organization* (pp. 61–68). Amsterdam: Elsevier.

Fugmann, R. (1994). Representational predictability: Key to the resolution of several pending issues in indexing and information supply. *Advances in Knowledge Organization, 4*, 414–422.

Føllesdal. *See* Foellesdal, D.

Gadamer, H.-G. (1975). *Truth and method*. London: Sheed & Ward. (Translated from the German original *Wahrheit und Methode*, 1960).

Garfield, E. (1980). Bradford's law and related statistical patterns. *Current Contents*, (19), 5–12.

Garfinkel, H. (1967). *Studies in ethnomethodology*. Cambridge: Polity Press.

Giesecke, H. (1981). *Indføring i pædagogik*. København: Nyt Nordisk Forlag Arnold Busch.

Gigerenzer, G., & Hug, K. (1992). Domain-specific reasoning: Social contracts, cheating, and perspective change. *Cognition, 43*(2), 127–171.

Gopinath, M. A. (1976). Colon classification. In A. Maltby (Ed.), *Classification in the 1970's: A second look* (Rev. ed., pp. 51–80). London, Clive Bingly.

Green, A. (1990). What do we mean by user needs. *British Journal of Academic Librarianship, 5*(2), 65–78.

Greenwood, J. D. (1991). *Relations and representations. An introduction to the philosophy of social psychological science*. London and New York: Routledge.

Griffith, B. C. (Ed.). (1980). *Key papers in information science*. New York: Knowledge Industry Publications.

Grolier, E. de (1992). Towards a syndetic information retrieval system. In N. J. Williamson & M. Hudson (Eds.), *Classification research for knowledge representation and organization. Proceedings of the 5th international study conference on classification research* (pp. 223–234). Amsterdam: Elsevier.

Gudiksen, J. (1979). Behovsopfattelser. *Biblioteksarbejde: Tidsskrift for Informations- og kulturformidling, 1*, 11–26.

Habermas, J. (1968). *Erkenntnis und Interesse*. Frankfurt am Main: Suhrkamp.

Hakkarainen, P. (1990). *Motivaatio, leikki ja toiminnan kohteellisuus* [Motivation, play and object-orientation of activity]. Helsinki: Orienta-Konsultit Oy.

Hansson, S.-O. (1984a). Biblioteken och pseudovetenskapen. *Biblioteksbladet*, (3), 48–50.

Hansson, S.-O. (1984b). En kämpande folkbildning måste ta ställning till vetenskapen. [Answer to Forsman, 1984]. *Biblioteksbladet*, (5), 112.

Harré, R. (1972). *The philosophies of science*. Oxford: Oxford University Press.

Harter, S. P. (1986). *Online information retrieval: Concepts, principles, and techniques*. San Diego: Academic Press.

Harter, S. P., Nisonger, T. E., & Weng, A. (1993). Semantic relationships between cited and citing articles in library and information science journals. *Journal of the American Society for Information Science, 44*, 543–552.

Henriksen, C. (1990). Two papers on "Fag(sprog)lig kommunikation." (Content: 1. Hvad skal vi med fagsprog som forskningsområde? 2. Communication strategies in scientific-technological discourse). *Rolig papir No. 46*. Roskilde: Roskilde Universitetscenter.

Hermann, J., & Gregersen, F. (1978). *Gennem sproget: Om undersøgelse af sprogbrug i samfundet*. København: Gyldendal.

Hielmcrone, H. von (1975). *Etisk argumentation*. København: Berlingske forlag.

Hirschfeld, L. A., & Gelman, S. A. (Eds.). (1994). *Mapping the mind: Domain specificity in cognition and culture*. Cambridge and New York: Cambridge University Press.

Hjerppe, R. (1994). A framework for the description of generalized documents. *Advances in Knowledge Organization, 4*, 173–180.

Hjørland, B. (1984). Psychology and information search strategy: "Information input overload." *Social Science Information Studies, 4*, 143–148.

Hjørland, B. (1987). Virksomhedsbegrebet i Psychological Abstracts. *Psykolog Nyt*, (6), 186–187.

Hjørland, B. (1988). Information retrieval in psychology: Implications of a case study. *Behavioral & Social Sciences Librarian*, 6(3/4), 39–64.

Hjørland, B. (1989). *Psykologi og grænseområder: Kilder til information.* (3rd rev. ed.). København: Det kongelige Bibliotek.

Hjørland, B. (1990a). Døde bøger og tomme hylder: Anmeldelse. *Biblioteksarbejde*, 11(29), 61–71.

Hjørland, B. (1990b). Indledende betragtninger over faglitteraturens typologi og udtryksformer. *Biblioteksarbejde*, 11(29), 35–50.

Hjørland, B. (1991). Det kognitive paradigme i biblioteks- og informationsvidenskaben. *Biblioteksarbejde*, 12(33), 5–37.

Hjørland, B. (1992a). The concept of "subject" in information science. *Journal of Documentation*, 48(2), 172–200.

Hjørland, B. (1992b). Kvalitetsbegrebet i faglitteratur og videnskab. *Svensk Biblioteksforskning*, (3), 17–37.

Hjørland, B. (1992c). Skitse til en emnedatateori. In *Teknologi och kompetens. Föredrag presenterade vid 8:de Nordiska Konferenscen för Information och Dokumentation 19–21/5 1992 i Helsingborg* (pp. 227–231). Stockholm: TLS.

Hjørland, B. (1993a). *Emnerepræsentation og informationssøgning: Bidrag til en teori på kundskabsteoretisk grundlag.* Göteborg: Valfrid, Publiceringsföreningen för inst Bibliotekshögskolan vid Högskolan i Borås och Centrum för biblioteks- och informationsvetenskap vid Göteborgs universitet.

Hjørland, B. (1993b). Litteratursøgning som en kvalitativ og kvantitativ forskningsmetode. In N. K. Rosenberg, K. V. Mortensen, E. Hougaard, S. Lunn, & Alice Theilgaard (Eds.), *Klinisk psykologisk forskning. En indføring i metoder og problemstillinger* (pp. 58–70). København: Dansk Psykologisk Forlag.

Hjørland, B. (1993c). *Toward a new horizon in information science (IS): Domainanalysis.* Oral presentation given at the 56th annual meeting of ASIS in Columbus, OH, October 25, 1993. (Available on audiocassette F248–4 from ASIS). (Abstract published in *ASIS '93: Proceedings of the 56th ASIS Annual Meeting, 1993, Vol. 30* [p. 290]. Medford, NJ: American Society for Information Science and Learned Information, Inc.)

Hjørland, B. (1994). Nine principles of knowledge organization. *Advances in Knowledge Organization*, 4, 91–100. (Proceedings of the Third International ISKO Conference, 20–24 June 1994, Copenhagen, Denmark).

Hjørland, B. (1995). *Informationsvidenskabelige grundbegreber 1–2.* (2nd ed.) (Fundamental concepts of information science). København: Danmarks Biblioteksskole.

Hjørland, B. (1996a). Overload, quality and changing conceptual frameworks. In J. Olaisen, E. Munch-Petersen, and P. Wilson (Eds.), *Information science: From the development of the discipline to social interaction* (pp. 35–67). Oslo: Scandinavian University Press. (This book represents in part the proceedings from a Nordic conference, 27–28 April 1993, at the University of Borås, Sweden).

Hjørland, B. (1996b). Rejoinder: A new horizon for information science. *Journal of the American Journal for Information Science*, 47(4), 333–335.

Hjørland, B., & Albrechtsen, H. (1995a). Information science education from the point of view of domain analysis. In M. Hancock-Beaulieu & N. O. Pors (Eds.), *Proceedings of the 1st British-Nordic Conference on Library and Information Studies,*

22–24 May 1995 in Copenhagen (pp. 115–120). Copenhagen: The Royal School of Librarianship, 1995. Internet edition: http://epip.lut.ac.uk/bailer/14–bhhal.htm

Hjørland, B., & Albrechtsen, H. (1995b). Toward a new horizon in information retrieval: Domain analysis. *Journal of the American Society for Information Science, 46*(6), 400–425.

Holmgren, H., Timpka, T., Goldkuhl, G., Nyce, J. M., & Sjoberg, C. (1992). Argumentative design of medical software: An essential part of action design. In P. Degoulet, T. E. Piemme, & O. Rienhoff (Eds.), *MEDINFO 92: Proceedings of the seventh world congress on medical informatics* (Vol. 2, pp. 1249–1253). Amsterdam: North-Holland.

Holzkamp, K. (1983). *Grundlegung der Psychologie*. Frankfurt: Campus.

Horner, D. S. (1992). Frameworks for technology analysis and classification. *Journal of Information Science, 18*, 57–68.

Horstmann, H. (1990). Objektivität. In H. J. Sandkühler (Ed.), *Europäische Enzyklopädie zu Philosophie und Wissenschaften* (Vol. 3, pp. 592–594). Hamburg: Felix Meiner Verlag.

Hutchins, W. J. (1975). *Languages of indexing and classification: A linguistic study of structures and functions*. London: Peter Peregrinus.

Hutchins, W. J. (1977). On the problem of "aboutness" in document analysis. *Journal of Informatics, 1*, 17–35.

Hutchins, W. J. (1978). The concept of "aboutness" in subject indexing. *Aslib Proceedings, 30*, 172–181.

Iivonen, M. (1987). Indeksoinnin suuntautumisesta [On the orientation of indexing]. *Kirjastotiede ja informatiikka, 6*(1), 25–30.

Informationsordbogen. (1991). Ordbog for informationshåndtering, bog og bibliotek. 2. udg. Udarbejdet af J.B. Friis-Hansen, T. Høst, P. Steen Larsen & H. Spang-Hanssen. [Hellerup]: Dansk Standardiseringsråd.

Ingwersen, P. (1976). *Materiale vedrørende emners beslægtethed og emnesøgning: Et forsøg på at skabe en associationsmodel beregnet for søgning*. København: Danmarks Biblioteksskole. [Mimeograph; unpublished teaching material].

Ingwersen, P. (1992). *Information retrieval interaction*. London: Taylor Graham. (New edition of the dissertation *Intermediary functions in information retrieval interaction*. København: Handelshøjskolen, 1991).

Ingwersen, P. (1994). Polyrepresentation of information needs and semantic entities: Elements of a cognitive theory for information retrieval interaction. In *ACM/SIGIR-94* (pp. 101–110). London: Springer.

Ingwersen, P. (1996). Cognitive perspectives of information retrieval interaction: Elements of a cognitive IR theory. *Journal of Documentation, 52*(1), 3–50.

Ingwersen, P., & Wormell, I. (1990). *Informationsformidling: teori og praksis*. København: Munksgaard.

International Standard Organization (1985). *Methods for examining documents, determining their subjects, and selecting indexing terms* (ISO Standard No. 5963). Geneva: International Standard Organisation.

Itoga, M. (1992). Seeking understanding beneath the unspecifiable: An alternative framework for mapping information needs in communication. *Libri, 42*(4), 330–344.

Jacob, E. K. (1994). Classification and crossdisciplinary communication: Breaching the boundaries imposed by classificatory structure. *Advances in Knowledge Organization*,

4, 101–108. (Proceedings of the third international ISKO conference, 20–24 June 1994, Copenhagen, Denmark).

Jacobsen, B. (1991). *Studier i dansk voksenundervisning og folkeoplysning: Socio-psykologiske analyser.* København: Akademisk Forlag.

Jaenecke, P. (1994). To what end knowledge organization? *Knowledge Organization, 21*(1), 3–11.

Johansen, T. (1975). *Indledende betragtninger over emners beslægtethed* [Mimeograph]. København, Danmarks Biblioteksskole.

Johansen, T. (1985). An outline of a non-linguistic approach to subject-relations. *International Classification, 12*(2), 73–79.

Johansen, T. (1987a). Elements of the non-linguistic approach to subject-relationships. *International Classification, 14*(1), 11–18.

Johansen, T. (1987b). On the relationships of material subjects. *International Classification, 14*(3), 138–144.

Johansen, T. (1989). Om sammensatte emners struktur. In O. Harbo & L. Kajberg (Eds.), *Orden i papirerne—en hilsen til J. B. Friis Hansen* (pp. 157–165). København: Danmarks Biblioteksskole.

Josselson, R., & Lieblich, A. (1996). Fettering the mind in the name of "science." *American Psychologist, 51*(6), 651–652.

Juul Jensen, U. (1992). Humanistisk sundhedsforskning: Videnskabsteoretiske overvejelser. *Udkast, 20*(2), 113–131.

Juul Nielsen, J. (1977). *Problemformulering og -relatering: Usystematisk og systematisk søgning.* København: Den kgl. Veterinær- og Landbohøjskole [Mimeograph].

Jørgensen, J. (1963). *Psykologi på biologisk grundlag.* København: Munksgaard.

Kaae, S. (1990). *Verbal emneindeksering i BASIS: En håndbog.* Ballerup: Bibliotekscentralens forlag.

Kagelmann, J. (1988, October). Psychomliteratur: Lieber ins Kino? *Psychologie Heute,* 86–87.

Kaptelinin, V. (1992). Human computer interaction in context: The activity theory perspective. In J. Gornostaev (Ed.), *Proceedings of the St. Petersburg international workshop on human-computer interaction* (Vol. 1, pp. 7–13). Moscow: International Centre for Scientific and Technological Information.

Kaptelinin, V. (1993). Activity theory: Implications for human computer interaction. In M. D. Brouwer-Janse, & T. L. Harrington (Eds.), *Proceedings of NATO Advanced Study Institute on basics of man-machine communication for the design of education systems, 16-26 Aug. 1993 in Eindhoven, Netherlands* (Vol. 1, pp. 5–15). Eindhoven, Netherlands: Institute for Perception Research.

Kaptelinin, V., Kuutti, K., & Bannon, L. (1995). Activity theory: Basic concepts and applications. In B. Blumenthal, J. Gornostaev, & C. Unger (Eds.), *Human-computer interaction. 5th international conference, EWHCI' 95. Selected papers* (pp. 189–201). Berlin: Springer-Verlag.

Karamüftüoglu, M. (1996). Semiotics of documentary information retrieval systems. In P. Ingwersen & N. O. Pors (Eds.), *Proceedings CoLIS 2: Second international conference on conceptions of library and information science: Integration in perspective. October 13–16, 1996* (pp. 85–97). Copenhagen: The Royal School of Librarianship.

Keil, F. C. (1989). *Concepts, kinds, and cognitive development.* Cambridge, MA: MIT Press.

Kierkegaard, S. (1850). Journal X3 A652. In H. V. Hong & E. H. Hong (Eds.), *Søren Kierkegaard's journals and papers* (p. 498; entry 4873). Bloomington: Indiana University Press. (Here cited from the English translation, 1975)

Klein, J. T. (1990). *Interdisciplinarity: History, theory, and practice*. Detroit: Wayne State University Press.

Krarup, K., & Boserup, I. (1982). *Reader-oriented indexing: An investigation into the exent to which subject specialists should be used for the indexing of documents by and for professional readers, based on a sample of sociological documents indexed with the help of the PRECIS indexing system* [Mimeograph]. Copenhagen: Royal Library.

Kristeva, J. (1974). *La révolution du language poétique*. Paris: Seuil.

Kröber, G., & Segeth, W. (1983). Beschreibung. In G. Klaus & M. Buhr (Eds.), *Wörterbuch der Philosophie*. Leipzig: VEB Bibliographisches Institut.

Kuhlthau, C. C. (1993). *Seeking meaning: A process approach to library and information services*. Norwood, NJ: Ablex Publishing Corporation.

Kuhn, T. S. (1970). *The structure of scientific revolutions* (2nd ed.). Chicago: University of Chicago Press. (Here cited from the Danish translation of the 2nd ed.: Videnskabens revolutioner. København: Fremad, 1973).

Kulkarni, D., & Simon, H. A. (1988). The processes of scientific discovery: The strategy of experimentation. *Cognitive Science, 12*, 139–175.

Kuutti, K. (1990). The activity theory as an alternative framework for HCI research and design. In *European Association of Cognitive Ergonomics: ECCE-5, Fifth European Conference on Cognitive Ergonomics proceedings, 3–6 Sept. 1990 in Urbino, Italy* (pp. 347–357). Amsterdam: Free University.

Kuutti, K. (1991). The concept of activity as a basic unit of analysis for CSCW research. In L. Bannon, M. Robinson, & K. Schmidt (Eds.), *Proceedings of the Second European Conference on Computer-Supported Cooperative Work. ECSCW '91* (pp. 249–264). Dordrecht, Netherlands: Kluwer Academic Publishers.

Kuutti, K. (1992). HCI research debate and activity theory position. In J. Gornostaev (Ed.), *Proceedings of the St. Petersburg International Workshop on Human-Computer Interaction, 4-8 Aug. 1992, St. Petersburg, USSR* (Vol. 1, pp. 13–22). Moscow: International Centre for Scientific and Technological Information.

Kuutti, K., & Arvonen, T. (1992). Identifying potential CSCW applications by means of activity theory concepts: A case example. In J. Turner, & R. Kraut (Eds.), *Proceedings of ACM 1992 Conference on Computer-Supported Cooperative Work: Sharing Perspectives, 31 Oct.–4 Nov. 1992, Toronto, Ont., Canada* (pp. 233–240). New York: ACM.

Kuutti, K., & Bannon, L. J. (1993). Searching for unity among diversity: Exploring the "interface" concept (Using the approach of activity theory). In *Proceedings of INTERCHI '93* (pp. 263–268). Amsterdam: IOS Press.

Lancaster, F. W. (1991). *Indexing and abstracting in theory and practice*. London: The Library Association.

Lancaster, F. W., Elliker, C., & Connell, T. H. (1989). Subject analysis. *Annual Review of Information Science and Technology, 24*, 35–84.

Lancaster, F. W., Zeter, M. J., & Metzler, L. (1992). Ranganathan's influence examined bibliometrically. *Libri, 42*(3), 268–281.

Langridge, D. W. (1976). *Classification and indexing in the humanities*. London: Butterworths.

Langridge, D. W. (1989). *Subject analysis: Principles and procedures*. London: Bowker-Saur.

Larson, R. R. (1991). The decline of subject searching: Long-term trends and patterns of index use in an online catalog. *Journal of the American Society for Information Science, 42*(3), 197–215.

Lave, J. (1988). *Cognition in practice*. Cambridge: Cambridge University Press.

Leontiev, A. N. (1981). *Problems in the development of the mind*. Moscow: Progress. (Translated from the Russian original of 1959).

Leontiev, A. (1983). *Virksomhed, bevidsthed, personlighed*. Moskva: Sputnik. (English edition: *Activity, consciousness, personality*. Englewood Cliffs, NJ: Prentice-Hall, 1978).

Liebenau, J., & Backhouse, J. (1990). *Understanding information: An introduction*. London: MacMillan.

Linard, M., & Zeiliger, R. (1995). Designing navigational support for educational software [using activity theory]. In B. Blumenthal, J. Gornostaev, & C. Unger (Eds.), *Human-Computer Interaction. 5th International Conference, EWHCI' 95. Selected Papers* (pp. 63–78). Berlin: Springer-Verlag.

Little, D. (1991). *Varieties of social explanation: An introduction to the philosophy of social science*. Oxford: Westview Press.

Lübcke, P. (Ed.). (1983). *Politikens filosofileksikon*. København: Politikens forlag.

Lynch, M. J. (1978). Reference interviews in public libraries. *The Library Quarterly, 48*, 119–142.

Machlup, F. (1983). Semantic quirks in studies of information. In F. Machlup & U. Mansfield (Eds.), *The study of information: Interdisciplinary messages*. New York: John Wiley.

McKinin, E. J., et al. (1991). The Medline/full-text research project. *Journal of the American Society for Information Science, 42*(4), 297–307.

MacRoberts, M. H., & MacRoberts, B. R. (1989). Problems of citation analysis: A critical review. *Journal of the American Society for Information Science, 40*(5), 342–349.

Madigan, R., Johnson, S., & Linton, P. (1995). The language of psychology: APA style as epistemology. *American Psychologist, 50*, 428–436.

Madigan, R., Linton, P., & Johnson, S. (1996). APA style: Quo vadis? *American Psychologist, 51*(6), 653–655.

Malmkjær, K. (1995a): Behaviourist linguistics. In K. Malmkjær (Ed.), *The linguistics encyclopedia* (pp. 53–57). London: Routledge.

Malmkjær, K. (1995b): Functionalist linguistics. In K. Malmkjær (Ed.), *The linguistics encyclopedia* (pp. 158–161). London: Routledge.

Malmkjær, K. (1995c): Genre analysis. In K. Malmkjær (Ed.), *The linguistics encyclopedia* (pp. 170–181). London: Routledge.

Malmkjær, K. (1995d): Rationalist linguistics. In K. Malmkjær (Ed.), *The linguistics encyclopedia* (pp. 375–379). London: Routledge.

Mammen, J. (1983). *Den menneskelige sans: Et essay om psykologiens genstandsområde*. København: Dansk Psykologisk Forlag.

Mammen, J. (1994). En realistisk begrebsteori: Om forholdet imellem virksomhedsteorien og den økologiske kognitive psykologi. In J. Mammen, & M. Hedegaard (Eds.), *Virksomhedsteori i udvikling* (pp. 43–58). Århus: Århus Universitet, Psykologisk Institut.

Mariscal, A. R. (1993). Quantification of information. *International Forum on Information and Documentation*, *18*(3–4), 21–23.

Mark Pejtersen, A. (1979). The meaning of "about" in fiction indexing and retrieval. *Aslib Proceedings*, *31*, 251–257.

Mark Pejtersen, A. (1980). Design of a classification scheme for fiction based on an analysis of actual user-librarian communication, and use of the scheme for control of librarians' search strategies. In O. Harbo & L. Kajberg (Eds.), *Theory and application of information research: Proceedings of the Second International Research Forum on Information Science, 3–6 August 1977, Royal School of Librarianship, Copenhagen* (pp. 146–159). London: Mansell.

Markey, K. (1981). Levels of question formulation in negotiation of information need during the online presearch interview: A proposed model. *Information Processing and Management*, *17*(5), 215–225.

Maron, M. E. (1977). On indexing, retrieval and the meaning of about. *Journal of the American Society for Information Science*, *28*, 38–43.

Martin, L. M. W., Nelson, K., & Tobach, E. (Eds.). (1995). *Sociocultural psychology: Theory and practice of doing and knowing*. New York: Cambridge University Press.

Merton, R. K. (1968). *Social theory and social structure*. New York: The Free Press.

Metcalfe, J. (1973). When is a subject not a subject? In C. H. Rawski (Ed.), *Towards a theory of librarianship*. New York: Scarecrow Press.

Michajlov, A. I., Cernyj, A. I., & Giljarevskij, R. S. (1980). *Wissenschaftliche Kommunikation und Informatik*. Leipzig: VEB Bibliographisches Institut. (Translated from the Russian edition of 1976).

Middleton, D., & Edwards, D. (Eds.). (1990). *Collective remembering*. London: SAGE Publications.

Miksa, F. (1983a). Melvil Dewey and the corporate ideal. In G. Stevenson & J. Kramer-Greene (Eds.), *Melvil Dewey: The man and the classification* (pp. 49–100). Albany, NY: Forest Press.

Miksa, F. (1983b). *The subject in the dictionary catalog from Cutter to the present*. Chicago: American Library Association.

Mingers, J. C. (1996). An evaluation of theories of information with regard to the semantic and pragmatic aspects of information systems. *Systems Practice*, *9*, 187–209.

Misiak, H., & Sexton, V. S. (1966). *History of psychology: An overview*. New York: Grune & Stratton.

Mogensen, P. (1992). Towards a prototyping approach in systems development [activity theory]. *Scandinavian Journal of Information Systems*, *4*, 31–53.

Molina, M. P. (1994). Interdisciplinary approaches to the concept and practice of written text documentary content analysis. *Journal of Documentation*, *50*(2), 111–133.

Moneta, G. B. (1993). A model of scientists' creative potential—the matching of cognitive structure and domain-structure. *Philosophical Psychology*, *6*(1), 23–39.

Mooers, C. (1951). Zatocoding applied to mechanical organization of knowledge. *American Documentation*, *2*, 20–30.

Mos, L. P., & Boodt, C. P. (1992). Mediating between mentalism and objectivism: The conventionality of language. In C. W. Tolman (Ed.), *Positivism in psychology: Historical and contemporary problems* (pp. 185–216). Berlin: Springer-Verlag.

Moser, P. K., & Trout, J. D. (Eds.). (1995). *Contemporary materialism: A reader*. London & New York: Routledge.

Mote, L. J. B. (1962). Reasons for the variations in the information needs of scientists. *Journal of Documentation, 18*(4), 169–175.

Munch-Petersen, E. (1980). *Bibliografiens teori: En introduktion.* København: Danmarks Biblioteksskole.

Mustelin. O. (1988). Källhänvisningar och fotnoter i svenskspråkiga Åbodissertationer under 1700-talet. In *Bøger, biblioteker, mennesker. Et nordisk Festskrift tilegnet Torben Nielsen Universitetsbiblioteket i København* (pp. 105–126). København: Det kgl. Bibliotek i samarbejde med Det danske Sprog- og Litteraturselskab.

Myers, G. (1990). *Writing biology: Texts in the social construction of knowledge.* Madison: University of Wisconsin Press.

Mørch, F. (1985). Bidrag til en analyse af referenceinterviewet i folkebibliotekerne. *Bogens Verden, 67*(8), 519–524.

Nardi, B. A. (1992). Studying context: A comparison of activity theory, situated action models, and distributed cognition. In J. Gornostaev (Ed.), *Proceedings of the St. Petersburg International Workshop on Human-Computer Interaction* (Vol. 2, pp. 352–359). Moscow: International Centre for Scientific and Technological Information.

Nardi, B. A. (1996). *Context & consciousness: Activity theory & human-computer interaction.* Cambridge, MA & London: The MIT Press.

Neisser, U. (1967). *Cognitive psychology.* New York: Appleton-Century-Crofts.

Nissen, H.-E., Klein, H. K., & Hirschheim, R. (Eds.). (1991). *Information systems research: Contemporary approaches and emergent traditions. Proceedings of the IFIP TC8/WG 8.2 Working Conference on the Information Systems Research Arena of the 90's: Challenges, perceptions and alternative approaches, 14–16 Dec. 1990, Copenhagen, Denmark.* Amsterdam: NorthHolland.

Novack, G. (1975). *Pragmatism versus Marxism: An appraisal of John Dewey's philosophy.* New York: Pathfinder Press.

Nystrand, M., Greene, S., & Wiemelt, J. (1993). Where did composition studies come from? *Written Communication, 10*(3), 267–333.

Nystrand, M., & Wiemelt, J. (1991). When is a text explicit: Formalist and dialogical conceptions. *Text, 11,* 25–41.

Olaisen, J. (1991). Pluralism or positivistic trivialism: Important trends in contemporary philosophy of science. In H.-E. Nissen, H. K. Klein, & R. Hirschheim (Eds.), *Information systems research: Contemporary approaches and emergent traditions* (pp. 235–265). Amsterdam: Elsevier Science Publishers B.V (North-Holland).

Pao, M. L. (1993). Term and citation retrieval: A field study. *Information Processing & Management, 29*(1), 95–112.

Pao, M. L., & Worthen, D. B. (1989). Retrieval effectiveness by semantic and pragmatic relevance. *Journal of the American Society for Information Science, 40*(4), 226–235.

Peters, P. E. (1977). Philosophy of science. In A. Kent & H. Lancour (Eds.), *Encyclopedia of Library and Information Science* (Vol. 22, pp. 183–207). New York: Marcel Dekker.

Petrilli, S. (1993). Signs and values: For a critique of cognitive semiotics. *Journal of Pragmatics, 20*(3), 239–251.

Pirkola, A., & Järvelin, K. (1996). The effect of anapehor and ellipsis resolution on proximity searching in a text database. *Information Processing and Management, 32*(2), 199–216.

Popper, K. R. (1972). *Objective knowledge: An evolutionary approach.* Oxford: Clarendon Press.

Poulsen, C. (1987). *Begrundelse for at anvende deltekstrepræsentation af metalitteratur til emnesøgning*. København: Danmarks pædagogiske Bibliotek.

Poulsen, C. (1994). *Informationens skygge og foran: Informationskvalitet, informations-eksplosion og online kataloger*. Roskilde: Roskilde Universitetscenter, Institut for Datalogi, Kommunikation og Uddannelsesforskning.

Price, D. J. de Solla. (1972). Science and technology: Distinctions and interrelationships. In B. Barnes (Ed.). *Sociology of science: Selected readings* (pp. 166–180). Harmondsworth, England: Penguin. (Reprinted from W. Gruber & G. Marquis [Eds.], *Factors in the transfer of technology*. Cambridge: MIT Press, 1969).

Prieto, L. J., & Dascal, M. (1994). Relevance. In Sebeok, T. A. (Ed.), *Encyclopedic dictionary of semiotics* (2nd ed., pp. 794–797). Berlin & New York: Mouton de Gruyter.

Prieto-Diaz, R. (1992). Applying faceted classification to domain analysis. *Proceedings of the ASIS Annual Meeting* (Vol. 29, pp. 316–317). (Meeting abstracts).

Prætorius, N. (1981). *Subjekt og objekt: En afhandling om psykologiens grundlagsproblemer*. København: Thaning & Appel.

Putnam, H. (1975). *Mind, language, and reality* (Philosophical papers, Vol. 1). Cambridge: Cambridge University Press.

Putnam, H. (1990). *Realism with a human face*. Cambridge, MA: Harvard University Press.

Putnam, H. (1992). *Renewing philosophy*. Cambridge, MA: Harvard University Press.

Radnitzky, G. (1970). *Contemporary schools of metascience*. (Vols. 1–2). København: Munksgaard.

Ramoni, M., Stefanelli, M., Magnani, L., & Barosi, G. (1992). An epistemological framework for medical knowledge-based systems. *IEEE Transactions on Systems Man and Cybernetics*, 22(6), 1361–1375.

Ranganathan, S. R. (1963). *Documentation and its facets*. London: Asia Publishing House.

Ranganathan, S. R. (1967). *Prolegomena to library classification*. London: Asia Publishing House.

Ransdell, J. (1994). Peirce, Charles Sanders. In Sebeok, T. A. (Ed.), *Encyclopedic dictionary of semiotics* (2nd ed., pp. 673–695). Berlin & New York: Mouton de Gruyter.

Ratner, C. (1993). Reconstructing the unconscious: A sociohistorical account. *Udkast*, 21(2), 111–132.

Ravetz, J. R. (1973). *Scientific knowledge and its social problems*. Harmondsworth, England: Penguin Books, 1973.

Rayward, W. B. (1994). Visions of Xanadu: Paul Otlet (1868–1944) and hypertext. *Journal of the American Society for Information Science*, 45(4), 235–250.

Reed, E. S. (1996). The challenge of historical materialist epistemology. In I. Parker & R. Spears (Eds.), *Psychology and society. Radical theory and practice* (pp. 21–34). London: Pluto Press.

Reich, R. B. (1993). *The work of nations: Preparing ourselves for 21st century capitalism*. New York: Vintage Books.

Rescher, N. (1979). *Cognitive systematization. A system-theoretic approach to a coherentist theory of knowledge*. Oxford: Blackwell.

Rescher, N. (1987). *Scientific realism. A critical reappraisal*. Dordrecht: D. Reidel.

Rescher, N. (1995). Pragmatism. In T. Honderich (Ed.), *The Oxford companion to philosophy* (pp. 710–713). Oxford: Oxford University Press.

Resnick, L. B., Levine, J. M., & Teasley, S. D. (Eds.). (1991). *Perspectives on socially shared cognition*. Washington, DC: American Psychological Association.

Riesthuis, G. J. A. (1991). Thesaurification of the UDC. *Advances in Knowledge Organization, 2*, 109–117.

Riis, J. F. (1993). *Erkendelsesteori: En indføring*. København: Museum Tusculanums forlag.

Roberts, N. (1985). Concepts, structures and retrieval in the social sciences up to c. 1970. *Social Science Information Studies, 5*, 55–67.

Rogers, T. B. (1992). Antecedents of operationalism: A case history in radical positivism. In C. W. Tolman (Ed.), *Positivism in psychology: Historical and contemporary problems* (pp. 57–65). Berlin: Springer-Verlag.

Ross, A. (1955). Kritiske bemærkninger til prof. Tranekjær Rasmussens emnelære. *Nordisk Psykologi, 7*, 49–64.

Rowley, J. E. (1987). *Organizing knowledge: Introduction to information retrieval.* Ashgate, England: Gower Publications.

Rudd, D. (1983). Do we really need World III? Information science with or without Popper. *Journal of Information Science Principles & Practice, 7*, 99–105.

Ryle, G. (1949): *The concept of mind*. London: Hutchinson.

Salem, S. (1982). Towards "coring" and "aboutness": An approach to some aspects of in-depth indexing. *Journal of Information Science Principles & Practice, 4*, 167–170.

Saracevic, T. (1975). Relevance: A review of and a framework for the thinking on the notion in information science. *Journal of the American Society for Information Science, 26*, 321–343.

Sarvimäki, A. (1988). *Knowledge in interactive practice disciplines: An analysis of knowledge in education and health care*. Helsinki: University of Helsinki, Department of Education.

Schamber, L., Eisenberg, M. B., & Nilan, M. S. (1990). A re-examination of relevance: Toward a dynamic, situational definition. *Information Processing & Management, 26*(6), 755–766.

Schmidt, L.-H. (1991). *Det videnskabelige perspektiv: Videnskabsteoretiske tekster*. København: Akademisk Forlag.

Schultz, E. (1988). *Personlighedspsykologi på erkendelsesteoretisk grundlag—eller mysteriet om personen, der forsvandt*. København: Dansk Psykologisk Forlag.

Schwartz, C. A. (1992). Research significance: Behavior patterns and outcome characteristics. *The Library Quarterly, 62*(2), 123–149.

Sebeok, T. A. (Ed.) (1994). *Encyclopedic dictionary of semiotics* (2nd ed.). Berlin & New York: Mouton de Gruyter.

Segeth, W. (1983). Prädikat. In G. Klaus & M. Buhr (Eds.), *Wörterbuch der Philosophie*. Leipzig: VEB Bibliographisches Institut.

Seglen, P. O. (1996). Bruk av siteringer og tidsskriftimpaktfaktor til forskningsevaluering. *Biblioteksarbejde, 17*(48), 27–34.

Shapere, D. (1977). Scientific theories and their domains. In F. Suppe (Ed.), *The structure of scientific theories* (2nd ed., pp. 518–599). Urbana: University of Illinois Press.

Shapere, D. (1984). *Reason and the search for knowledge: Investigations in the philosophy of science* (Boston Studies in the Philosophy of Science, vol. 78). Dordrecht: D. Reidel.

Shapere, D. (1989). Evolution and continuity in scientific change. *Philosophy of Science*, *56*, 419–437.

Sharp, H. (1991). The role of domain knowledge in software design. *Behaviour and Information Technology*, *10*(5), 383–401.

Shute, S. J., & Smith, P. J. (1993). Knowledge-based search tactics. *Information Processing & Management*, *29*(1), 29–45.

Siegler, R. S. (1989). How domain-general and domain-specific knowledge interact to produce strategy choices. *Merril-Palmer Quarterly Journal of Developmental Psychology*, *35*(1), 1–26.

Sinha, C. (1988). *Language and representation. A socio-naturalistic approach to human development*. London: Harvester.

Small, H. G. (1977). A co-citation model of a scientific speciality: A longitudinal study of collagen research. *Social Studies of Science*, *7*. Here cited from: B. C. Griffith (Ed.), *Key Papers in Information Science* (pp. 211–238). New York: Knowledge Industry Publications, 1980.

Smith, E. E. (1989). Concepts and induction. In M. I. Posner (Ed.), *Foundations of cognitive science* (pp. 501–526). London: MIT Press.

Smith, L. (1981). Citation analysis. *Library Trends*, *30*, 83–106.

Soergel, D. (1985). *Organizing information: Principles of data base and retrieval systems*. London: Academic Press.

Solla Price, D. J. de. See Price, D. J. de Solla.

Spang-Hanssen, H. (1970). *How to teach about information as related to documentation*. Unpublished manuscript.

Spang-Hanssen, H. (1974). Kunnskapsorganisasjon, informasjonsgjenfinning, automatisering og språk. In *Kunnskapsorganisasjon og informasjonsgjenfinning*. Seminar arrangert 3.–7.desember 1973 i samarbeid mellom Norsk hovedkomite' for klassifikasjon, Statens Biblioteksskole og Norsk Dokumentasjonsgruppe (pp. 11–61). (Skrifter fra Riksbibliotektjenesten, Nr. 2). Oslo: Riksbibliotekstjenesten.

Spang-Hanssen, H. (1989). Registre på brugernes niveau. In O. Harbo & L. Kajberg (Eds.), *Orden i papirerne—en hilsen til J. B. Friis Hansen* (pp. 149–155). København: Danmarks Biblioteksskole.

Sparck Jones, K. (1987). Architecture problems in the construction of expert systems for document retrieval. In I. Wormell (Ed.), *Knowledge engineering: Expert systems and information retrieval* (pp. 7–33). London: Taylor Graham.

Sparck Jones, K. (1992). Information retrieval. In S. C. Shapiro (Ed.), *Encyclopedia of artificial intelligence* (2nd ed., Vol. 1). New York: John Wiley & Sons, Inc.

Sparck Jones, K., & Kay, M. (1973). Fact retrieval. *Linguistics and information science* (chap. 7, pp. 174–194). London: Academic Press.

Steiger, R. (1973). Zu philosophisch-weltanschaulichen Fragen der Informationssprachen. *Informatik*, *20*, 52–55.

Stern, P. (1996). *Prisoners of the crystal palace: Mapping and understanding the social and cognitive organization of scientific research fields*. Umea: Borea Bokforlag.

Stone, S. (1982). Humanities scholars: Information needs and uses. *Journal of Documentation*, *38*, 292–313.

Suchman, L. (1987). *Plans and situated actions: The problem of human-machine communication.* Cambridge: Cambridge University Press.

Swales, J. (1990). *Genre analysis: English in academic and research settings.* Cambridge: Cambridge University Press.

Swanson, D. R. (1977). Information retrieval as a trial-and-error process. *Library Quarterly, 47*(2). Here cited from: B. C. Griffith (Ed.), *Key papers in information science* (pp. 328–348). New York: Knowledge Industry Publications, 1980.

Swanson. D. R. (1986a). Subjective versus objective relevance in bibliographic retrieval systems. *Library Quarterly, 56,* 389–398.

Swanson, D. R. (1986b). Undiscovered public knowledge. *Library Quarterly, 56,* 103–118.

Swanson, D. R. (1988). Historical note: Information retrieval and the future of an illusion. *Journal of the American Society for Information Science, 39*(2), 92–98.

Swift, D. F., Winn, V., & Bramer, D. (1978). "Aboutness" as a strategy for retrieval in the social sciences. *Aslib Proceedings, 30,* 182–187.

Taylor, R. S. (1962). The process of asking questions. *American Documentation, 13,* 391–396.

Taylor, R. S. (1967). *Question negotiation and information seeking in libraries* (Studies in the Man-System Interface in Libraries No. 3). Bethlehem, PA: Lehigh University, Center for the Information Sciences.

Taylor, R. S. (1968). Question-negotiation and information seeking in libraries. *College and Research Libraries, 29,* 178–194.

Taylor, R. S. (1985a). This week's citation classic. [About the author's article from 1968]. *Current Contents, 17*(47), 24.

Taylor, R. S. (1985b). *Value-added processes in information systems.* Norwood, NJ: Aplex Publishing.

Thing Mortensen, A. (1972). *Perception og sprog: Et filosofisk essay.* København: Akademisk forlag.

Thorhauge, J. (1993). Fra bureaukrati til ad-hockrati—personaleudvikling og uddannelse. *Biblioteksarbejde, 14*(39), 89–94.

Tiles, J. E. (1988). *Dewey.* London: Routledge.

Timpka, T., & Nyce, J. M. (1991). Dilemmas at a primary health care center: A baseline study for computer-supported cooperative health care work. *Methods of Information in Medicine, 31*(3), 204–209.

Tippo, H. R. (1993). *Abstracting, information retrieval and the humanities: Providing access to historical literature.* Chicago: American Library Association.

Togeby, O. (1997). *Om sprog: En introduktionsbog.* København: Hans Reitzel.

Tolman, C. W. (Ed.). (1992). *Positivism in psychology: Historical and contemporary problems.* Berlin: Springer-Verlag.

Tranekjær Rasmussen, E. (1956). *Bevidsthedsliv og erkendelse: Nogle psykologisk-erkendelsesteoretiske betragtninger.* København: Københavns Universitet.

United Nations Educational, Scientific, and Cultural Organization and the International Council of Scientific Unions (1971). *Study report on the feasibility of a world science information system* ("UNISIST"). Paris: UNESCO.

Vakkari, P. (1996). Library and information science: Context and scope. In J. Olaisen, E. Munch-Petersen, and P. Wilson (Eds.), *Information science: From the development of the discipline to social interaction* (pp. 169–232). Oslo: Scandinavian University Press.)

Vammen, T. (1986). *Rent og urent: Hovedstadens piger og fruer 1880–1920*. København: Gyldendal.

van Rijsbergen, C. J. (1986). A new theoretical framework for information retrieval. In American Society for Computing Machinery, *Proceedings of the 1986 ACM Conference on research and development in information retrieval* (pp. 194–200). New York: ACM Press.

Vickery, B., & Vickery, A. (1987). *Information science in theory and practice*. London: Bowker-Saur.

Vipond, D. (1993). *Writing and psychology: Understanding writing and its teaching from the perspective of composition studies*. Westport, CT: Praeger.

Vipond, D. (1996). Problems with a monolithic APA style. *American Psychologist*, 51(6), 653.

Vygotsky, L. S. (1962). *Thought and language*. Cambridge, MA: MIT Press.

Vygotsky, L. S. (1978). *Mind in society: The development of higher psychological processes*. Cambridge, MA: Harvard University Press.

Vygotsky, L. S. (1982). *Tænkning og sprog* (Vols. 1–2). København: Hans Reitzel.

Webb, W. H. (1986). *Sources of information in the social sciences: A guide to the literature* (3rd ed.). Chicago: American Library Association.

Weinberg, B. H. (1988). Why indexing fails the researcher. *The Indexer*, 16(1), 3–6.

Welwert, C. (1984). *Läsa eller lyssna? Redovisning av jämförande undersökningar gjorda åren 1890–1980 rörande inläring vid auditiv och visuell presentation samt ett försök till utvärdering av resultaten*. Malmö, CWK Gleerup.

Wersig, G. (1973). *Informationssoziologie: Hinweise zu einem informationswissenschaftlichen Teilbereich*. Frankfurt am Main: Athenäum Fischer Taschenbuch Verlag.

Wersig, G. (1996). Information theory. In J. Feather, & P. Sturges (Eds.), *International encyclopedia of library and information science* (pp. 220–227). London & New York: Routledge.

Wertsch, J. V. (Ed.). (1981). *The concept of activity in soviet psychology*. Armonk, NY: M. E. Sharpe.

Wertsch, J. V., del Rio, P. & Alvarez, A. (Eds.). (1995). *Sociocultural studies of mind*. Cambridge: Cambridge University Press.

White, H. D. (1992). Literary forms in information work. In H. D. White, M. J. Bates, & P. Wilson (Eds.), *For information specialists: Interpretations of reference and bibliographic work* (pp. 131–149). Norwood, NJ: Ablex Publishing Corporation.

Whitley, R. D. (1984). *Intellectual and social organization of the sciences*. Oxford: Clarendon.

Wicklund, R. A. (1990). *Zero-variable theories and the psychology of the explainer*. Berlin: Springer.

Widell, P. (1982). Habermas: Enheden af teori og praksis. In P. Lübcke (Ed.), *Vor tids filosofi: Engagement og forståelse* (pp. 271–279). København: Politikens forlag.

Wilson, P. (1968). *Two kinds of power: An essay on bibliographical control*. Berkeley: University of California Press.

Wilson, P. (1993). Communication efficiency in research and development. *Journal of the American Society for Information Science*, 44(7), 376–382.

Wilson, P. (1996). Some consequences of information overload and rapid conceptual change In J. Olaisen, E. Munch-Petersen, and P. Wilson (Eds.), *Information science: From the development of the discipline to social interaction* (pp. 21–34). Oslo: Scandinavian University Press.

Wilson, T. D. (1981). On user studies and information needs. *Journal of Documentation*, *37*(1), 3–15.

Winograd, T., & Flores, F. (1987). *Understanding computers and cognition: A new foundation for design*. New York: Addison-Wesley.

Winther-Jensen, T. (1989). *Undervisning og menneskesyn belyst gennem studier af Platon, Comenius, Rousseau og Dewey—En antropologisk betragtningsmåde*. København: Akademisk Forlag.

Wold, A. H. (Ed.). (1992). *The dialogical alternative*. Oslo: Scandinavian University Press.

Wormell, I. (1985). *Subject access project—SAP: Improved subject retrieval for monographic publications*. Lund: Lund University.

Wulff, H. R. (1985). Assessment of progress in medicine. In T. Hagerstrand (Ed.), *Identification of progress in learning* (pp. 69–90). New York: Cambridge University Press.

Yitzhaki, M. (1996). Informativity of journal article titles: The ratio of "significant" words. In P. Ingwersen & N. O. Pors (Eds.), *Proceedings CoLIS2: Second international conference on conceptions of library and information science, integration in perspective, October 13–16, 1996* (pp. 447–458). Copenhagen: The Royal School of Librarianship.

Øhrgaard, P. (1992). Hvad taler vi om, når vi taler om kvalitet. *Dansk pædagogisk Tidsskrift*, (3), 119–127.

Index

About the Author

BIRGER HJØRLAND is Associate Professor and Head of the Department of Humanities and Social Sciences Information Studies at the Royal School of Librarianship in Copenhagen.

ISBN 0-313-29893-9

9 780313 298936

HARDCOVER BAR CODE